watercolor wanderlust

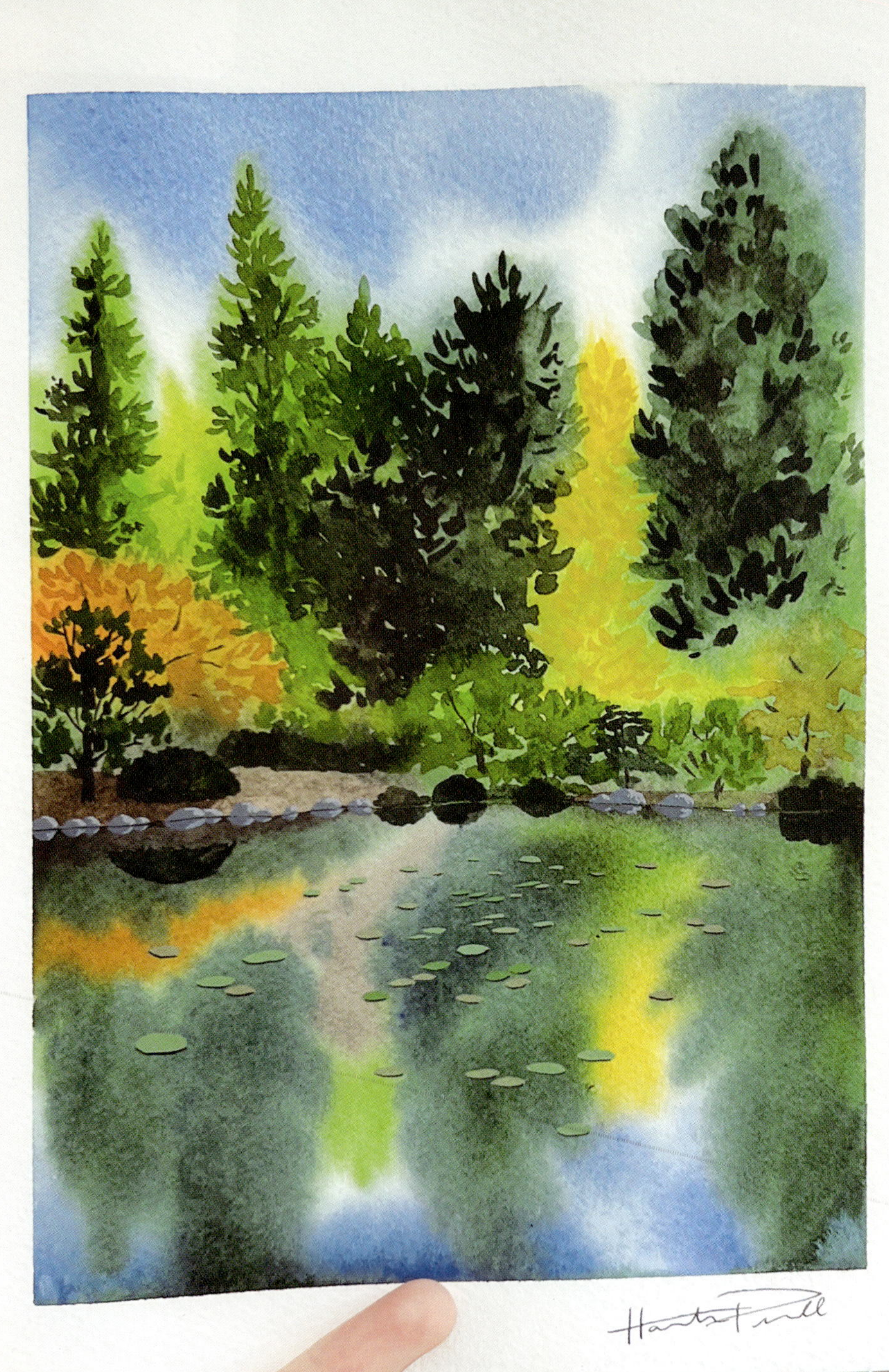

watercolor wanderlust

The Ultimate Guide to Painting Beautiful Landscapes

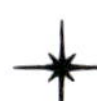

20+ Comprehensive Tutorials for Mountains, Forests, Deserts, Seascapes & More

Hannah M. Pickerill

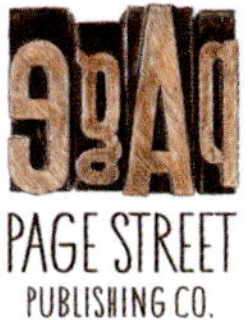

PAGE STREET PUBLISHING CO.

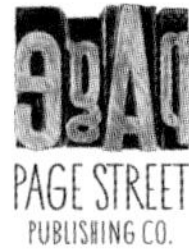

First published in 2024 by
Page Street Publishing Co.
27 Congress Street, Suite 1511
Salem, MA 01970
www.pagestreetpublishing.com

Distributed by Macmillan, sales in Canada by The Canadian Manda Group.

30 29 28 27 26 4 5 6 7 8

ISBN-13: 978-1-645-67952-3
ISBN-10: 1-64567-952-7

Library of Congress Control Number: 2023937271

Edited by Sadie Hofmeester
Cover and book design by Emma Hardy for Page Street Publishing Co.
Photography by Hannah M. Pickerill

Photo credits for reference photos:
Oregon Plains (page 28) by Dianne Pickerill
Golden Palouse (page 42) by Jarred Decker (Unsplash)
Moroccan Sand Dunes (page 52) by Donna Payne
The Grandest Canyon (page 57) by Alan Pickerill
Sedona Courthouse Butte (page 65) by Alan Pickerill
Autumn Reflections (page 106) by Dianne Pickerill
Great Smoky Mountains (page 131) by Div Pithadia (Unsplash)
El Capitan (page 144) by Adrienne Pickerill
Sailboat on Sunlit Water (page 180) by Vidar Nordli-Mathisen (Unsplash)
Colorful Galaxy (page 204) by ESA (European Space Agency)/Hubble & NASA, A. Filippenko
Mr. Moon (page 210) by Mike Petrucci (Unsplash)

Printed and bound in China

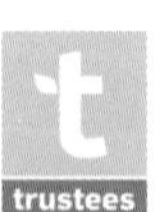

Page Street Publishing protects our planet by donating to nonprofits like The Trustees, which focuses on local land conservation.

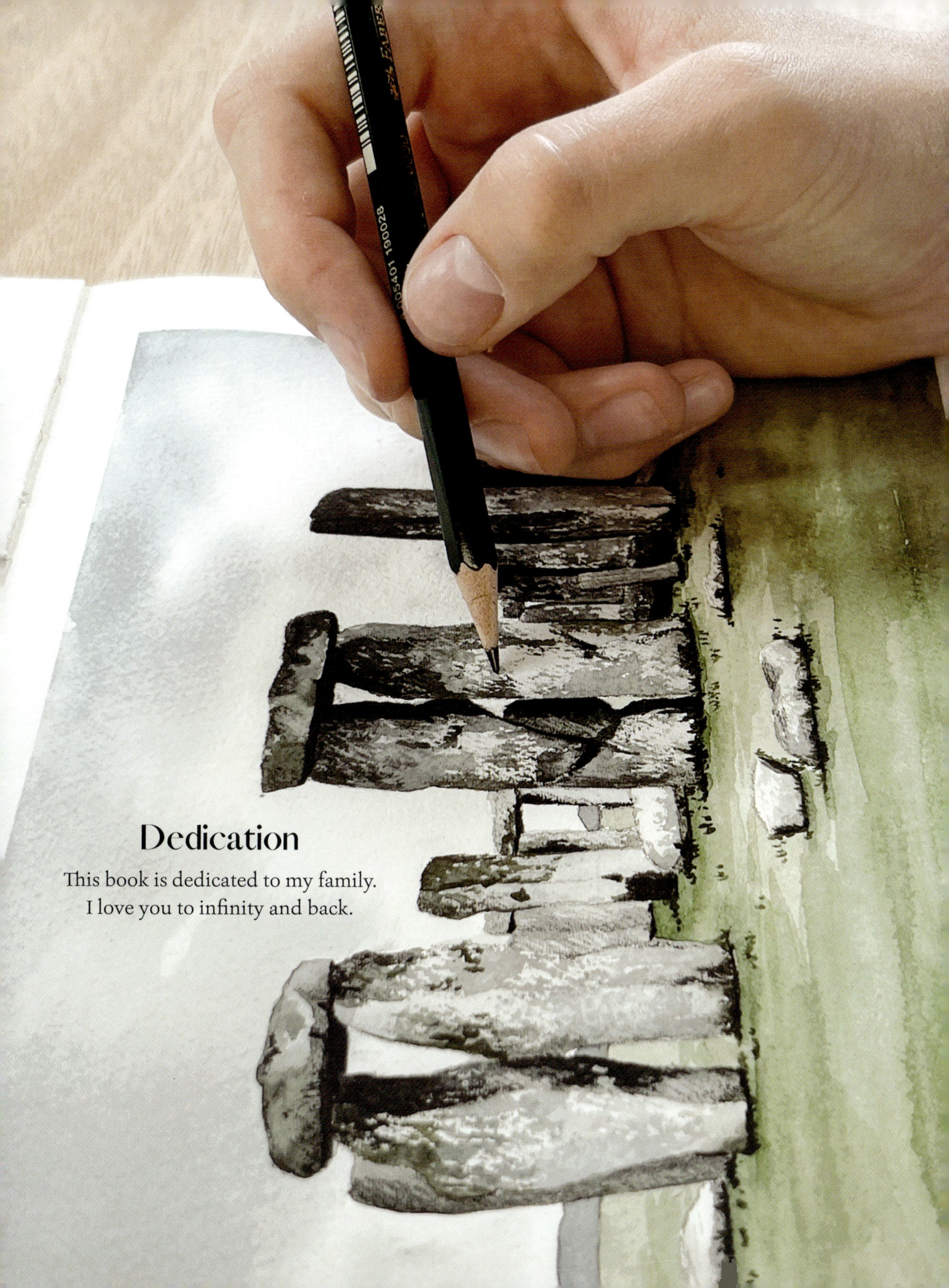

Dedication

This book is dedicated to my family.
I love you to infinity and back.

table of contents

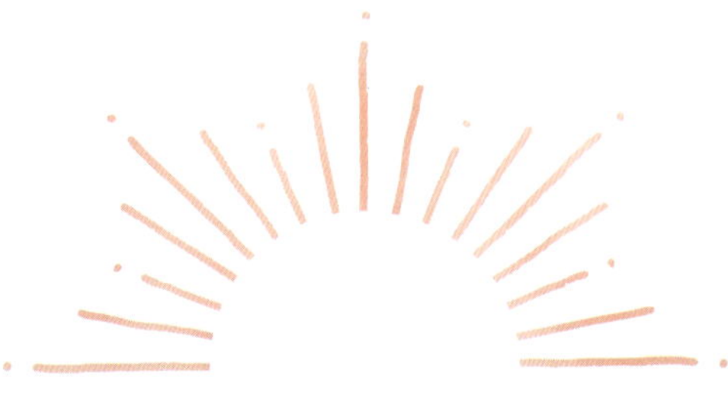

introduction

Welcome, dear artist, to *Watercolor Wanderlust*! My name is Hannah, and I'll be your tour guide, teacher and (occasionally) drill sergeant as you paint your way through this book. A little bit about me before we get started: I grew up near Seattle, Washington, surrounded by gorgeous landscapes that still inspire my art today. I was an adventurous, sporty and happy kid who loved being outside (not much has changed there), and I've been painting from the time I could hold a brush in my chubby little baby hands. Don't get me wrong here; I am no savant. My childhood drawings probably looked very much like yours. What was different for me was how much I loved the experience—I could lose myself, my endless thoughts and hours of time in a drawing or a painting, and that feeling is what has kept me practicing art for my entire life.

Once I got to college, I chose to major in psychology but added a minor in fine art purely so that I could continue taking classes and carving out time to create. When I graduated college, I moved to Cincinnati, Ohio, and started working in psychology research. I was quite reluctantly starting the application process for a Ph.D. when the pandemic hit and derailed all my plans. With the extra time, I was able to draw and paint more consistently and reevaluate my life and what I wanted it to look like. I began posting my work on social media and, over the next several months, started to make real money with my art. Finally, by October of 2021, I was able to quit my research job and become a professional, full-time artist (cue the angels singing).

The last few years have been the best adventure of my life so far, and despite all of the challenges that have come with it, I'm the happiest I've ever been and so content with the path I've chosen. That leads us here, to this book sitting in front of you now. I truly hope you enjoy learning some of the things I've picked up along the way, and I hope this book serves you as a stepping stone to a new passion for watercolor.

While the foundation of this book is my love for watercolor painting and teaching, the inspiration for the individual projects is my own wanderlust. Most of the lessons are based on my photography or that of friends and family (with a few exceptions of course; I haven't had the chance to go *everywhere* yet). I've been very lucky to be able to visit some amazing places throughout my life, and the reference photos I take on these adventures inspire most of my paintings. We'll be journeying to all sorts of beautiful and unique locations together throughout this book, and I hope you find a new appreciation for the billions of beautiful landscapes throughout the world that you might otherwise pass over. More importantly, I hope it inspires your love for nature, and a passion to take care of this Earth with your own small actions, so that future generations can continue to see these landscapes in real life rather than just in photos or paintings.

One VERY IMPORTANT note before we get started: an advantage to starting art while you are young is that you're not afraid to fail—as a child you're learning everything for the first time, and you're expected to fail and work through problems until you've got it figured out. When starting something as adults, we tend to expect perfection on the first try and give up if we don't achieve it. I want you to keep this in mind as you begin your art journey: Every artist that's ever lived has made SO MANY BAD PAINTINGS! Like, so many. It's (unfortunately) how humans have to learn new skills, and practice is the *only* way to improve. So, if I can force one thing into your brain as you work through this book and continue on your art journey, it's this: **Let go of the pressure to make "good" art.** Make so many bad paintings and give yourself forgiveness and understanding when you do. Paint for the enjoyment of the process, seeing the colors blend together in a pretty way, an hour of peace and quiet or an appreciation for the landscape you're recreating. You'll find the process so much more enjoyable this way, and before you know it, the paintings you're proud of will be stacking up on your desk.

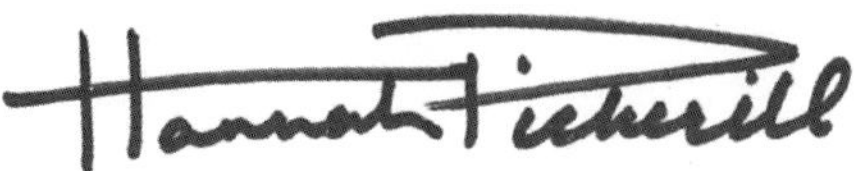

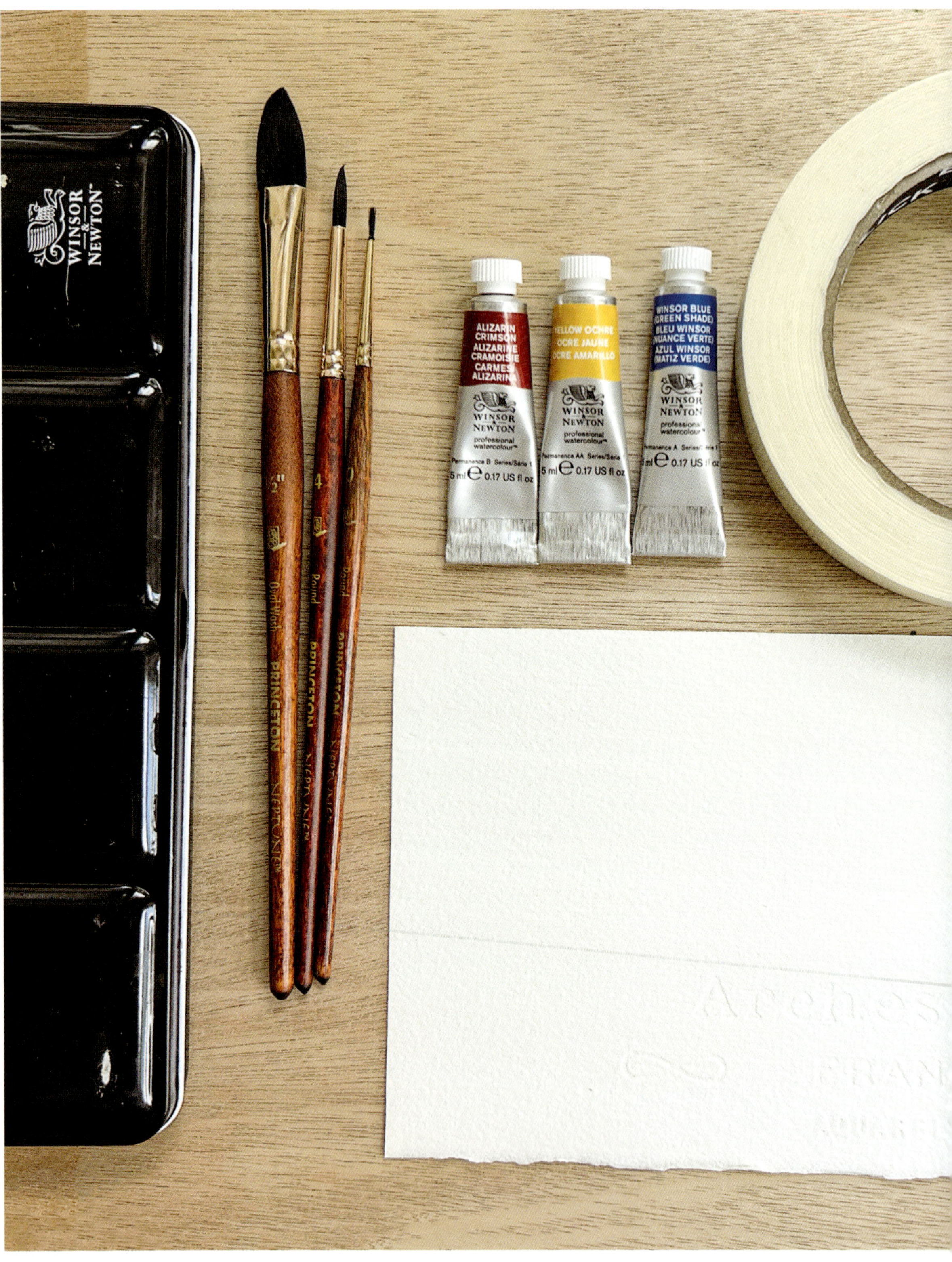
WINSOR & NEWTON
PRINCETON NEPTUNE
Oval Wash
Round
ALIZARIN CRIMSON
ALIZARINE CRAMOISIE
CARMESI ALIZARINA
YELLOW OCHRE
OCRE JAUNE
OCRE AMARILLO
WINSOR BLUE (GREEN SHADE)
BLEU WINSOR (NUANCE VERTE)
AZUL WINSOR (MATIZ VERDE)
WINSOR & NEWTON
professional watercolour
5 ml e 0.17 US fl oz

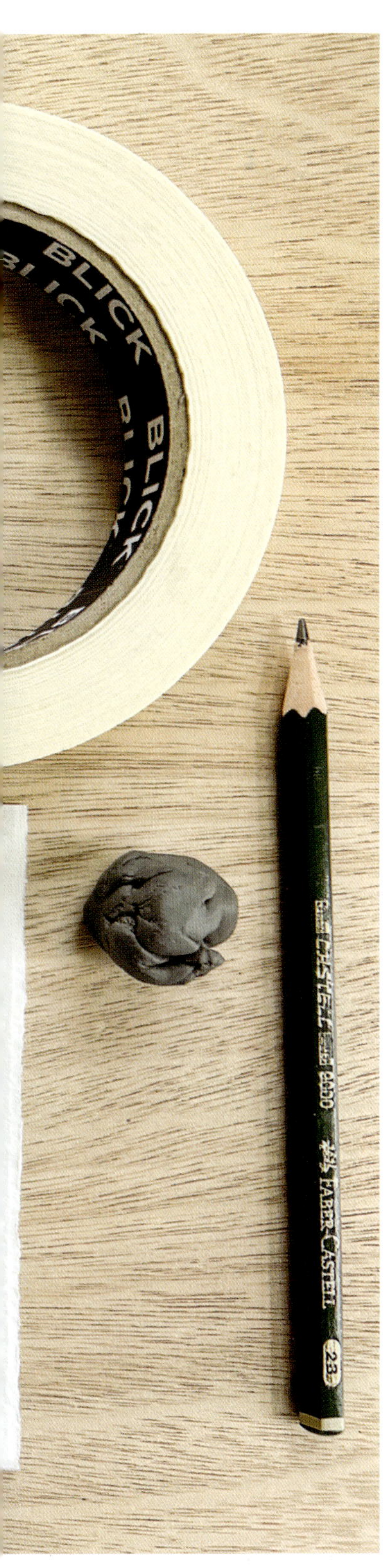

chapter 1
before you start

Let's briefly discuss some administrative items before we get to the good stuff. First, this book is organized into chapters by types of landscapes, such as water scenes, deserts or forests. Within each chapter, there are four to six projects that increase in difficulty. If you're feeling confident, feel free to flip through the book with reckless abandon and find projects that inspire you in the moment. If you're feeling more tentative, I recommend you work through it in order.

Art supplies: The paints I used to create these landscapes are Winsor & Newton professional watercolors. I like to buy individual tubes of watercolor and squeeze them into the pans in my watercolor set and let them dry; it's more cost effective this way, and I can simply replace one color when I run out rather than buying an entire new set. My watercolor paper is by Fabriano Artistico in a watercolor sketchbook from Etchr, or Arches watercolor paper, and my brushes are by Princeton Neptune.

I've tried a lot of art supplies over the years, and these are some of my personal favorites; however, **you can use any watercolor supplies you like to create these landscapes**. To a certain degree, more expensive paints, paper and brushes can be higher quality and may give you better results, but from my own experience, your success is way less dependent on the quality of your supplies and more dependent on your commitment to practicing your skills.

Colors: I used sixteen total colors for the landscapes in this book, and you will likely find all of these colors (or very similar substitutes) in any watercolor set you happen to buy. You can see these colors below, and throughout the book, I'll be using the official color names when referring to them. Paint sets sometimes differ in their color names, so if the color names in your paint set don't match mine, take a moment to identify colors in your palette that look similar to these so that you can follow the color recipes throughout the book!

Color recipes: Throughout this book, I will provide you with the paint combinations I used to mix each color, along with a swatch. These are just general guidelines for your reference—you don't need to follow them exactly, and your colors can look different from mine!

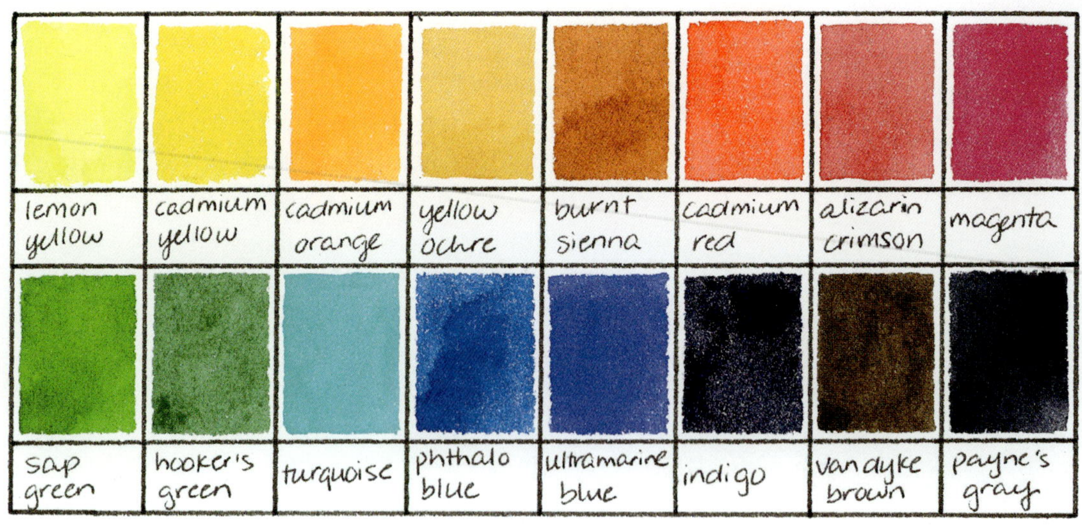

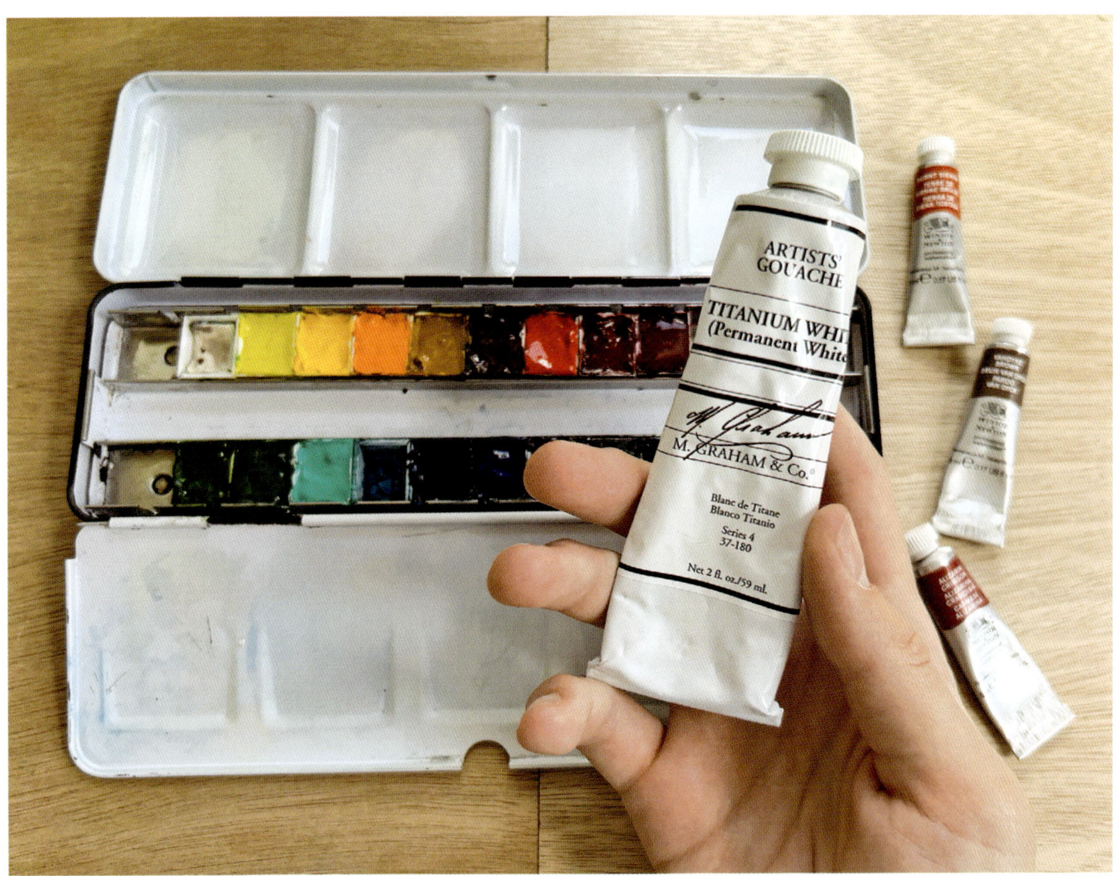

Gouache: I LOVE GOUACHE! If you've never heard of it, it's kind of like an opaque watercolor paint. I strongly recommend having a small tube of white gouache handy (You can find it at any art store or online. Just avoid any gouache labeled "acryla" or "acrylic" as it won't mix as well with your watercolors). M. Graham is my personal favorite brand for adding white highlights to your painting at the end.

Because of its composition, gouache can also be mixed with your watercolor paint to create an opaque paint. Since watercolor paint is translucent, you can't paint light on top of dark, so I love using gouache to add some lighter details to my paintings. You can find examples of this in projects like Motion of the Ocean (page 156) or Autumn Reflections (page 106).

Household materials: For the sake of your patience and sanity, I strongly recommend having a hairdryer around when watercolor painting to dry the paint between layers. It cuts down on a ton of drying time and lets you move on to the next steps so much quicker! Other household items that will be useful are a cup for water, paper towels for drying your brushes, a pencil and eraser, a ruler and masking tape or masking fluid.

Paper set up: In the beginning of each project, I tell you to set up your paper how you like. I prefer to tape my paper down at the edges using masking tape (which can be found in your local art store or hardware store) because I like a clean border around the outside of the painting. If you do this, I strongly recommend taping your paper to something movable (a large book, a board, some cardboard, etc.) so that you can pick up the painting and move it around, rather than taping it to the table you're working on. That being said, your paper set up is completely up to your personal taste. If you prefer the natural border around the outside, or prefer to paint all the way to the edge of the paper, that's your prerogative. You can also use whatever size paper you're comfortable with!

TIP: If you ever find the tape is ripping your paper when peeling it, heat it up with a hairdryer for a few seconds first! The heat melts the glue on the tape and helps it release the paper.

At the start of each project, I will also note the orientation of the painting. **Landscape** means the long side of your paper is horizontal, and **portrait** means the long side is vertical.

Reference photos: These are super common tools in realistic art, and I absolutely recommend using them. I'll provide reference photos for many of the projects in this book, and I suggest you use them to inspire your own painting in conjunction with my instructions. Don't get too caught up here though—your painting doesn't have to look exactly like (or even remotely like) the reference photo for it to be a good painting. Use it to inspire you but know that it's totally okay to change or ignore certain elements for your painting.

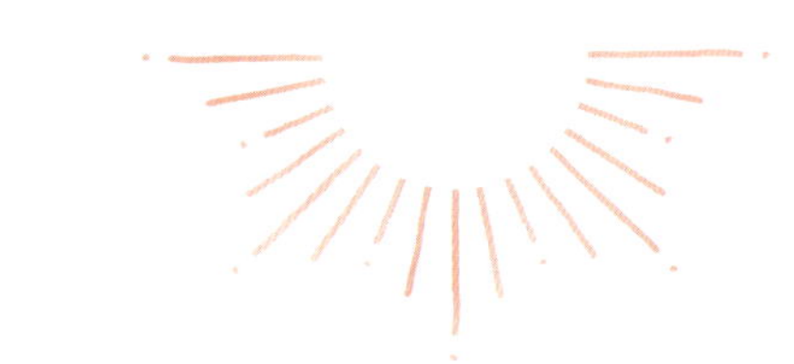

Basic Terms and Techniques

Flat wash: Start by mixing enough paint for the area you need to cover. My favorite trick is to alternate adding water from your cup and paint to your mixing area until you've built up enough paint to cover the area you're working with. Don't be gentle with your watercolor paints here—dig your brush into the paint to really load it up! Once your color is mixed, use a large brush to cover the area with your paint, working somewhat quickly to get a smooth wash. I like using either horizontal or vertical brush strokes when possible as this helps reduce the texture of the paint.

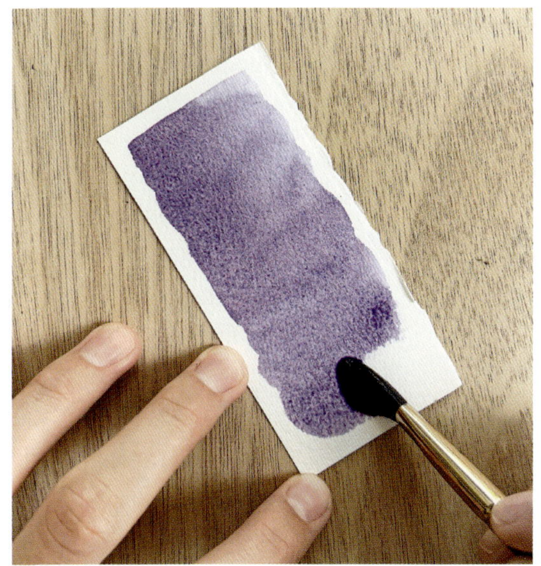

Flat wash

Gradient to white: Start by covering about a third of the area with paint. Then, quickly mix more water into the paint on your palette and continue painting another third of the area. Finally, clean off your brush and use plain water to cover the last third. You can use a clean, damp brush to pass over the whole area again to smooth out the blend. I like using horizontal brushstrokes when painting things like sky or water, but sometimes vertical brush strokes might be better for certain objects or areas.

Gradient to white

Gradient between colors: Cover one side of the area with one color and cover the other side with your other color, allowing them to meet in the middle. Use a clean damp brush to blend the area where the colors meet until it's smooth. I like using horizontal or vertical brush strokes when possible.

Gradient between colors

Dry brush: Add paint to your brush, then touch your brush to a paper towel for a few seconds to remove paint until your brush is nearly dry. Then, hold your brush almost parallel to your paper and quickly and lightly scrape the side of your brush along the paper so the paint breaks over the texture of the paper. This is an amazing technique for adding texture in all sorts of landscapes and water scenes.

Wet-on-wet: Cover the area you're working on with a substantial layer of plain water, but try to avoid creating huge lakes. Then drop in the color(s) you want in the area using dotting or sweeping motions with your brush. Keep in mind your colors will be diluted by the water on the paper, so I suggest dropping in quite saturated colors. They will all blend and run on the paper in beautiful, unique ways, and you can even pick up and tilt your painting in different directions to encourage the blending. If you end up with large puddles on your page after adding color, use a completely dry brush to draw up the excess. This will help it dry evenly and quickly. This technique is great for skies, distant backgrounds and preliminary layers of paintings.

Lifting: After adding paint to your paper, use a completely dry brush and tap or drag your brush to lift pigment off the paper. Dry your brush with a paper towel every few seconds as you work. Note that this is only possible while the paint is still wet. This technique is great for clouds, highlights and water texture.

Dry brush

Wet-on-wet

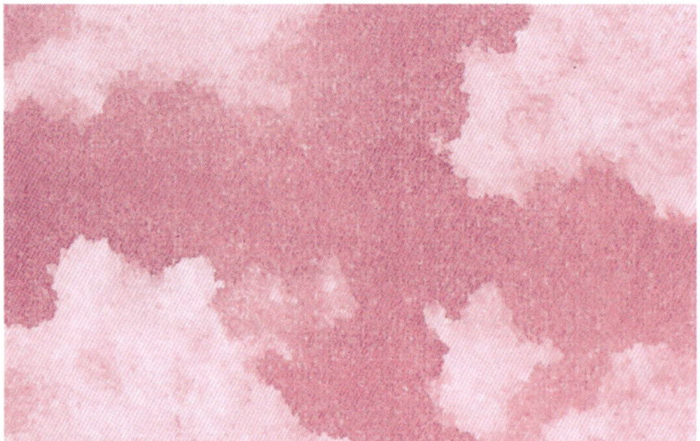

Lifting

I have one last SUPER important note for you before you embark on your journey through this book. When painting with watercolor, you'll often end up in what's called the Ugly Stage. This typically happens when you're right in the middle of your painting, and it can be quite discouraging to feel like your painting isn't turning out right. You may think you're a bad artist or that you can't paint (not true, silly), and this is often when beginner artists quit. It is SO important to understand that this is completely normal, pretty much every artist experiences this when painting (including me), and it doesn't mean you're a bad artist. The Ugly Stage is just a stage, and I promise if you keep working and adding detail and practicing, you'll often escape the Ugly Stage and create a painting you're happy with.

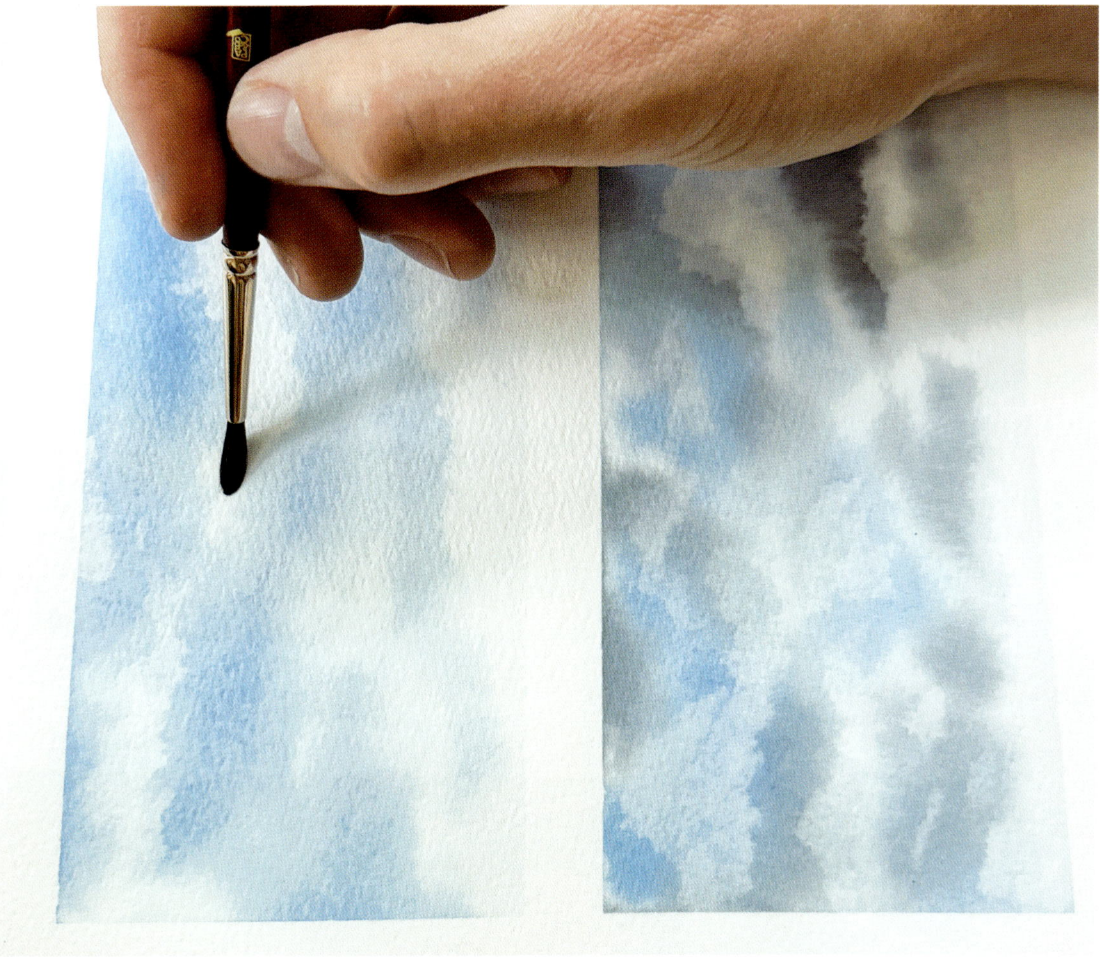

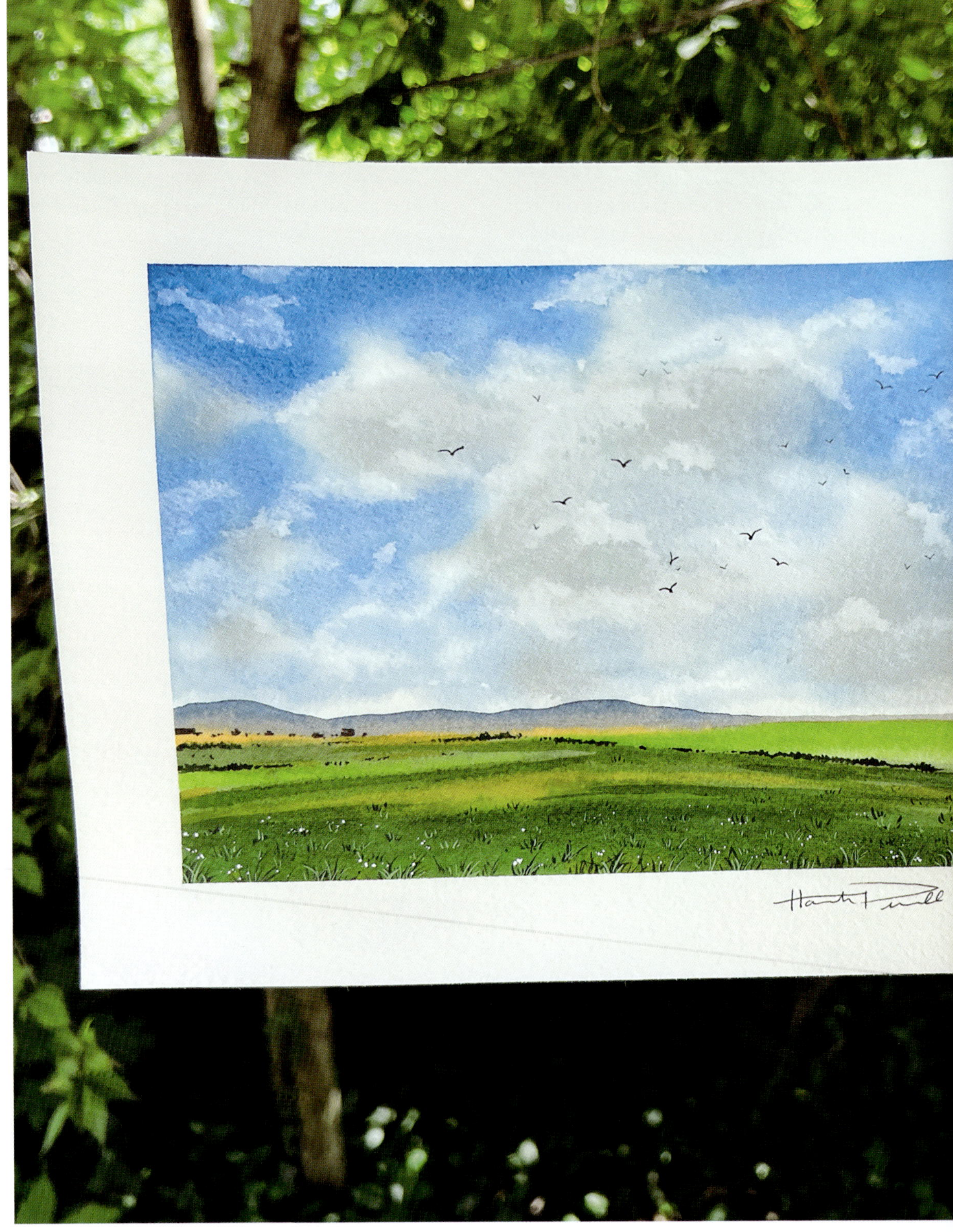

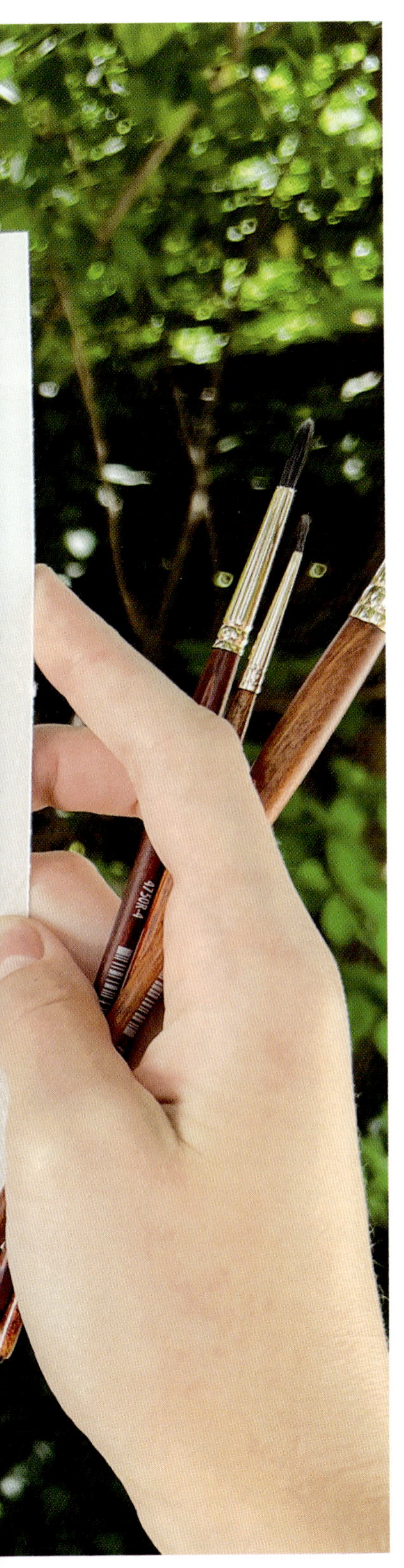

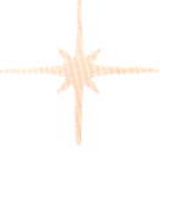

chapter 2

prairies, plains and palouse (oh my)

In this chapter, we will delve into the beautiful simplicity of expansive fields and lush, rolling hills under wide, dramatic skies. I felt like this would be a great chapter to start with because these types of landscapes will give you practice with your watercolor washes, color mixing and sky techniques, without bogging you down with complicated subject matter right off the bat. If you're a watercolor newbie, or maybe not as confident in your skills yet, these projects should help you gain some confidence and get some good watercolor practice!

rolling hills

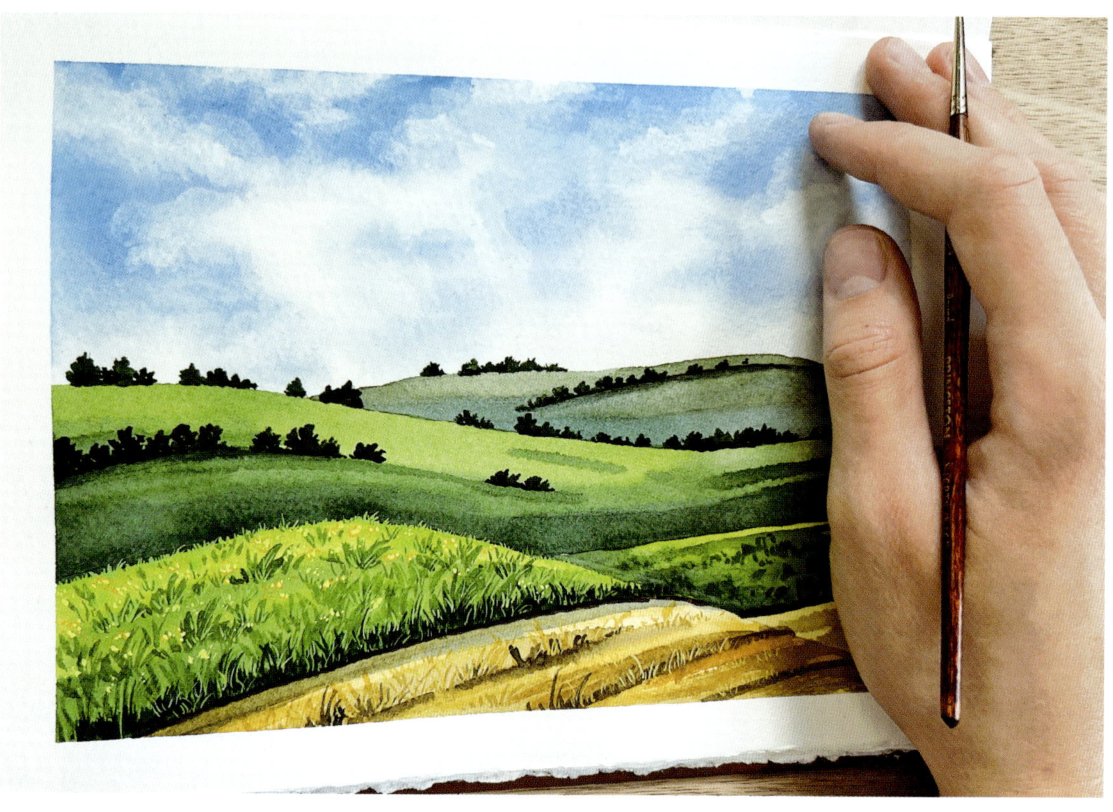

This fun project is a great way to begin. Rolling hills are a very forgiving subject—they aren't too complicated, and they can look a ton of different ways! The ones I've painted here are inspired by the rolling hills of the English countryside, but there's such a wide variety of landscapes like this one in the world that it could really be anywhere. These hills are offset by an atmospheric summer sky, which adds a bit of drama without adding a ton of time. We won't be using a reference photo this time (though feel free to find one that you like on the internet if you need more structure), so this is a great opportunity to be loose, creative and expressive with your paints.

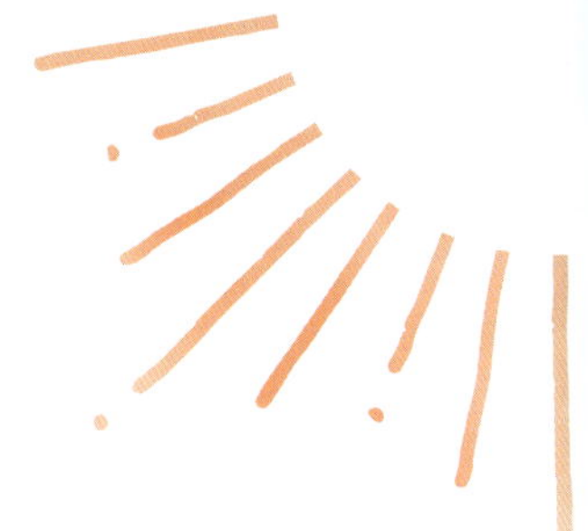

materials

Watercolor paints

- Cadmium Yellow, Yellow Ochre, Ultramarine Blue, Phthalo Blue, Hooker's Green, Sap Green and Van Dyke Brown
- White gouache (optional)

Watercolor paper of your choice

- I used my cold press Fabriano Artistico sketchbook size 6 x 8 inches (15 x 20 cm)

Brushes

- one larger brush (I used a ½ inch oval) and one detail brush (I used a size 0 round)

Orientation

- landscape

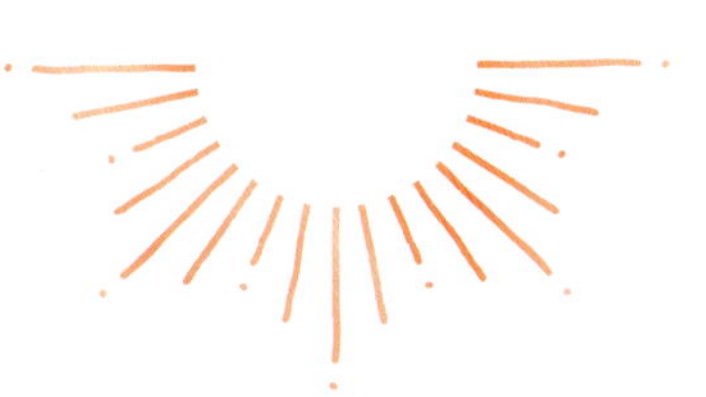

Set up your paper as you like and make sure to add a drop or two of water to your colors, so they start to soften.

Sketch

Sketch a few hills using loose, wavy lines in the bottom half of the page. Feel free to adjust the horizon line if you'd like more sky or more land in your painting. As you can see in the photo, I ended up with four sections, and I wouldn't recommend making too many more than that.

NOTE: Skies are almost always the first thing I'll paint when painting a landscape. They set the mood for the rest of the painting, and when painted correctly, they perfectly complement the rest of the landscape in a believable way. There are probably a million different ways to paint a sky, but I have a few tried and tested strategies that I use nearly every time I paint a landscape; this particular sky is one I call my "Perfect Summer Sky."

Sky Blue
Ultramarine Blue +
Phthalo Blue

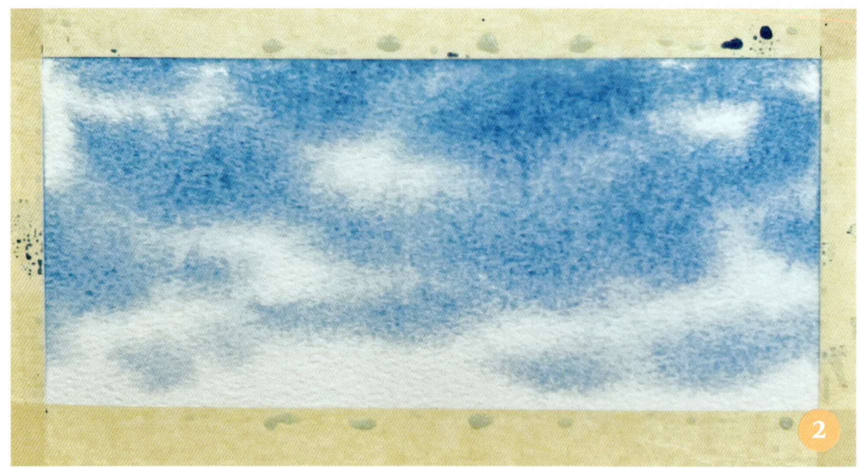

PAUSE: Please read through Steps 1-4 before you start so that you can work quickly without stopping to read.

Step 1

Using a large brush, cover the entire sky section of your paper with clean water. Tilt your head to see the light reflected off the water on your paper to see any spots you've missed. Try not to create any huge lakes on your paper, but do make sure to cover it with a good layer of water.

Step 2

Mix your Sky Blue and load up a large brush with paint. Start at the top of your paper and paint in some sweeping brush strokes, making sure to leave some blank spots where the white paper still shows through. Don't over-think or paint too slowly–movement and "imperfections" are great for this technique.

You'll notice your brush will start to run out of paint after you've painted a few spots. Feel free to grab more Sky Blue paint, but as you work to the bottom of your sky section, **let your brush run out of paint**. This will make the sky lighter towards the horizon line, which gives the painting atmospheric perspective (the feeling of distance). Your sky should overlap the tops of your hills just a little bit; this will help the rest of the painting look cleaner and more polished.

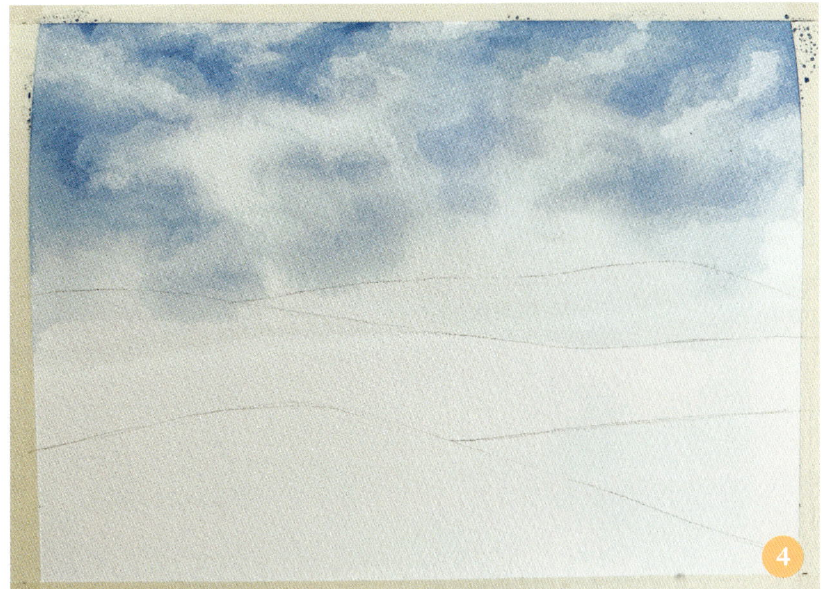

Step 3

Pick up your painting from the table and tilt it in different directions. This will cause the paint to slowly spread around the paper, and it creates really soft, beautiful blends. Try not to overdo this—if you keep blending you'll lose the white spots. Once you're happy with the blend, set your paper back on the table. You can use a slightly damp brush to blend instead, if you'd prefer.

Step 4

Now we will add the final detail—clouds! Use a completely dry brush and a tapping motion to pick up pigment and create fluffy cloud shapes. I like to focus the cloud shapes on the areas that are still white (or lighter blue) on my paper. Use your paper towel to dry off your brush often as you do this. It only works when the brush is totally dry and the paint is still wet, so work quickly with this and don't overthink. Clouds often look better and more natural when you let go of control.

Once you're happy with your clouds (or your painting has dried), you're all done with your sky! Let this fully dry before moving on.

Muted Green

Hooker's Green + Van Dyke Brown + water

Muted Blue-Green

Hooker's Green + Ultramarine Blue + Van Dyke Brown + water

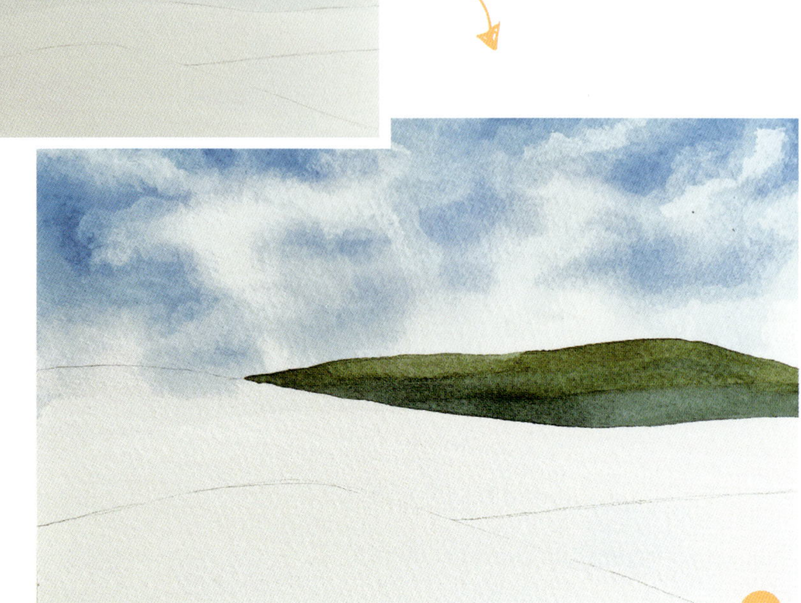

Step 5

For the hills themselves, we will work back to front, so start with the very top layer of your rolling hills. Mix up two muted green colors for this section; this will help it look further in the distance. Water these down a bit—we don't want saturated colors yet.

Use a bigger brush and the Muted Green color to fill in the top outline of the furthest hill and a few contours within that section. Quickly (no need to clean your brush) pick up the Muted Blue-Green color and fill in the rest of the section. If you do this quickly enough, the colors will blend and create cool textures.

Let this fully dry before moving on.

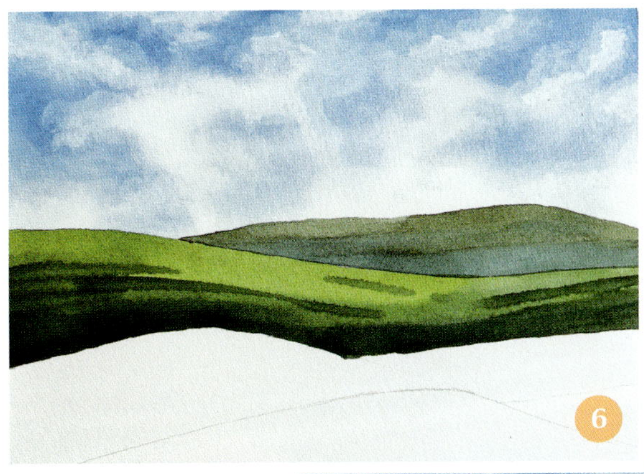

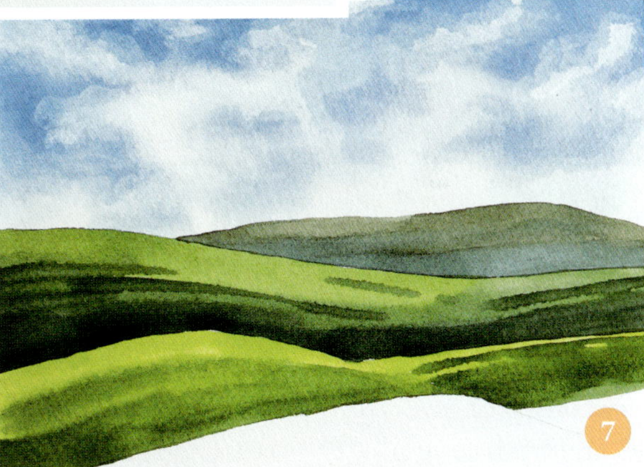

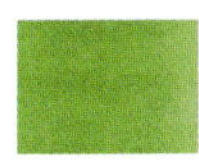

Green
Sap Green

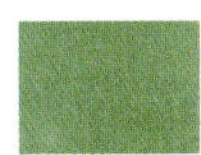

Blue-Green
Sap Green + little Ultramarine Blue + little Van Dyke Brown

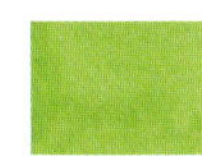

Light Green
Sap Green + Cadmium Yellow

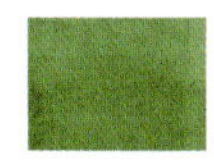

Dark Green
Sap Green + Ultramarine Blue

Step 6

Now we will fill in the next section in the same way. Mix some new green colors (Green and Blue-Green)—they should be slightly more bright and saturated than the colors from the previous step (for the Blue-Green, use more green paint and less blue and brown paint in your mix). Use the Green to fill in the top of the next hill section, plus a few contours within the section. Quickly transition to the Blue-Green and fill in the rest of the section. Let this fully dry before moving on.

Step 7

You probably get where we're going with this by now. Mix the next colors and make these the most saturated greens yet. Fill in your next section with the Light Green and Dark Green, the same way as with the previous layers. Make sure this section is completely dry before moving on.

Yellow
Yellow Ochre +
Cadmium Yellow

Brown
Van Dyke Brown

Extra Dark Green
Sap Green +
Ultramarine Blue +
Van Dyke Brown

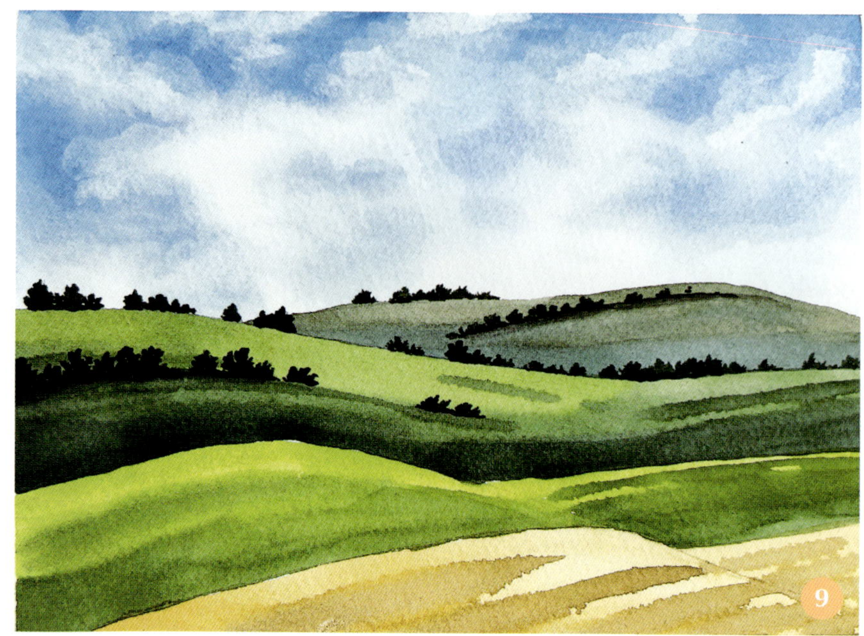

Step 8

You'll notice I left a section blank at the bottom—I chose to create a contrasting section of yellow grass (Could be dead or could be harvested. Who knows?) in the very front of the painting. This is optional, and if you'd like to stick to the greens from Step 5 for your painting, feel free. If not, mix up a Yellow and a Brown color.

Fill in the section with the Yellow color you mixed, then quickly use the Brown color to drop in some curving, horizontal lines to look like rows of grass. Let the colors do what they want to do; though if you find they're running together too much, you can use a completely dry brush to lift extra paint and define the contours better.

Step 9

Next, we will add some detail to those more distant hills. Mix a saturated, Extra Dark Green by mixing together Sap Green, Ultramarine Blue and Van Dyke Brown, using very little water in your paint mixture.

Use this color and a detail brush to add some lines of small trees in the distance. I like to use these to disguise the "seam" between the layers of hills or any funky spots. Keep in mind, these small trees should only be painted in the more distant layers—if you put them in too close, the perspective of the painting won't read correctly.

For bonus points, use a watered-down version of this same Green to add a thin, subtle shadow underneath these trees.

If you need help or more guidance with painting these distant trees, check out the One Tree at a Time project on page 84.

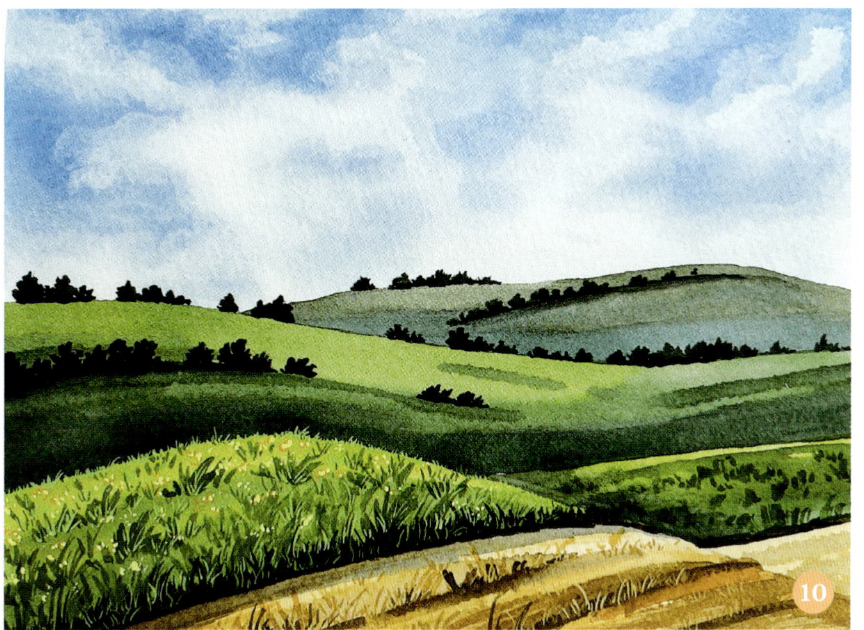

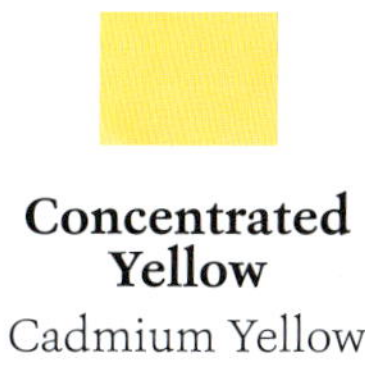

Concentrated Yellow
Cadmium Yellow

Step 10

The last step is to add detail to the foreground. This is the section where we can see individual blades of grass or flowers. Use the same colors from earlier in this project and your detail brush to add clumps of grass. Add Extra Dark Green grass in the border between the yellow grass section and the green grass. And use some Concentrated Yellow to put in a few wildflowers in the foreground grass section (the one you painted in Step 7).

If you find that this is all you need to create a painting that you're happy with, that's all you need to do! If you're looking for a little extra sparkle, mix some white gouache with Sap Green watercolor and add some lighter grassy texture to the foreground. You can also mix Yellow Ochre with white gouache to add some grassy highlights in the yellow grass section! For a final optional detail, you can also mix Cadmium Yellow with white gouache and add light yellow dots to enhance the look of the wildflowers.

Once you've added all the texture and detail you want to this section, you're all done! Take off the tape, sign and date your painting and admire your work!

oregon plains

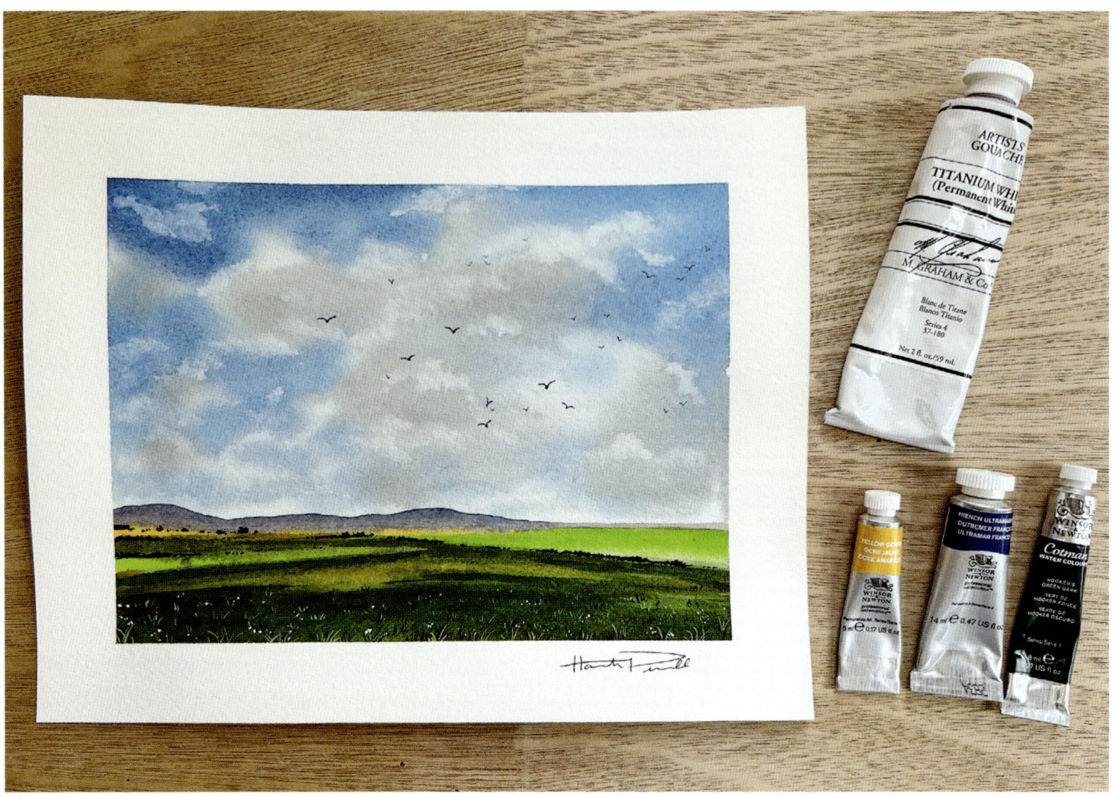

When my mom texted me this picture from her road trip to northeastern Oregon, I immediately knew it had a place in my book. I loved recreating the fluffy clouds and the vibrant green fields, and the simple composition is compelling and peaceful. Landscapes like these can be great practice for your sky techniques because the sky often takes up a lot of the page. You'll also get practice with distance and perspective with those fields that seem to go on forever. I hope you enjoy painting this one along with me!

materials

Watercolor paints

- Cadmium Yellow, Yellow Ochre, Burnt Sienna, Sap Green, Ultramarine Blue, Phthalo Blue, Payne's Gray and Van Dyke Brown
- White gouache (optional)

Watercolor paper of your choice

- I used a piece of Arches cold press watercolor paper size 6 x 8 inches (15 x 20 cm)

Brushes

- one larger brush (I used a ½ inch oval), one medium brush (I used a size 4 round) and one detail brush (I used a size 0 round)

Orientation

- landscape

Set up your paper as you like and make sure to add a drop or two of water to your colors so they start to soften.

Reference photo

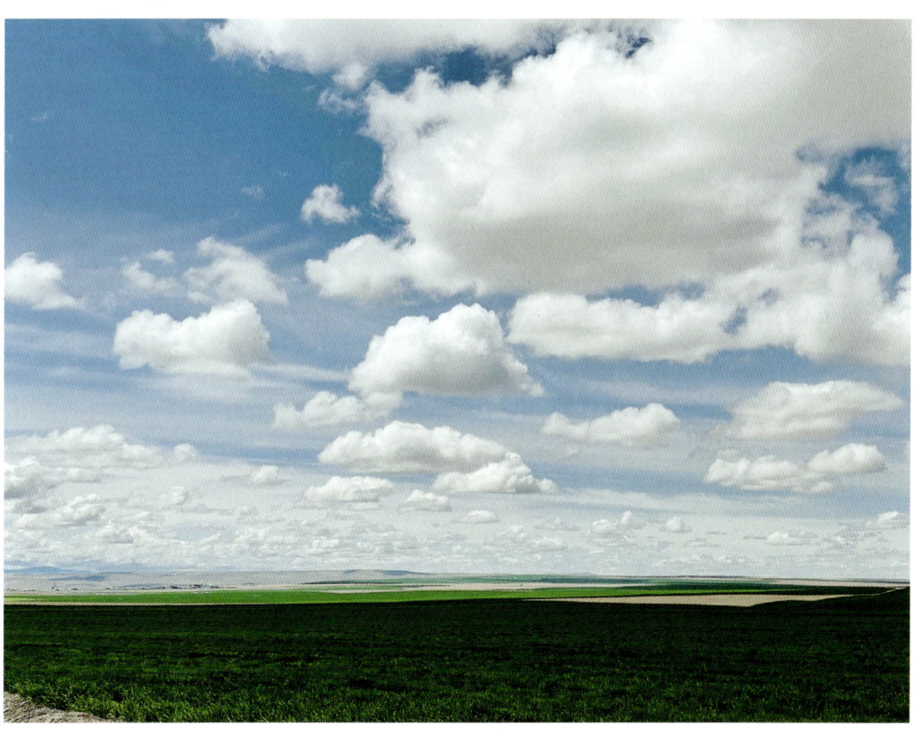

Sky Blue
Ultramarine Blue +
Phthalo Blue

Gray
Payne's Gray +
little Van Dyke
Brown

Sketch

Sketch your horizon line a little less than one-third of the way up the paper. Feel free to use a ruler to get a perfectly straight horizon line or eyeball it.

PAUSE: Please read through Steps 1–5 before you start so that you can work quickly without stopping to read.

Step 1

To create the blue and gray cloudy sky, we'll use exactly the same technique as the summer sky in the Rolling Hills project (page 20), except we'll add in gray paint along with the blue paint. Mix a Sky Blue color and a Gray color.

Put a piece of masking tape under the horizon line so you keep a clean edge. Cover your paper above the horizon line with a layer of clean water. Try not to create any lakes on your paper, but do make sure to cover with a decent layer of water.

Step 2

Using a large brush and working from top to bottom, add in sweeping brush strokes with your Sky Blue, letting the color fade out as you work toward the bottom of your paper.

Step 3

Go back to the top and add in the Gray color in the same manner. Feel free to overlap the blue paint and try to still leave some white areas.

Step 4

Slowly tilt your paper in different directions (or use a damp brush) to softly blend the colors together. When they are sufficiently blended, set your paper down flat to stop the blending.

Step 5

Use a completely dry brush to pick up paint and create fluffy cloud shapes. I find a tapping motion works best for this. Make sure to do this while the painting is still wet and make sure to continuously dry your brush with a paper towel as you work.

Once you're happy with your clouds (or your painting has dried), you're all done! Make sure the sky section is fully dry before moving on.

PAUSE: Please read through the following instructions before you start so that you can work quickly without stopping to read.

Step 6

Now we will block in the colors in the bottom of the painting. Mix the 5 colors swatched on the next page before you begin.

We will complete this section from top to bottom, starting at the horizon line and ending at the bottom of the page. I switched between my 4 round brush and my larger ½-inch oval brush depending on how much detail I needed and how much space I needed to cover.

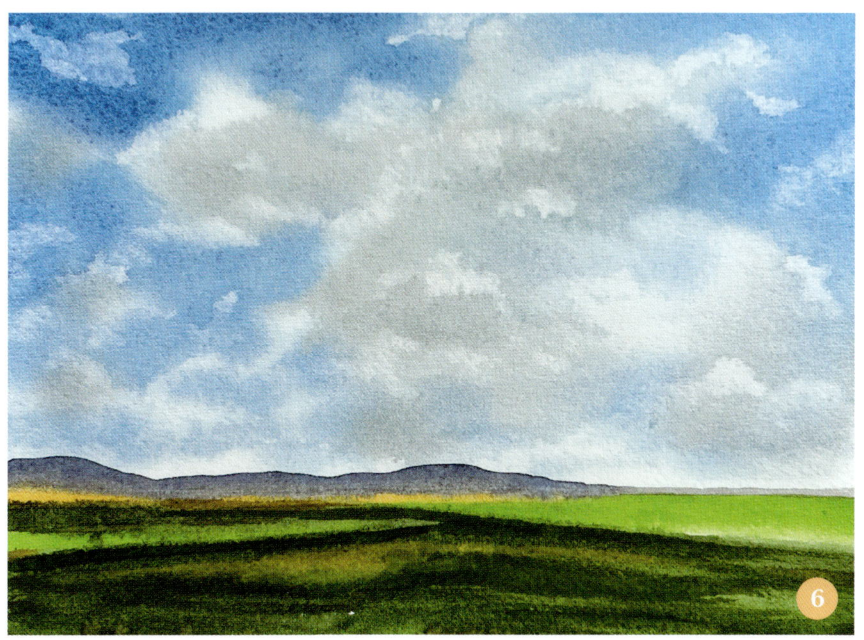

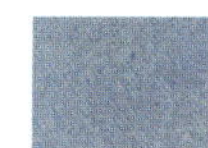

Mountain Gray
Ultramarine Blue + little Van Dyke Brown

Mountain Brown
Van Dyke Brown + little Ultramarine Blue

Yellow
Cadmium Yellow + Yellow Ochre

Light Green
Sap Green + Cadmium Yellow

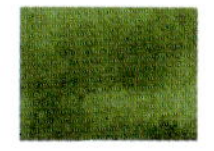

Dark Green
Sap Green + little Ultramarine Blue + little Van Dyke Brown

Start by using the Mountain Gray color to create a mountain range just above the horizon line. Start from the left and fade out the mountain range before you get to the right side of the page.

Next, switch to the Mountain Brown color and place a thin strip just under the mountain range so the colors blend together. Take the thin strip all the way across the horizon line.

Now, switch to your Yellow color. Place a thin strip of this just below the Mountain Brown.

Then, switch to the Light Green color. Place this underneath the Yellow and in a couple other places around the landscape. Feel free to make geometric shapes or random brush strokes.

Fill in any blank areas with the Dark Green. All of the colors should be blending together a bit.

Last, while it's still wet, go back over the painting and drop in some colors randomly–drop some Yellow among the greens, a little Light Green among the Dark Green, etc.

Once you're happy with it, let it dry completely.

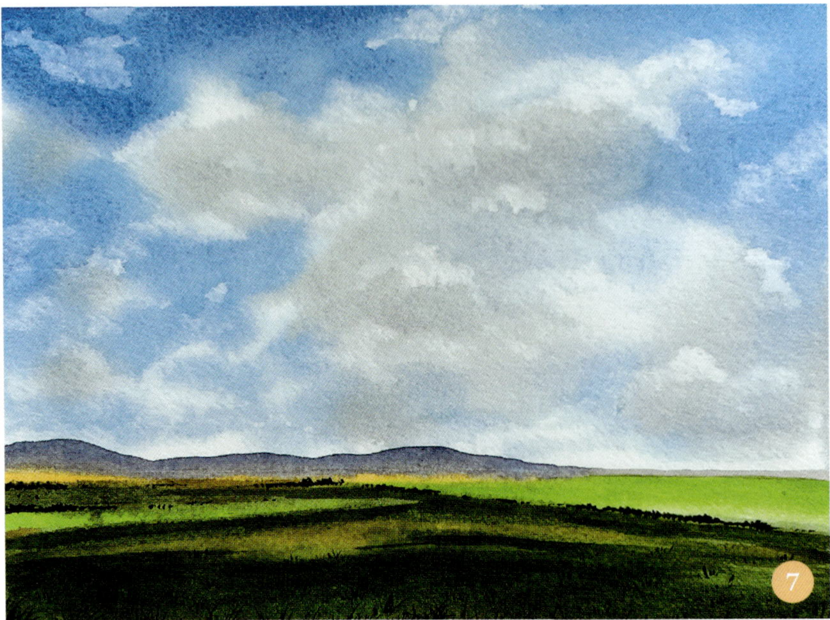

Step 7

Now let's add some detail to this field of ours. Use a detail brush and your Dark Green color from Step 2 to add:

- Some additional washes. If you have any spaces in the field that you want to look darker and more saturated, add another wash with the Dark Green from Step 6. I did this in the foreground to deepen the color there. You can blend out the edges of these washes with a clean, damp brush, so that the new wash blends into the background.
- Some tiny bushes or trees in the distance. I like to add small clusters of these at any obvious seams between two colors in the field, but feel free to add them anywhere. I use a dotting motion with my smallest brush to develop small lumpy shapes—no need to add much detail.
- Some short blades of grass in the foreground. The key here is to use a super light touch and vary your brushstrokes—make some longer and some shorter and make them go in all different directions. I like to cluster some grass clumps together when I do this rather than spacing out each individual stroke.

Step 8 (optional)

We have some optional final details for the foreground which require gouache. First, mix up your white gouache with some Sap Green to make a lighter green color. Use this color and a detail brush to add more grass texture to the foreground, concentrating this detail at the very bottom of the page.

Next, use some plain white gouache to add random dots around the foreground. Cluster them together or spread them out randomly.

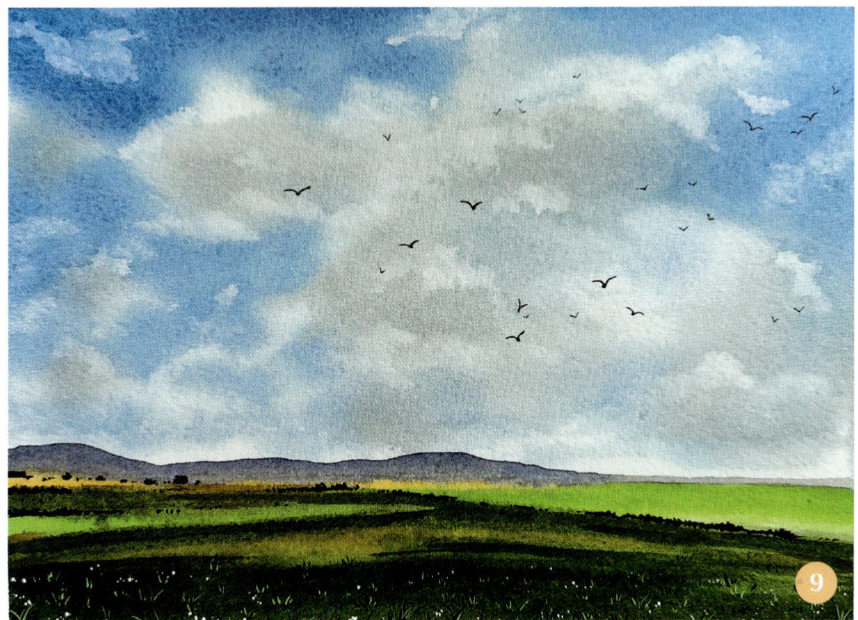

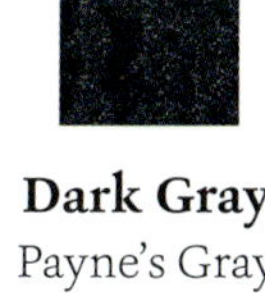

Dark Gray
Payne's Gray

This should look like some little wildflowers growing in the field. This isn't something that's in the reference photo, but I thought it would be cute and add interest to the piece.

Step 9

The final step is to add some birds flying in the sky. This also isn't in the reference photo, but I love adding birds to compositions with a lot of sky like this one. Use a Dark Gray color and your detail brush to add some little V shapes. A couple keys here:

- Change the angle of the V shapes. Some should be very shallow, and some should be more extreme. You can also change the orientation of the V shapes; make some of them lean one direction or the other.
- Make some larger and some much smaller. This is SO important in adding depth to the painting. It makes some birds look closer and some look far away.
- To the larger birds, add a small dot or short horizontal dash at the base of the V shape. This will look like the body of the bird.

Don't go overboard! It's so easy to just keep adding birds, but you will reach a "too many birds" point. I'd recommend pausing after making 20 birds of varying sizes and really examining if you need to add more.

And that's it! Take off the tape, sign and date your painting and admire your work!

yellowstone bison

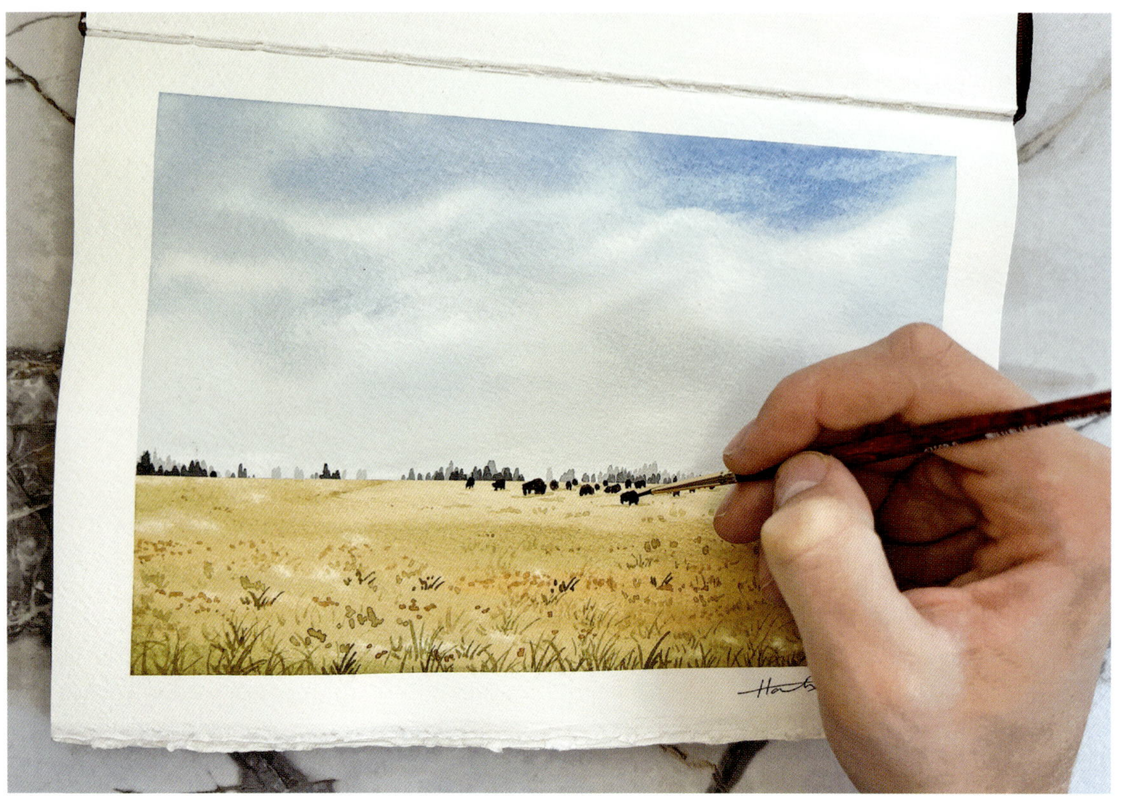

Yellowstone National Park is one of the coolest places I've ever visited, with vast grassy landscapes, mountains, colorful hot springs and bison roaming around everywhere! While having a quick lunch, I spied this herd of bison in the distance and took a few pictures. This fun project will give you even more practice with expansive skies, distance and perspective and a chance to try out painting some realistic-looking bison in the distance.

materials

Watercolor paints

- Yellow Ochre, Burnt Sienna, Sap Green, Ultramarine Blue, Phthalo Blue, Payne's Gray and Van Dyke Brown

Watercolor paper of your choice

- I used my cold press Fabriano Artistico sketchbook size 6 x 8.5 inches (15 x 21.5 cm)

Brushes

- one larger brush (I used a ½ inch oval), one medium brush (I used a size 4 round) and one detail brush (I used a size 0 round)

Orientation

- landscape

Set up your paper as you like and make sure to add a drop or two of water to your colors so they start to soften.

Reference photo

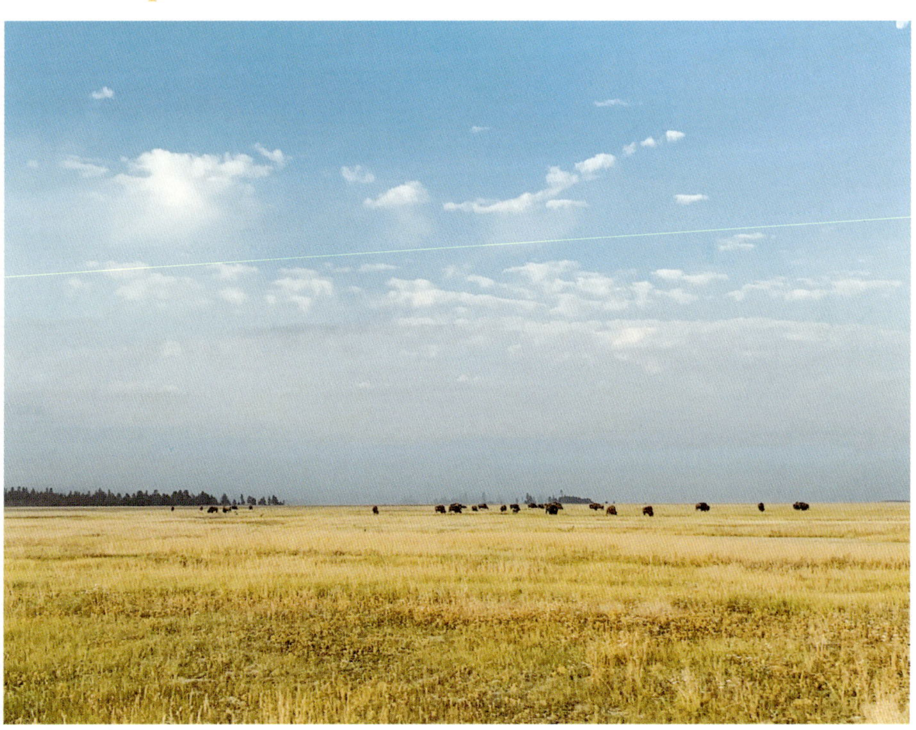

Sky Blue
Ultramarine Blue +
Phthalo Blue

Sketch

Draw a horizon line about one-third of the way from the bottom of the paper and feel free to add tape at the horizon line to get a straight line.

Step 1

As usual, we will start with the sky. This technique will be exactly the same as in the Rolling Hills project earlier in this chapter (on page 20), so feel free to refer back there for more detail. Mix your Sky Blue color first.

Using your large brush, cover the top section of paper (everything above the horizon line) with a layer of water. Then use sweeping motions to add in the Sky Blue paint, starting at the top of the page and working your way down. Allow your brush to run out of paint as you get close to the horizon line and leave a few pockets of white paper showing through.

Tilt your paper in different directions to blend the blue paint in with the clear water on the paper. Then, use a completely dry brush to lift the wet paint and add in some clouds. Pay attention to the reference photo here—these clouds are wispy and have lots of movement to them. Try to imitate that with your brush! Let this fully dry before moving on.

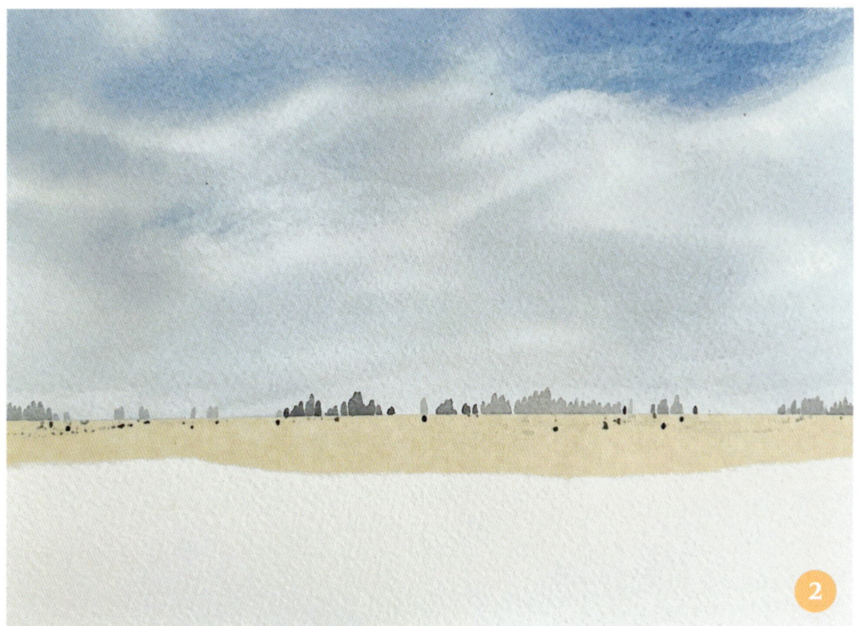

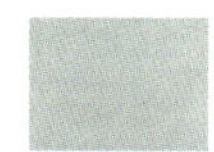

Light Gray-Green

Payne's Gray + Sap Green + Ultramarine Blue + more water

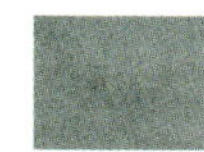

Dark Gray-Green

Payne's Gray + Sap Green + Ultramarine Blue + less water

Step 2

Next, we will add some distant trees. You'll need a gray-green color for this step, but you'll need two different saturations (amounts of water). Using a smaller brush (I used my 4 round), use the Light Gray-Green color and add a few distant trees right at the horizon line on your paper. Create these trees by painting short vertical brush strokes clumped together. Feel free to add as few or as many as you like, but I like leaving a few areas without trees.

Once the light gray trees have dried, use the Dark Gray-Green color to layer slightly darker trees on top of the previous ones. This adds depth to this section and makes some trees look closer and others look far away.

Once you're done adding trees, you can remove the tape at the horizon line. Fully dry this section before moving on.

Yellow
Yellow Ochre + little Van Dyke Brown + water

Orange
Burnt Sienna + Yellow Ochre

Green
Sap Green + Van Dyke Brown + Yellow Ochre

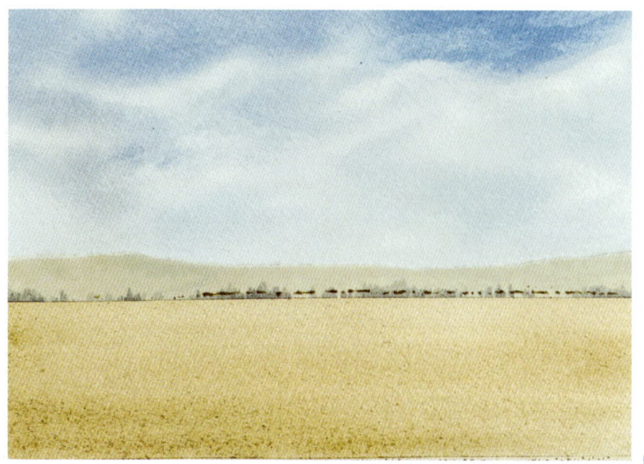

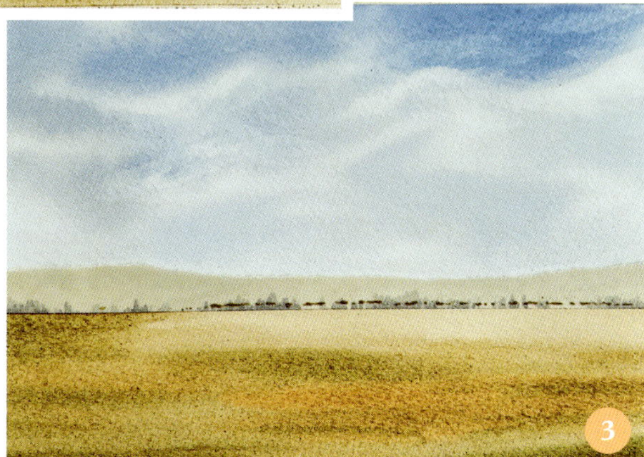

Step 3

Next, we will add our first layer of the grassy field. Mix the Yellow, Orange and Green colors swatched above before starting on this step. Use a big brush and cover the entire bottom section with the Yellow color. While it's still wet, sweep the Orange color over the Yellow in a few places to add variety. Clean your brush and do the same with the Green color. I concentrated the Green in the bottom half of the grass section, but feel free to put it wherever you feel like it! Before this section dries, use a completely dry brush to pick up the paint from a few spots to add highlights.

Step 4

Now we will start adding details to the grassy field using the same colors from Step 3. Use your smallest detail brush and start adding in little clusters of dots with the Orange color to look like distant bushes or grasses. Use the Green to add small tufts of grass, plus some larger grass blades at the very bottom of the painting.

There shouldn't be any details in the top third of the grassy section. Then there should be small suggestions of detail in the middle third, and then your more obvious grasses and bushes can be painted in the bottom third of this section. This will give the effect of distance in the painting!

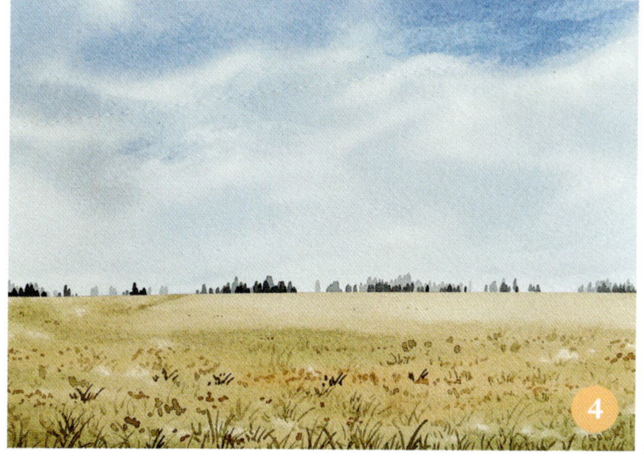

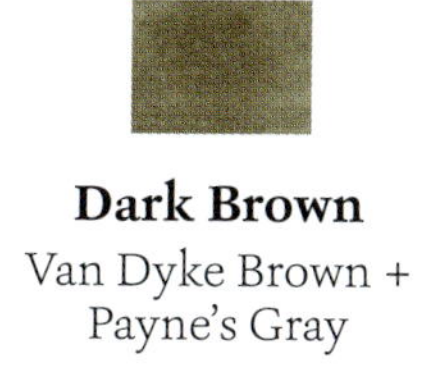

Dark Brown
Van Dyke Brown +
Payne's Gray

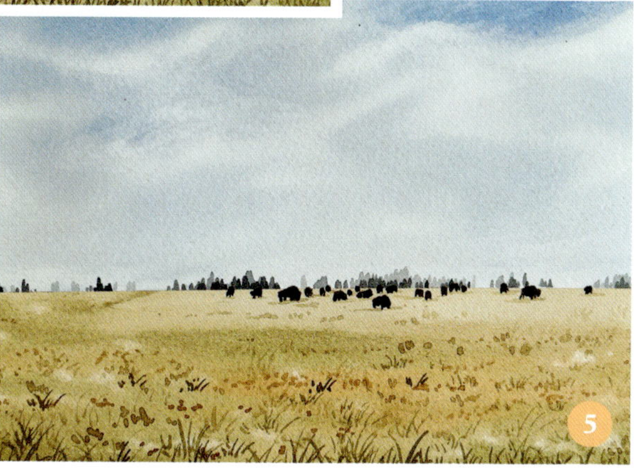

Step 5

The last step of this painting is to add our herd of bison! Don't panic–since these bison are quite far away, we won't have to include too much detail for them to look like bison. First, mix the Dark Brown color shown above and grab your detail brush (I used my 0 round).

The bison that are facing away or toward us can be painted simply as small vertical ovals with two legs. You can also add a few laying down by painting little lumps without legs. The ones facing sideways are horizontal ovals, plus a small vertical oval on one side for the head, plus four legs. Add as many or as few as you like, concentrating them closer to the horizon line. Add them in clusters, add a few on their own, make a few overlap, etc.

For the final details, use a bit of the Yellow color from Step 3 and a detail brush to add a small horizontal line under each bison to give them shadows and integrate them into the landscape.

Once you're happy with your bison, you're all done! Take off the tape, sign and date your painting and admire your work!

golden palouse

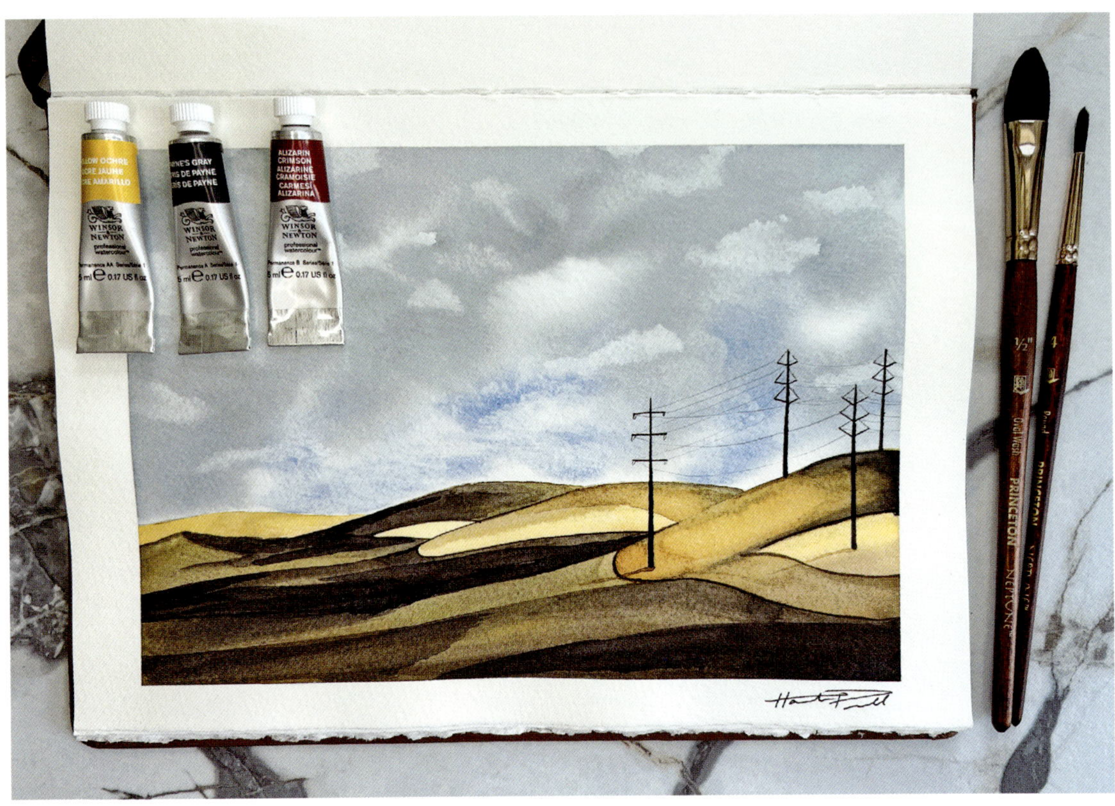

The Palouse region is a unique area located in southeastern Washington and south central Idaho, the homelands of the Palus and Nez Perce peoples. The beautiful rolling hills seem to go on forever, with only the occasional barn or farmhouse to break up the vast stretches of grasslands and wheat fields. This land is a stark contrast to the temperate rainforests and mountains of Western Washington. Our reference photo for this project features those golden rolling hills and a dramatic cloudy sky, with a few telephone pole details. We will be practicing the wet-on-wet technique for the sky, and a layering technique for the foreground.

materials

Watercolor paints

- Cadmium Yellow, Yellow Ochre, Burnt Sienna, Alizarin Crimson, Ultramarine Blue, Van Dyke Brown and Payne's Gray

Watercolor paper of your choice

- I used my cold press Fabriano Artistico sketchbook size 6 x 8.5 inches (15 x 21.5 cm)

Brushes

- one larger brush (I used a ½ inch oval) and one detail brush (I used a size 0 round)

Orientation

- landscape

Set up your paper as you like and make sure to add a drop or two of water to your colors so they start to soften.

Reference photo

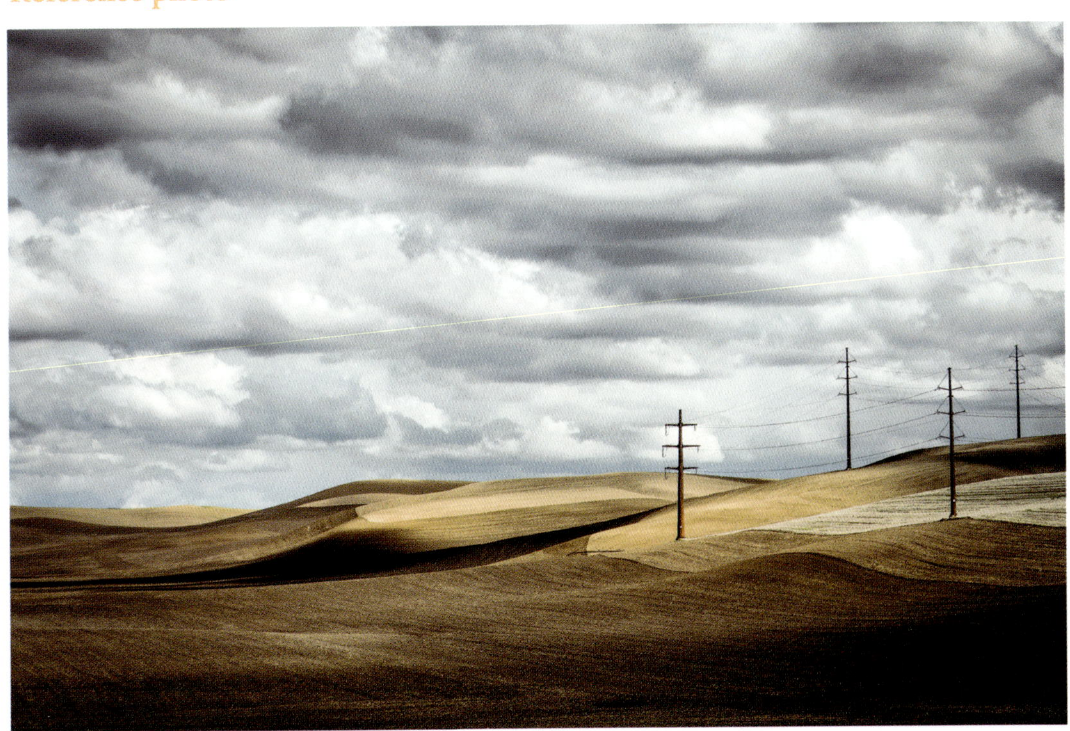

Gray
Payne's Gray + a little Van Dyke Brown

Blue
Ultramarine Blue

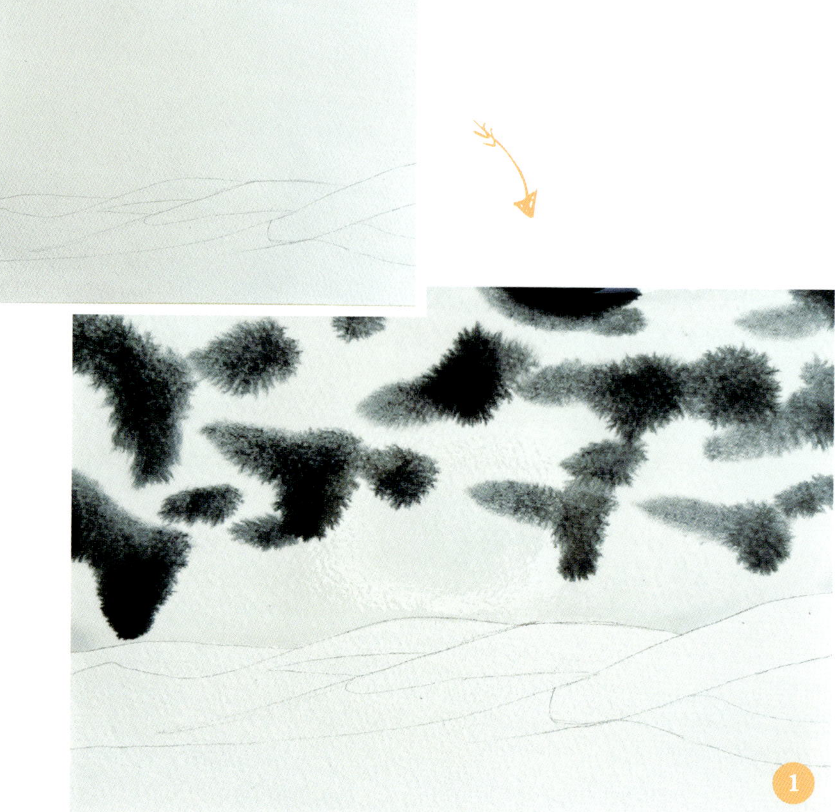

Sketch

Sketch the rolling hills about one-third of the way up the paper and focus on finding a few major shapes in the reference photo to bring into the painting. It might be tempting to try to recreate every shape you see, but we want to simplify this reference a bit. Squint your eyes to pick out the most obvious shapes and bring those to your paper. Don't sketch the telephone poles yet—we'll do that at the end. Once you're happy with the sketch, lighten your lines with an eraser.

Step 1

As usual, we will start with the sky section, following a similar procedure as in the Oregon Plains project earlier in this chapter (see page 28). Prepare your Gray and Blue colors first.

Cover the paper above the rolling hills with a layer of water. Pick up your Gray color and start adding short sweeping strokes in the sky section, making sure to leave some areas blank.

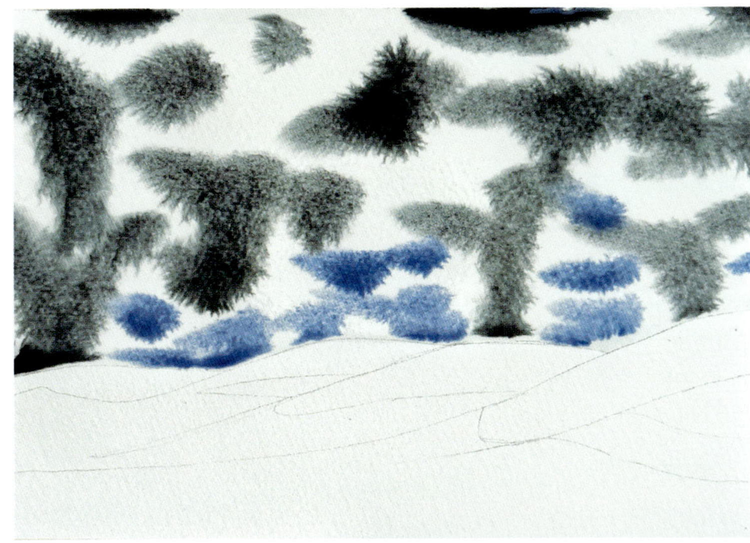

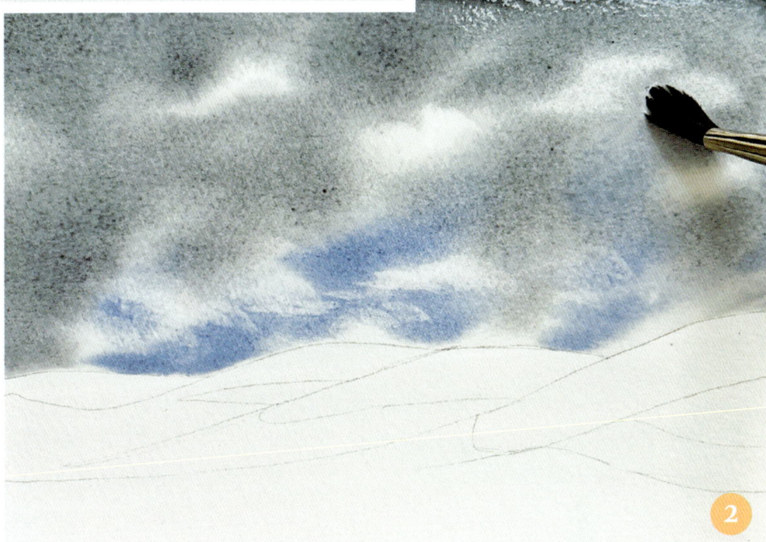

Step 2

Once you've added enough Gray, add a few strokes of Blue closer to the horizon.

Now you can tilt your paper in different directions to blend the colors more or use a clean damp brush to blend (still making sure to leave some lighter spots).

Use a completely dry brush to pick up some paint and create cloud shapes. I like to use a tapping motion with my brush to create fluffy clouds. Fully dry this section before moving on.

Yellow
Cadmium Yellow + Yellow Ochre + water

Orange
Yellow Ochre + Burnt Sienna + water

Brown
Burnt Sienna + Van Dyke Brown + water

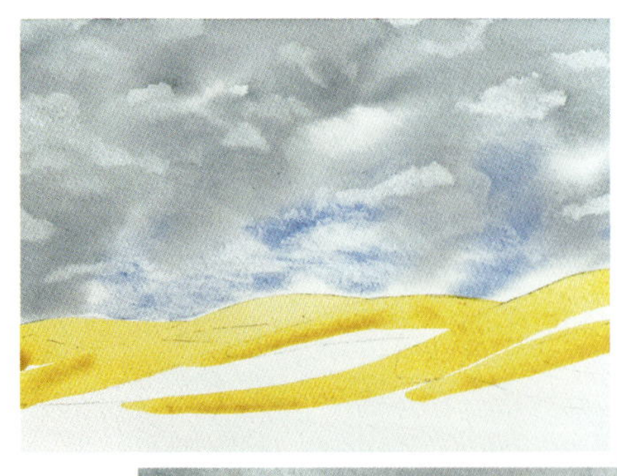

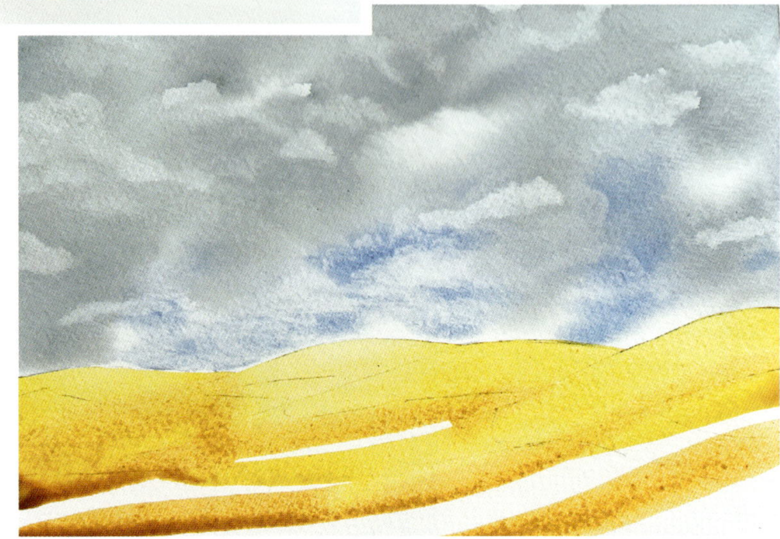

Step 3

We will work on our first layer of the rolling hills. You'll need three colors for this section: Yellow, Orange and Brown.

PAUSE: Please read through the following instructions before you start so you can work quickly without stopping to read.

First, take a look at your reference photo. Make a mental note of the areas that are lightest in value, the midtone areas and the darkest areas. Use a larger brush to sweep the Yellow color where you want the lightest areas to be. Make sure to follow the contours and direction of the rolling hills with your brush strokes.

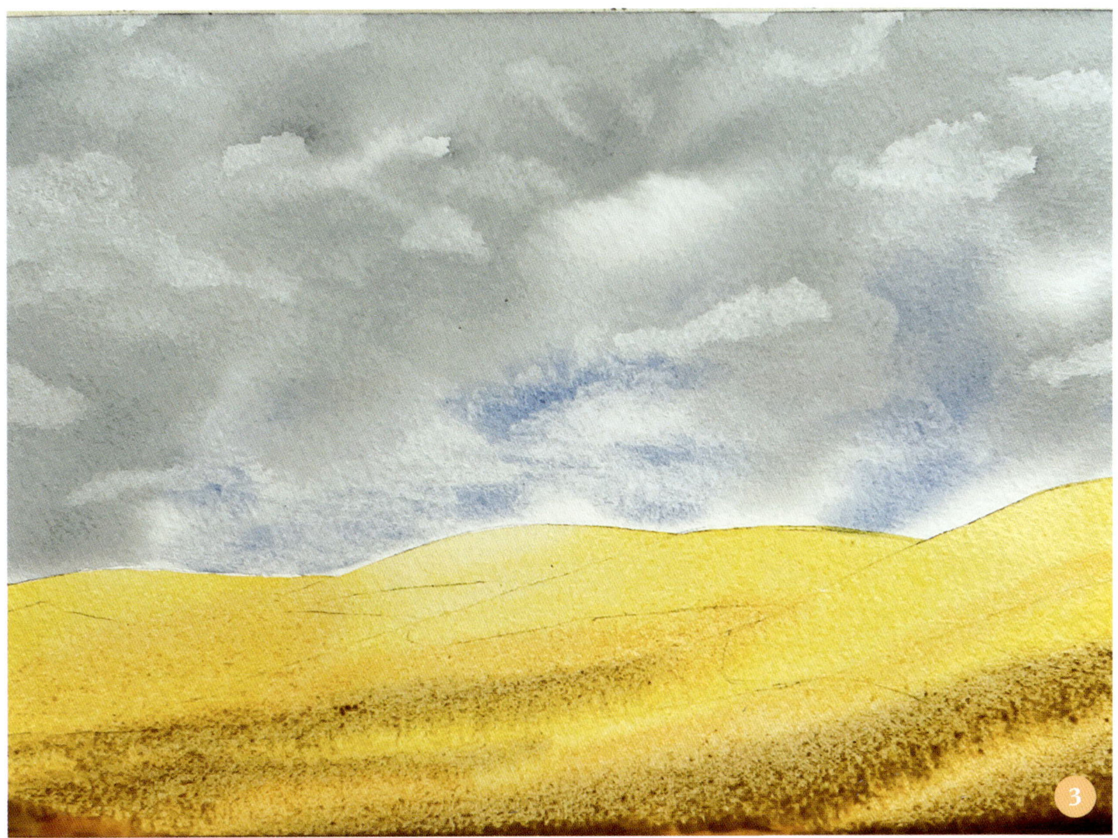

Without washing your brush, pick up your Orange color and use it to add some midtones. The Orange should blend with the Yellow in places where they meet.

Finally, take your Brown color and fill in the rest of the rolling fields where you see some darker areas and shadows. Your colors should all be blending together a bit, though it's okay if you have areas that don't blend.

Fully dry this section before moving on.

Dark Brown
Burnt Sienna +
Van Dyke Brown +
little Ultramarine
Blue

Purple
Burnt Sienna +
Alizarin Crimson +
Ultramarine Blue

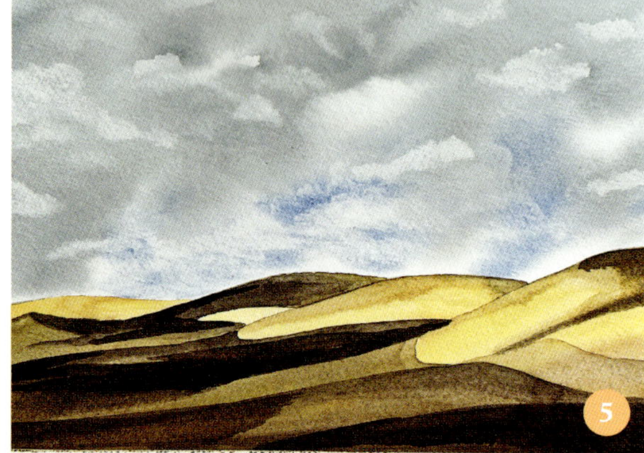

Step 4

Next, we will add some shadows and dimensions to these hills with a Dark Brown color. Use the same Brown color that you used in Step 3 but add a little Ultramarine Blue to darken it.

Now, take a look at the reference photo and notice where the main shadows are: mostly on the left side of the page with some shadows in between the hills. Lay down a flat wash of Dark Brown everywhere there are shadows. Feel free to water down this color a bit if you need a lighter shadow in certain areas.

Fully dry this section before moving on.

Step 5

To define the shadow areas even more, mix a dark Purple color. Since purple is the complementary color of yellow, this will provide a really nice contrast between the purple shadows and yellow highlights of the hills.

Use this Purple color to add depth to the areas where you want the darkest shadows. I did this in a few places in between the hills and a small section towards the bottom of the page. You can leave the sharp edges of these shadow shapes, or you can use a clean damp brush to softly blend one or more edges of those shadow shapes while they're still wet.

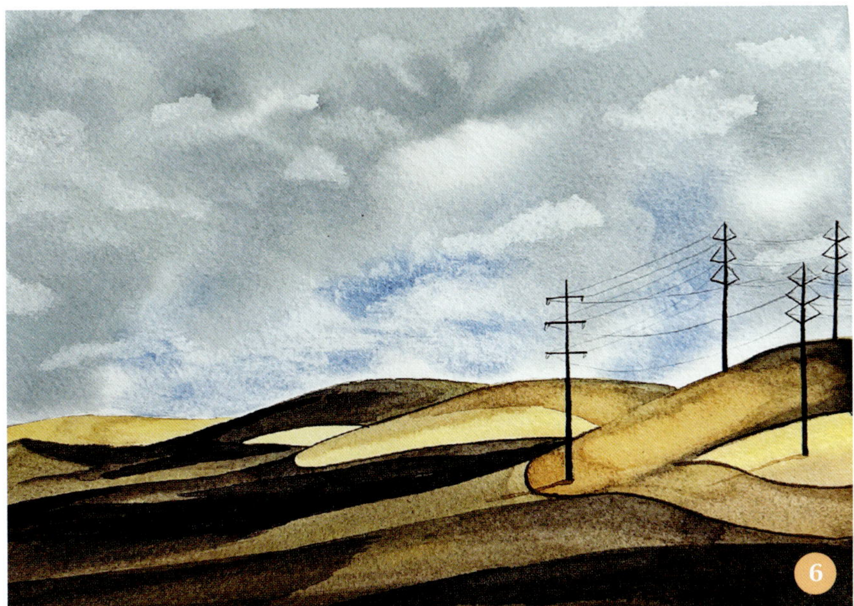

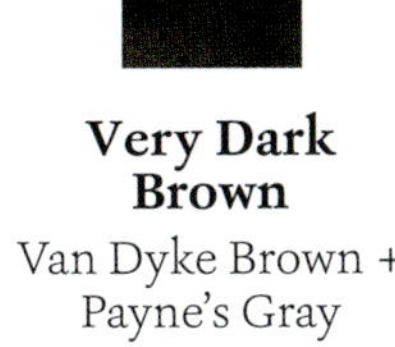

Very Dark Brown
Van Dyke Brown +
Payne's Gray

Step 6

Now on to our final details. If you wish, you can use any of the previous colors to add more details to the lighter areas of the hills. I used the Orange and Brown colors from Step 3 to define and darken a couple of areas, using the reference photo to guide me. Make sure you dry any details you add here before moving on.

Finally, mix up a Very Dark Brown and use your smallest detail brush to paint in the telephone pole shapes. You're welcome to sketch these out first if that helps you. Use the reference photo as a guide while doing this.

For the wires between the telephone poles, **water down the Dark Brown color you just used**. This will help the wires look thin and far away. Then use your smallest brush to paint in a few of the wires between the poles. Don't feel like you have to paint every single one–just a few is enough of a suggestion.

Take off the tape, sign and date your painting and admire your work!

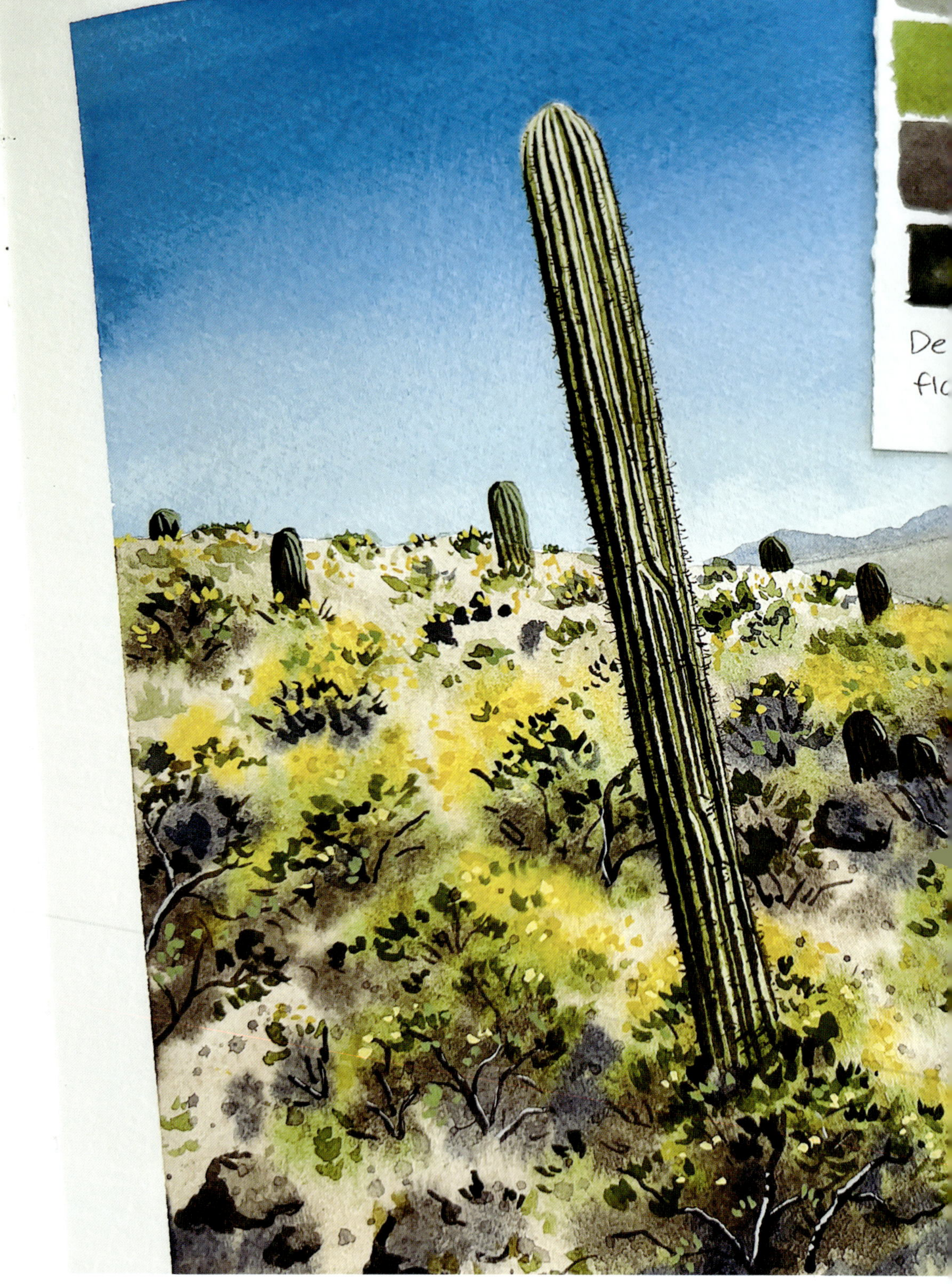

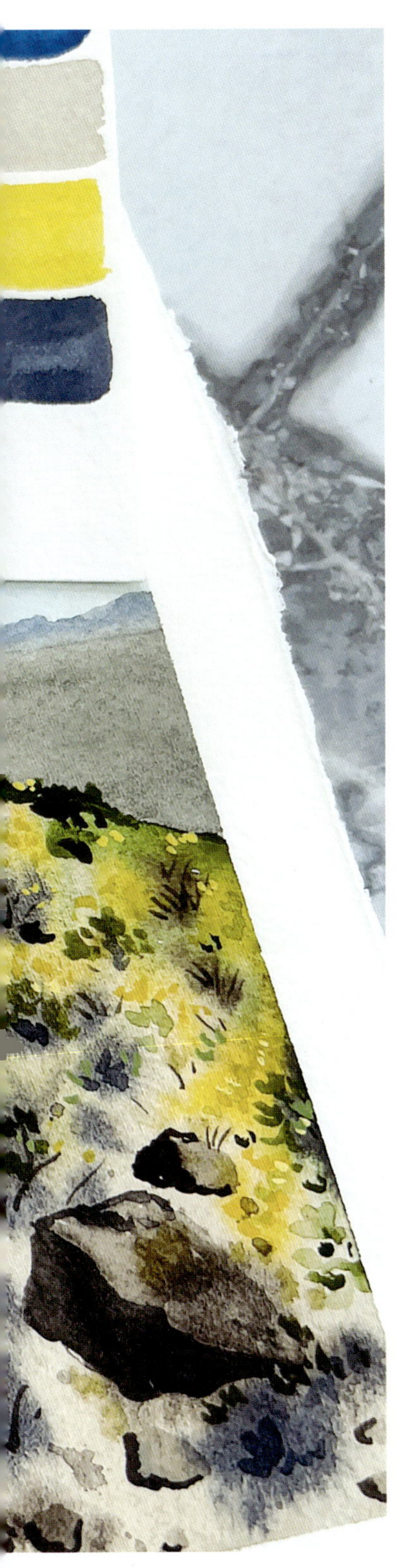

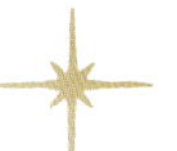

chapter 3 desert lands

The next destination in our watercolor journey is the desert. There are many different kinds of deserts, from completely dry, arid landscapes like those in northern Africa, to lusher landscapes like the Sonoran Desert in Arizona. These landscapes are so unique and fun to paint, and I did my best to give you a good variety in this chapter. We'll be using lots of dry brushing in this chapter, so feel free to brush up (pun definitely intended) on that technique on page 16. I hope you enjoy working your way through these desert landscapes with me!

moroccan sand dunes

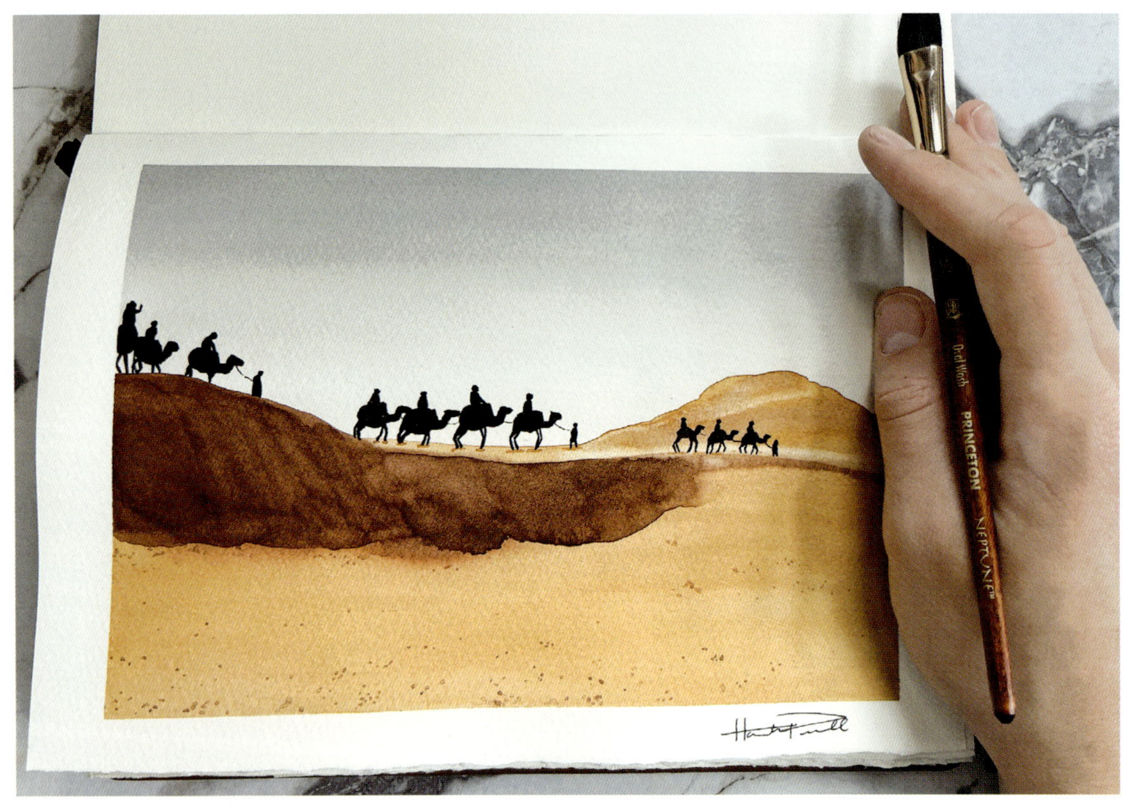

I absolutely love the simplicity of this reference photo—the vibrant orange sand dunes contrast so well with the gray sky, and I just love the lines of camels walking across the scene. These types of landscapes, while simple, are super pleasing to the viewer (in my opinion). Plus, creating those sharp shadow shapes in the sand dunes really make them look three-dimensional. I hope you enjoy creating this desert scene with me!

materials

Watercolor paints

- Yellow Ochre, Cadmium Red, Burnt Sienna, Ultramarine Blue, Payne's Gray and Van Dyke Brown

Watercolor paper of your choice

- I used my cold press Fabriano Artistico sketchbook size 6 x 8.5 inches (15 x 21.5 cm)

Brushes

- one larger brush (I used a ½ inch oval) and one detail brush (I used a size 0 round)

Orientation

- landscape

Set up your paper as you like and make sure to add a drop or two of water to your colors so they start to soften.

Reference photo

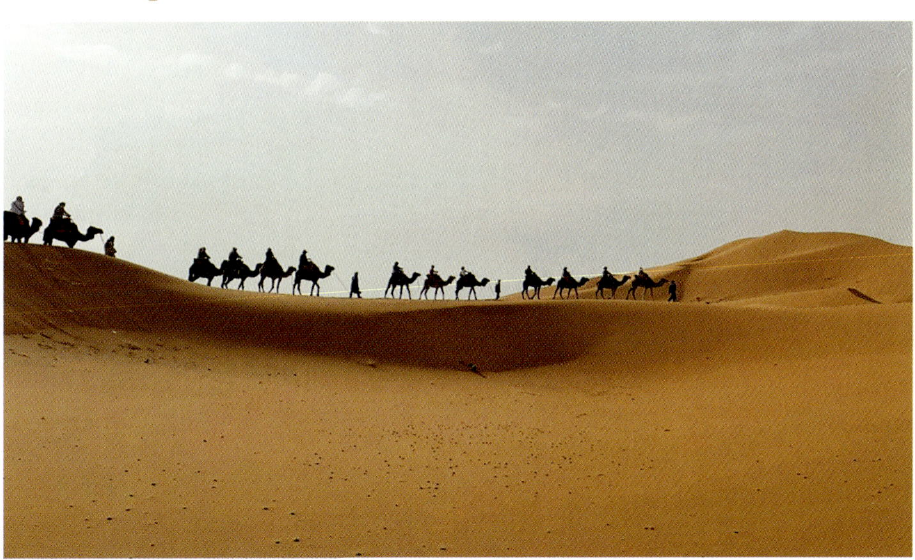

Gray
Payne's Gray + little Burnt Sienna + little Ultramarine Blue + water

Sketch

If you prefer, sketch out the outline of the sand dune and the shadow shapes. I chose to just paint the dunes directly on the paper without sketching, but you're welcome to sketch first if that's more comfortable for you!

Step 1

Let's start with that light gray sky in the background. First, mix up a warm Gray color for the sky.

Use a large brush and create a gradient, starting with the original Gray color at the top and fading to the white paper about halfway down the page. If you need additional details for this step, check out page 15, and just use this Gray color instead of Blue.

Let this fully dry before moving on.

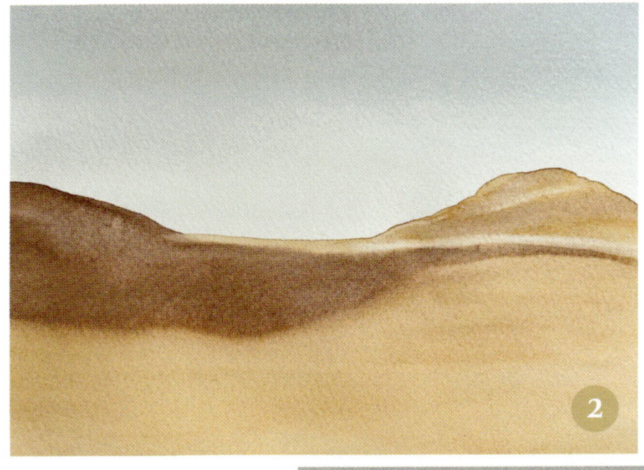

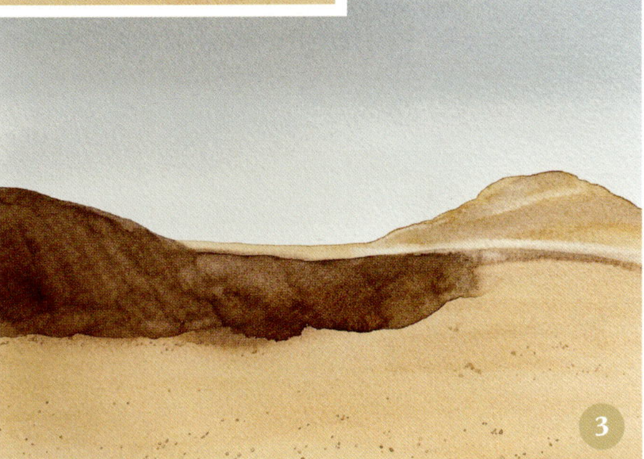

Rust
Yellow Ochre + little Cadmium Red + little Van Dyke Brown + little Ultramarine Blue

Orange
Yellow Ochre + little Cadmium Red + little Burnt Sienna

Step 2

Mix up a Rust and an Orange color for the sand dunes.

Use your large brush and the Rust color to paint in the general shadow shape you can see in the left side of the reference photo about halfway up the paper. Then use the Orange color to fill in everything else, including the little hill on the right side of the page and the rest of the dunes to the bottom of the paper. The colors should bleed together a bit.

While this is still wet, you can use a dry brush to pick up some highlights along the ridge of the sand dune, as well as in the little hill in the distance to add some dimension.

Let this fully dry before moving on.

Step 3

Use the same Rust color from the previous step to create a sharper and more saturated shadow shape.

Also, add some sand texture at the very bottom of the page. Using a detail brush and the Rust color, dot randomly around the bottom fourth of the page.

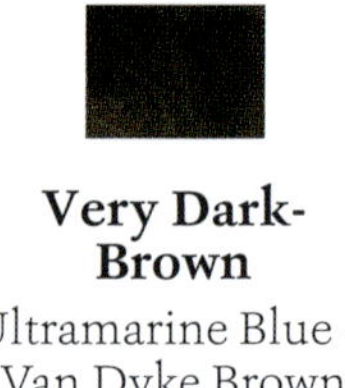

Very Dark-Brown
Ultramarine Blue + Van Dyke Brown

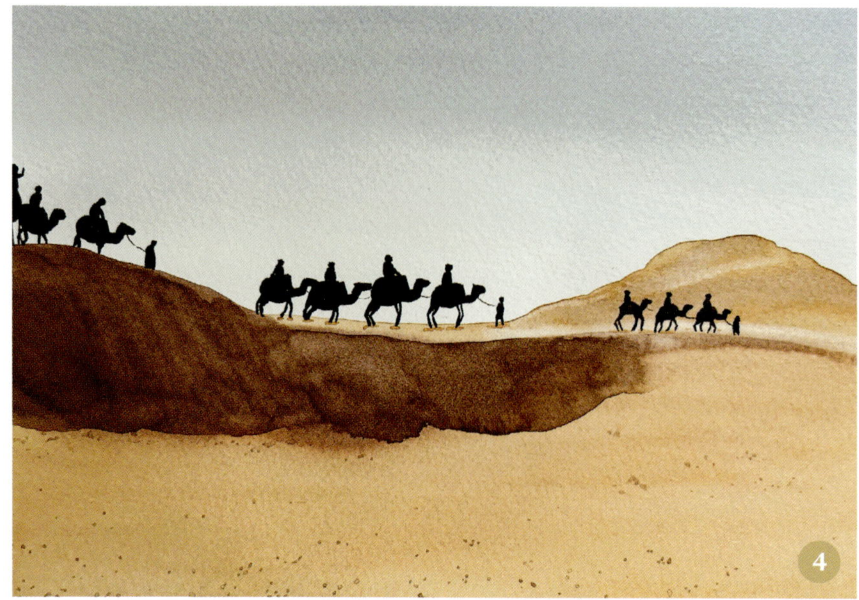

Step 4

Now let's add the main focal point of this piece: the camel silhouettes walking along the ridge of the sand dune. For this, I used a Very Dark Brown color. I started on the left side of the page (where the camels are closest to us and thus the largest) and used a detail brush to work my way from left to right, making the camels smaller as I went. I've included a small sketch with the general shapes I used:

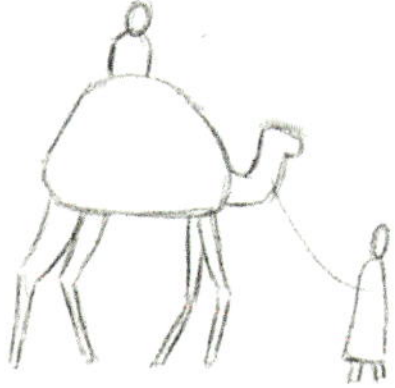

The main body of the camel is like a rock shape, with an "S" shape for the neck and head. The legs are long and skinny, with the back legs bending backwards and the front legs bending forward. I used a small oval and a narrow tombstone shape for the people riding the camels. You can follow this main blueprint for each of the camels and just change up the shape and leg position slightly each time. I painted these straight onto my paper, but you are welcome to start with a pencil sketch or practice on scrap paper if that's more comfortable for you.

Don't feel like you need to include every camel in the reference photo. I left some out, and I'd recommend the same for you! These may feel or look weird to you when you've only painted one or two, but I promise, as long as you're getting the general shape, they will look way more realistic once you're done!

Once you're happy with the camels you've painted, you're all done with this painting! Take off the tape, sign and date your painting and admire your work!

the grandest canyon

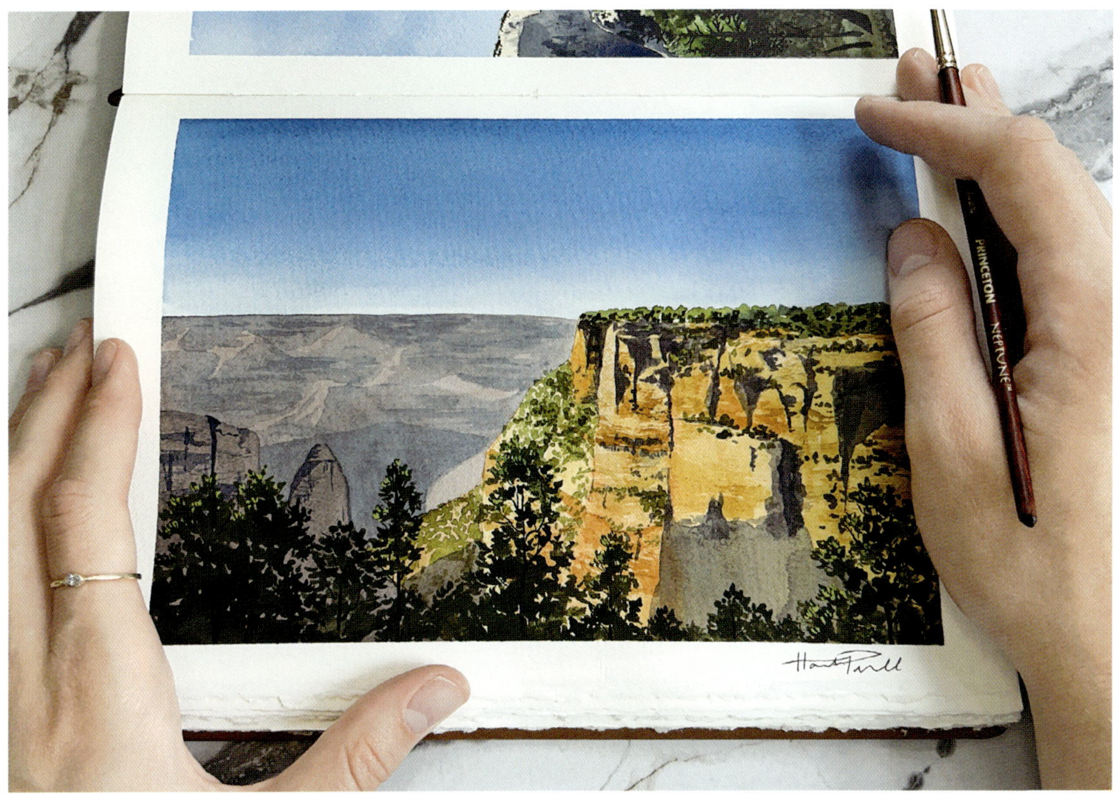

The Grand Canyon can be an incredibly difficult subject to capture in photographs or paintings. It's so hard to portray the grandiosity of the landscape, and the colors are often quite similar to each other so the details can be difficult to paint. Luckily, my dad took this reference photo (page 58) at sunset, which provides us with interesting light and color contrast. This will help us immensely in our quest to paint the Grand Canyon.

materials

Watercolor paints

- Yellow Ochre, Cadmium Red, Alizarin Crimson, Sap Green, Phthalo Blue, Ultramarine Blue and Van Dyke Brown
- White gouache (optional)

Watercolor paper of your choice

- I used my cold press Fabriano Artistico sketchbook size 6 x 8.5 inches (15 x 21.5 cm)

Brushes

- one larger brush (I used a ½ inch oval), one medium brush (I used 4 round) and one detail brush (I used a size 0 round)

Orientation

- landscape

Set up your paper as you like and make sure to add a drop or two of water to your colors so they start to soften.

Reference photo

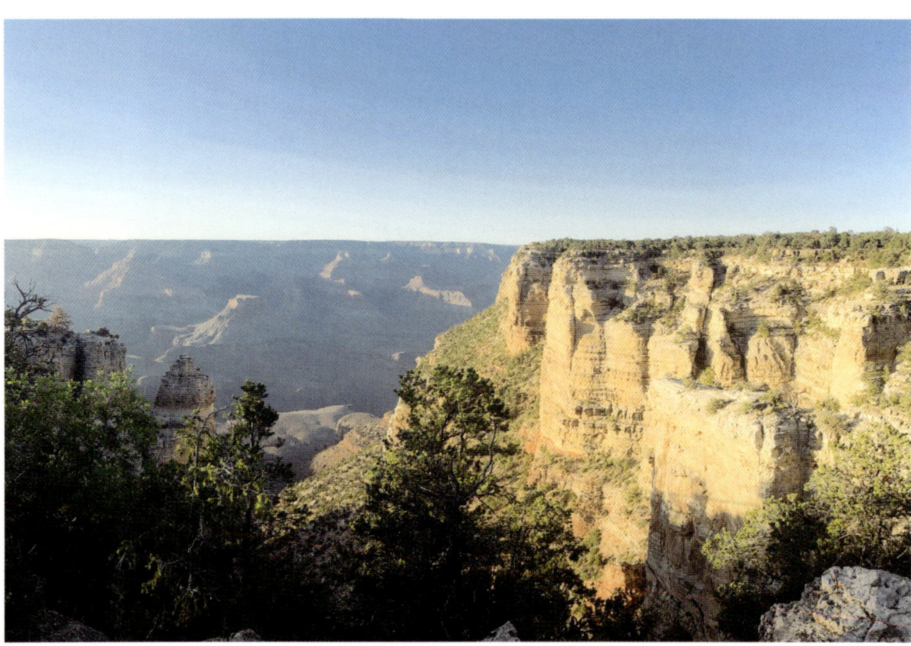

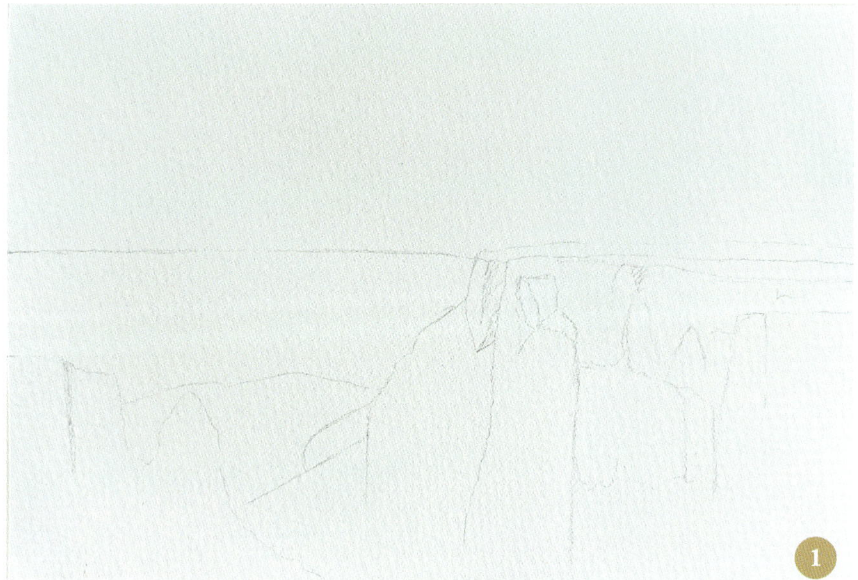

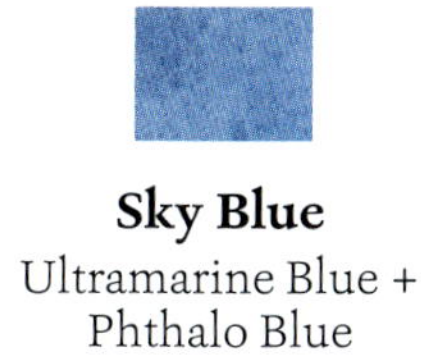

Sky Blue
Ultramarine Blue +
Phthalo Blue

Sketch

Sketch the horizon line a bit above halfway up the paper and the land formation on the right side of the composition, as well as the closer land formation on the bottom left if you want (it's somewhat hidden, so feel free to ignore it for simplicity). Feel free to lightly shade in some of the shadow shapes with your pencil here–those will be covered up with paint later.

Step 1

First, mix your Sky Blue. Add a little water to this mixture as well, and make sure you mix enough paint to cover your paper!

NOTE: One of the best backgrounds for any landscape is a clear blue sky. Having such a simple background allows the foreground to draw more attention, and it creates a sunny, warm feeling for the entire painting. In this project, we will practice painting a clear blue sky that lightens toward the horizon. This important detail gives the painting "atmospheric perspective," which is the feeling of distance and depth in a painting.

PAUSE: Please read through Steps 2–4 before you start so that you can work quickly without stopping to read.

Step 2

Load up a large brush with your blue paint. Start at the top of your paper and work your way down the sky section using horizontal stripes. Make sure to work somewhat quickly; if you take too long, the paint will start to dry, and you will end up with texture or streaks in your sky.

Step 3

After you've filled in about half of your sky section, pause and quickly add some water to the Sky Blue paint you have left. Continue your horizontal stripes with this watered-down Sky Blue until you're close to the horizon line.

Step 4

Once you are almost to the horizon line, rinse off your brush but don't dry it. Use this clean, wet brush for your last horizontal strokes to cover the rest of the sky section. This extra water should pull down a bit of the Sky Blue paint above it but remain fairly light, which gives the sky that atmospheric perspective that we talked about earlier.

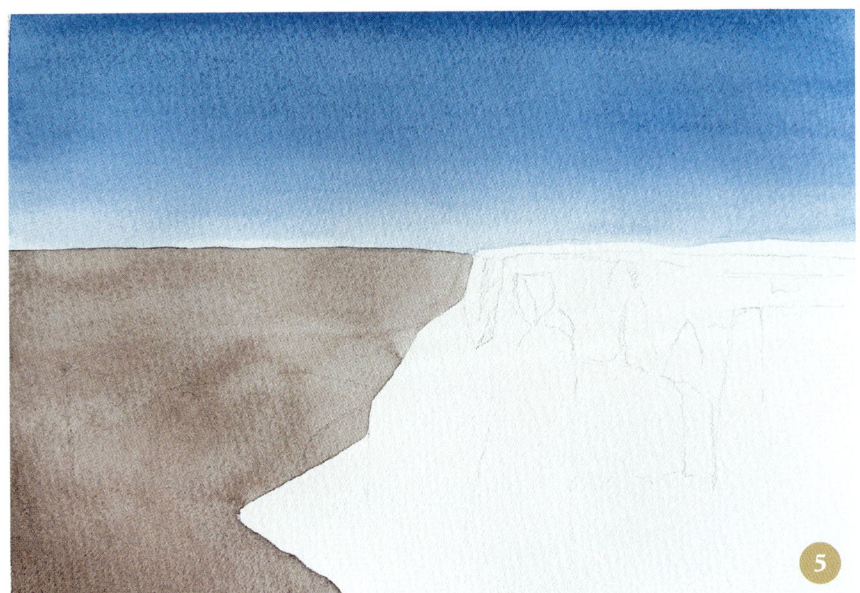

Warm Gray
Alizarin Crimson + Van Dyke Brown + Ultramarine Blue + water

Yellow
Yellow Ochre + water

If you notice some significant streaks or unevenness, and your painting is still wet, you can work in horizontal strokes with a clean, damp brush from bottom to top to blend. You **cannot** do this once some of the painting is dry, so check the reflection off the paper to see if it is still wet. I'd only recommend doing this once—after that you'll likely end up with more texture than less. It's okay to have some inconsistencies or streaks in your sky; once you paint in the foreground, they become much less noticeable.

Let this fully dry before moving on.

Step 5

Next, let's block in the general colors of the landscape. Mix a Warm Gray color and a Yellow color. Use the Warm Gray color and a large brush to fill in everything except the land formation on the right side of the composition with a flat wash. Let it dry completely, then use the Yellow color to fill in the land formation on the right with a flat wash.

Let this fully dry before moving on.

Lavender
Warm Gray + little Ultramarine Blue

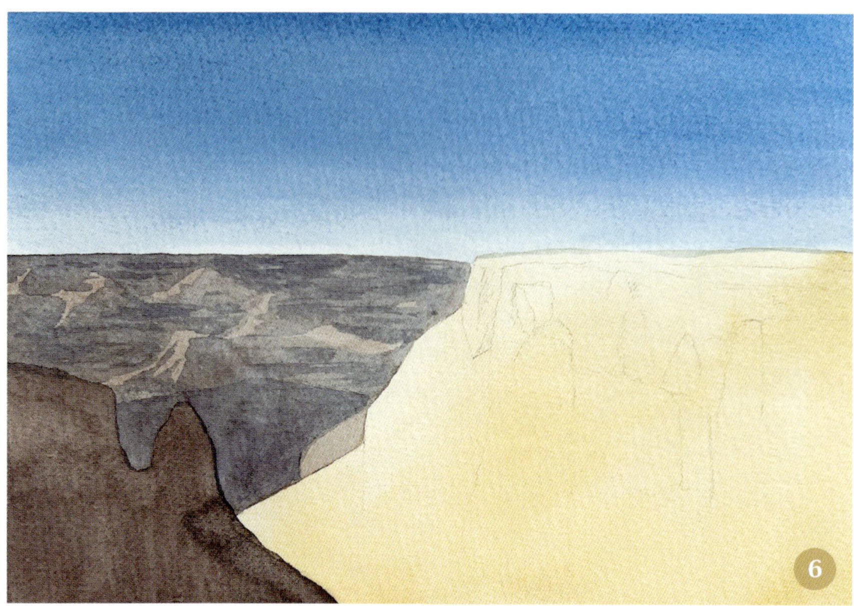

Step 6

Next, mix a little Ultramarine Blue into the Warm Gray color from Step 5 to create a Lavender color.

Take a look at the reference photo here. Notice how the contours of the distant canyon are very subtle, basically just a few hills and valleys in the distance. Use a smaller brush and your new color to pick out a few of these hills and contours. Don't overthink it here–leave a few spaces blank as "highlights" where the Warm Gray color shows through, and paint around those blank spaces to create shadows. Feel free to add some horizontal strokes and/or dry brushing strokes to add to the texture.

You can also use this color as a flat wash on that smaller land formation at the bottom right (if you included it); this will darken it and bring it closer to the foreground.

Step 7

Now let's work on the foreground a bit. Use the Yellow color from Step 5, plus the four colors swatched on page 63. With the Light Green and Dark Green colors and a detail brush, let's start adding some of the shrubs growing on top of the rock formation. I like to start with the Light Green and use a dotting motion to fill up the space, then switch to the Dark Green and continue dotting to add some detail and shadow. Do this all over the top of the right-side rock formation, as well as on the sloped ledges.

Next, use the Blue-Gray color to start picking out the shadows and crevices on the rock face. Do this with both of the foreground rock formations.

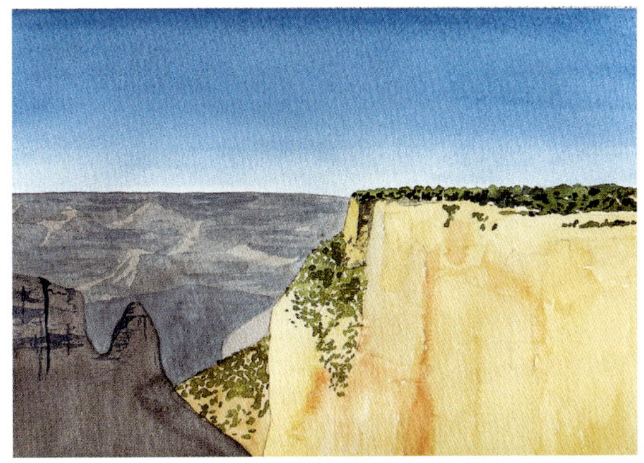

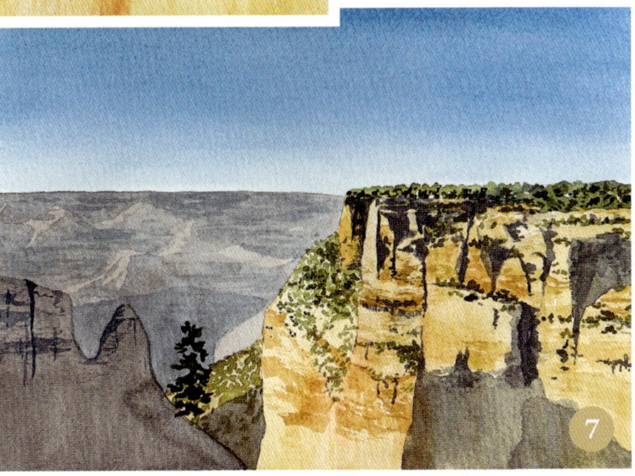

Light Green
Sap Green + Yellow Ochre

Dark Green
Sap Green + Ultramarine Blue + Van Dyke Brown

Blue-Gray
Ultramarine Blue + little Van Dyke Brown

Orange
Yellow Ochre + Cadmium Red

Use the reference photo here to help you pick out the shapes and locations of these crevices but feel free to deviate from the reference and add more or fewer details here. You can also water down this color for lighter shadows and textures!

Finally, use the Yellow (from Step 5) and Orange colors to add some extra texture to the rock face. I used a dry brushing technique (see page 16) with my 4 round brush to scrape the paint along the paper, following the contours of the rock. You can also add flat washes of Orange and Yellow in certain areas to increase the saturation.

Continue with this combination of details until you're happy with how the rock formations look. Don't worry too much about what's happening at the bottom of the paper; this will be covered with trees in the next step.

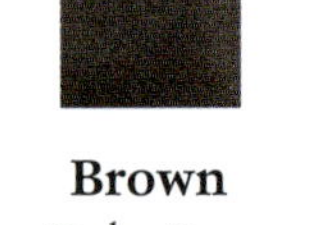

Brown
Van Dyke Brown +
little Payne's Gray

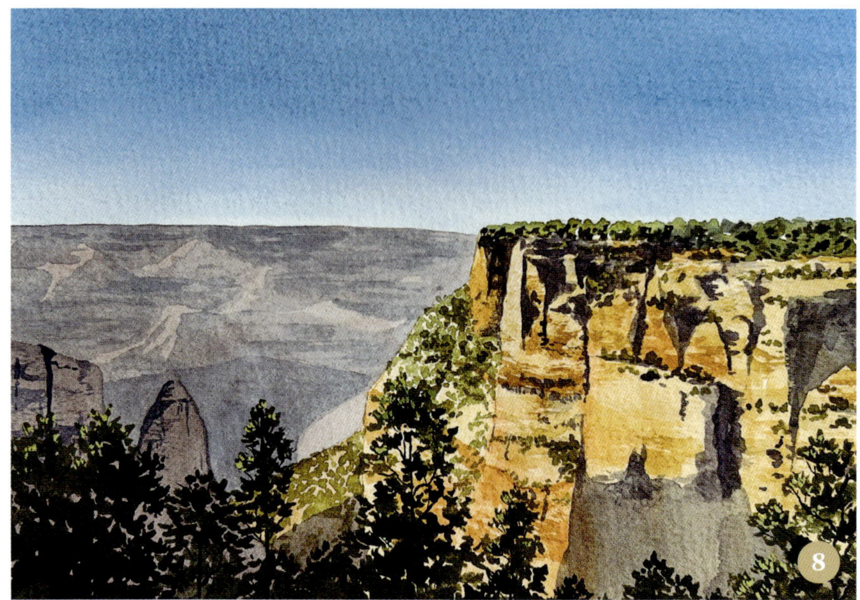

Step 8

Use the same Dark Green from Step 7 to create the trees at the very bottom of the page. I like to use my detail brush and dot in some clumps in the general shape of the tree, leaving room for the trunk or branches to peek through later.

Mix up a Brown color to add a trunk and some branches peeking through the leaves of each of these trees.

Finally, if you want a little extra sparkle, mix your white gouache with Sap Green, and add a few dots of this opaque light green to the tops of your trees with a detail brush!

Once you're happy with your trees take off the tape, sign and date your painting and admire your work!

sedona courthouse butte

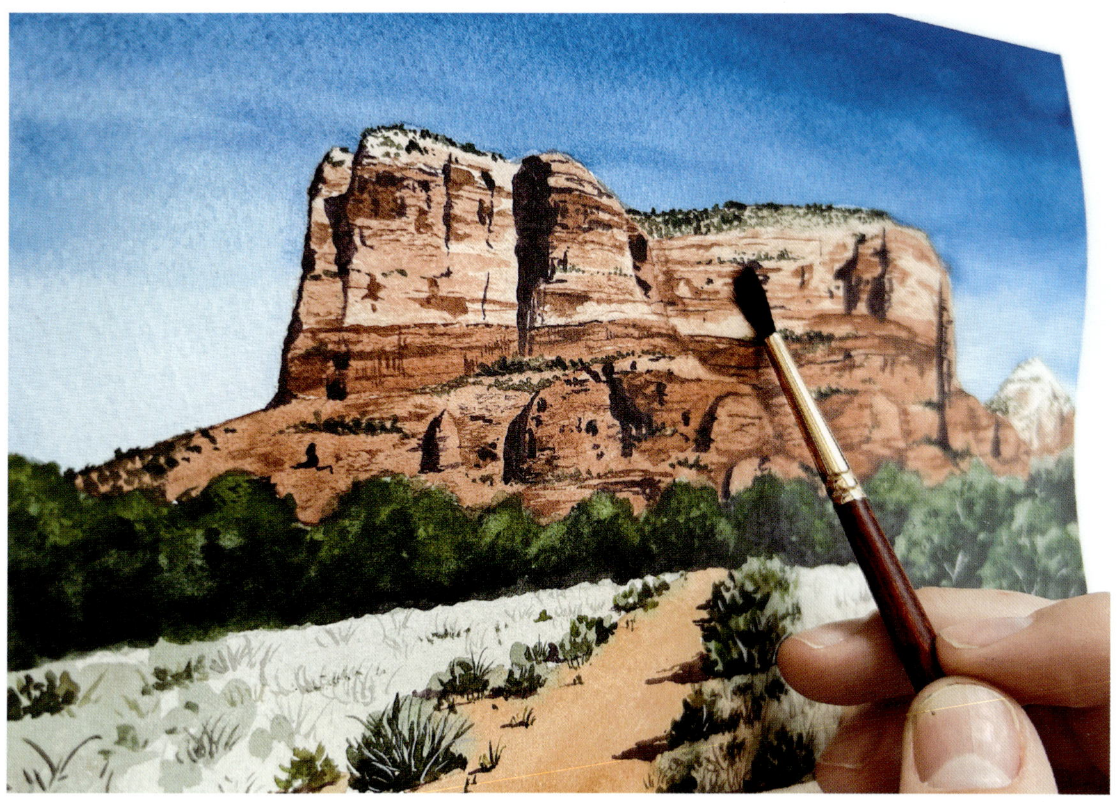

I like big buttes, and I cannot lie! Courthouse Butte is located in Sedona, Arizona, where there's an abundance of impressive landscapes like this. Rock formations like these are incredibly fun to paint; you'll get lots of practice with dry brushing and with building up color and contrast to make the formation look three-dimensional. And though landscapes like these may seem intimidating at first, I promise we'll break it down into doable steps. Walk with me . . .

materials

Watercolor paints

- Yellow Ochre, Cadmium Red, Burnt Sienna, Sap Green, Ultramarine Blue, Phthalo Blue and Van Dyke Brown
- White gouache (optional)

Watercolor paper of your choice

- I used my cold press Fabriano Artistico sketchbook size size 6 x 8.5 inches (15 x 21.5 cm)

Brushes

- one larger brush (I used a ½ inch oval), one medium brush (I used 4 round) and one detail brush (I used a size 0 round)

Orientation

- landscape

Set up your paper as you like and make sure to add a drop or two of water to your colors so they start to soften.

Reference photo

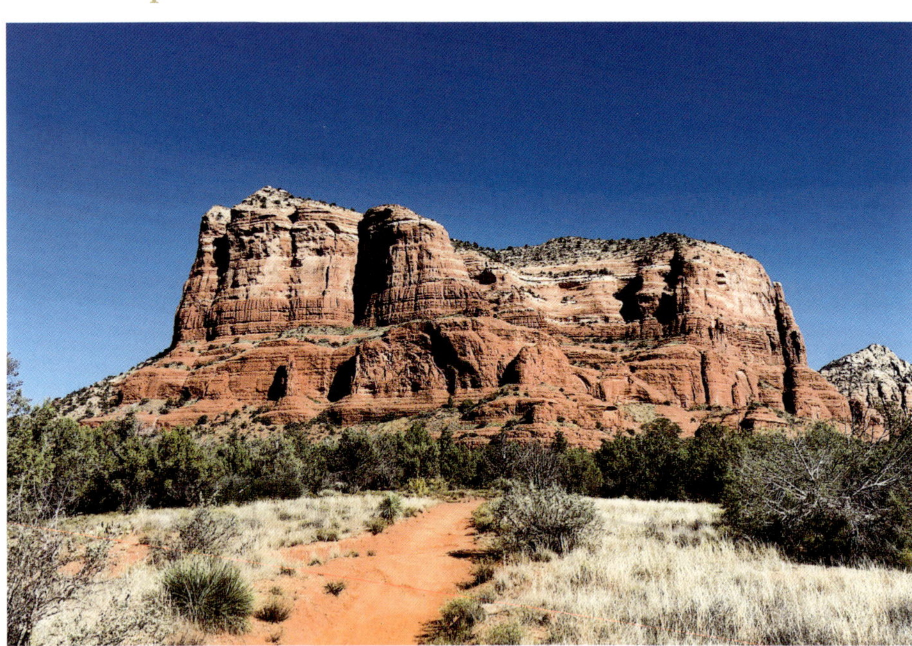

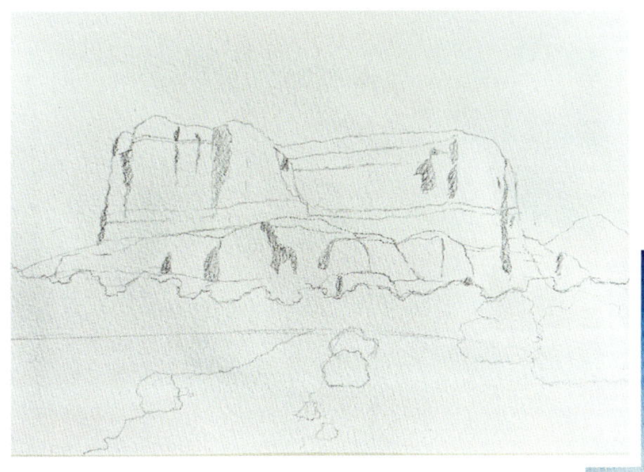

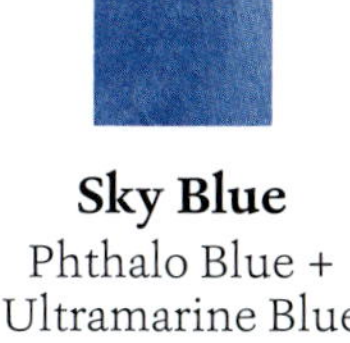

Sky Blue
Phthalo Blue +
Ultramarine Blue

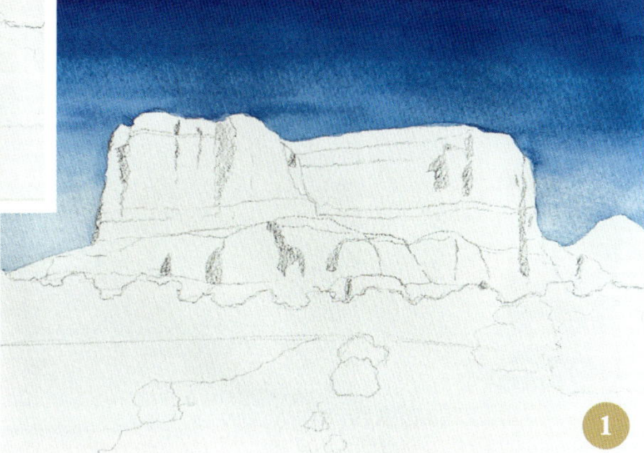

Sketch

Sketch the horizon line where the grass meets the trees, just under one-third of the way up the paper. Then sketch out the general outline of the butte, as well as the major shadow shapes. Feel free to shade with your pencil; the paint will cover up any pencil marks later. Don't forget the little path, the distant tree line and a couple of the larger trees on the right of the composition. Don't stress too much about getting everything perfect—it doesn't have to look exactly like the reference.

Step 1

We'll start by painting the sky a vibrant blue color. We will use the same technique as in the Grandest Canyon Project earlier in this chapter (page 57), so feel free to refer to that project for more detailed instructions. Mix your Sky Blue color before starting.

Using a large brush, start at the top of the page and fill in with horizontal strokes. Once you fill in about half of the sky section, start mixing clean water into the Sky Blue paint to get a lighter blue.

NOTE: Make sure you're painting **around** the rock formation. Don't paint over it!

Let this fully dry before moving on.

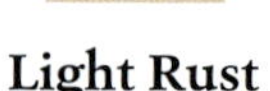

Light Rust
Burnt Sienna + Cadmium Red + Yellow Ochre + Van Dyke Brown + water

Green
Sap Green + Yellow Ochre + Ultramarine Blue + water

Tan
Burnt Sienna + Yellow Ochre + Ultramarine Blue + Van Dyke Brown + water

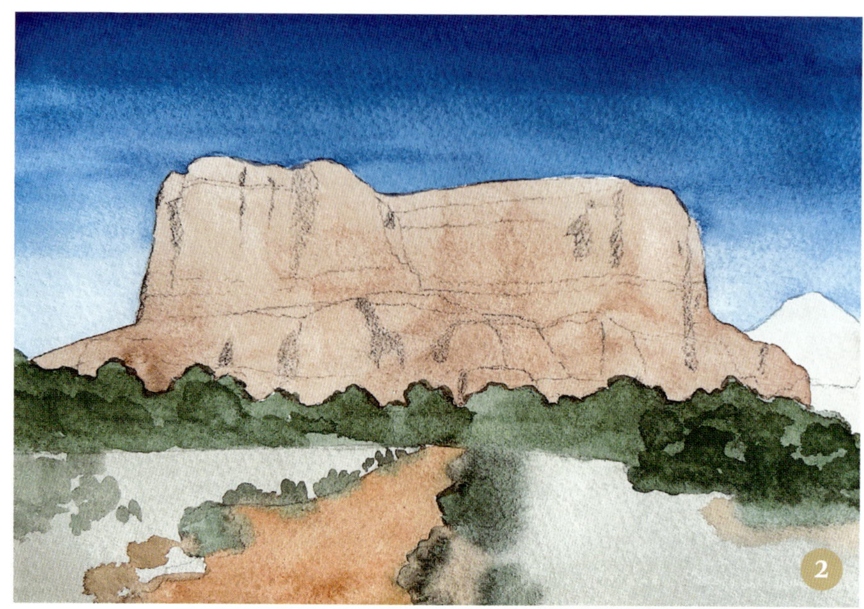

Step 2

Next, let's put down a preliminary layer of color over the rest of the painting. Mix up three colors: Light Rust, Green and Tan. Make sure to water these colors down a bit—we don't need super saturated colors yet.

Work quickly with this step so that all of the colors blend together on the page.

Use a large brush to fill in the general blocks of color. Use the Light Rust color to fill in the butte and the path. Then, use the Tan color to fill in the grass section and use the Green color to fill in the tree section. You can also add some Green dots on the sides of the path while the paint is still wet, and we can turn those into shrubs later.

Let this fully dry before moving on.

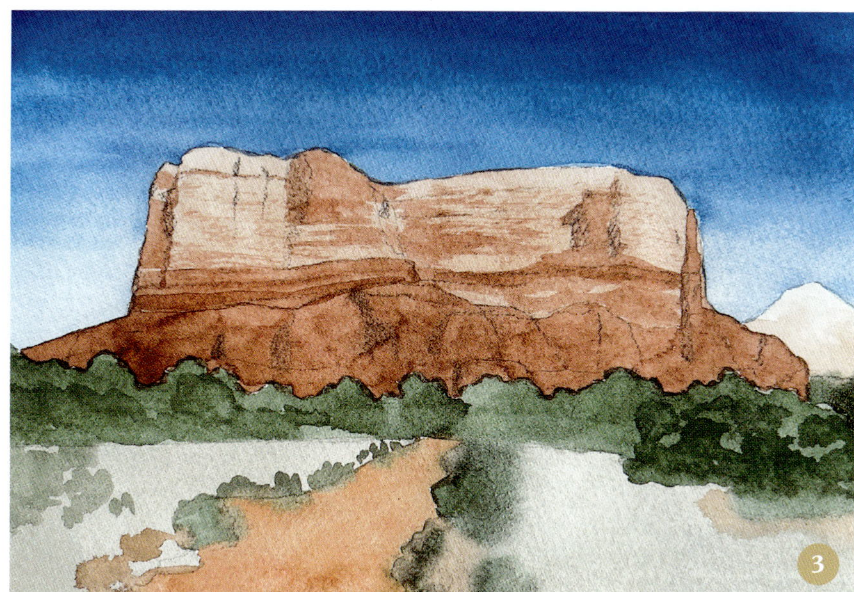

Rust
Burnt Sienna +
Cadmium Red +
Yellow Ochre +
Van Dyke Brown

Step 3

The butte is the focal point of this piece, so we'll spend the most time and effort on that section. Switch to your smaller brushes for this section; I used my size 4 round brush and my size 0 round detail brush.

With the Light Rust color from Step 2, start building up the saturation in certain sections of the butte. Notice in the reference photo that the bottom half of the formation is a bit darker than the top half, so add a flat wash over the bottom half on your painting. You can use a dry brushing technique (see page 16), as well as thin, wiggly horizontal and vertical lines to layer on some texture to the top half.

Create a more saturated Rust color (more paint, less water) and continue adding this texture.

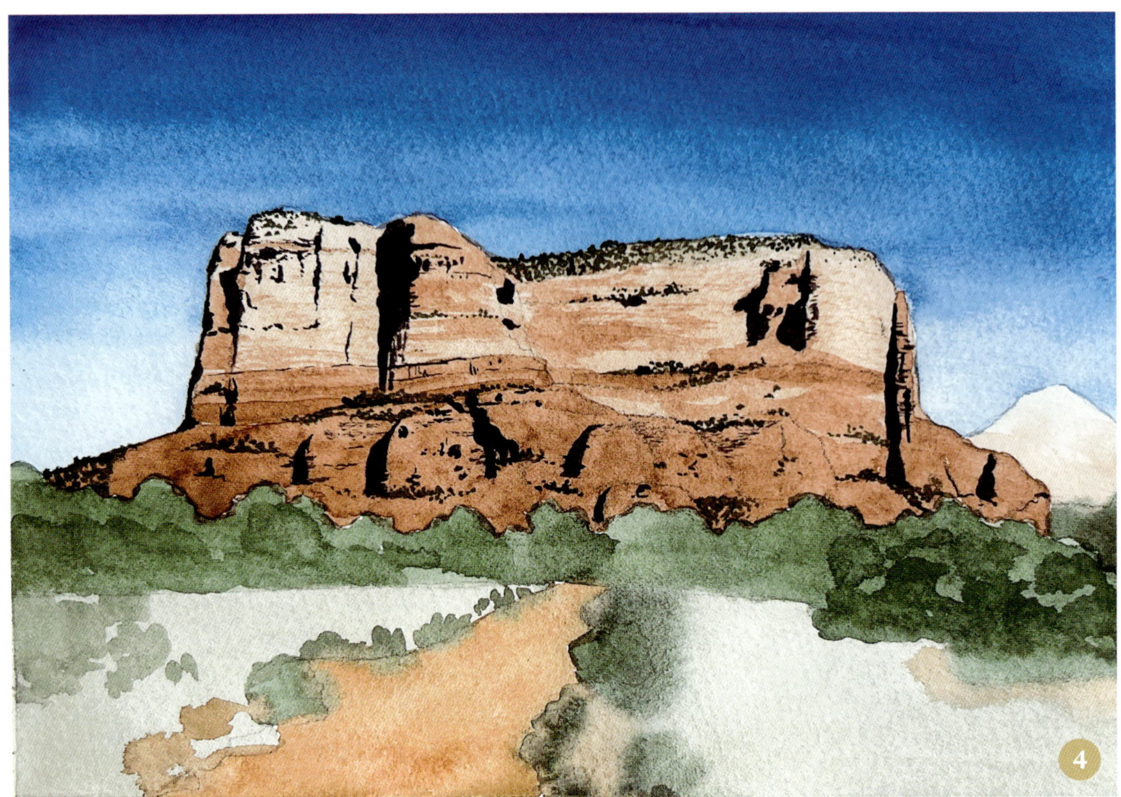

Step 4

Use a detail brush and a dotting motion with the Green color from Step 2 for the vegetation. Focus this on the top of the butte but add some smaller clusters on ledges across the face of the butte. You can layer green dots on top of each other to build texture and shadows on this element.

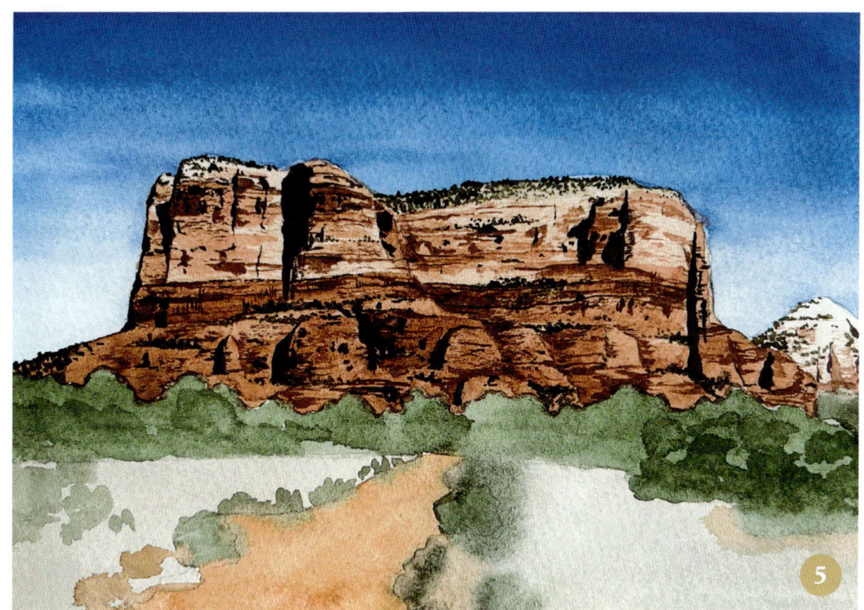

Dark Purple
Cadmium Red + Ultramarine Blue + Van Dyke Brown

Dark Green
Sap Green + Ultramarine Blue + (optional) Yellow Ochre

Step 5

Add the dark shadows across the formation with the Dark Purple color. Use the reference photo here to help you with the shapes and location. Add the large shadows, then feel free to add some smaller cracks, textures or little dots around the face. Use this Dark Purple color to dry brush some texture in certain areas but be sparing with this.

Continue cycling through Steps 3-5 until you're happy with the result.

Step 6

Now let's add some detail to those distant trees at the base of the butte. These trees are pretty far away, so we don't want any sharp details.

Mix up a Dark Green and dab in some shadows along the base of the trees using your medium brush (I used a 4 round). Fade out that detail towards the top of the trees. Once the paint is mostly dry, use a clean, damp brush and a circular scrubbing motion to blur out those details.

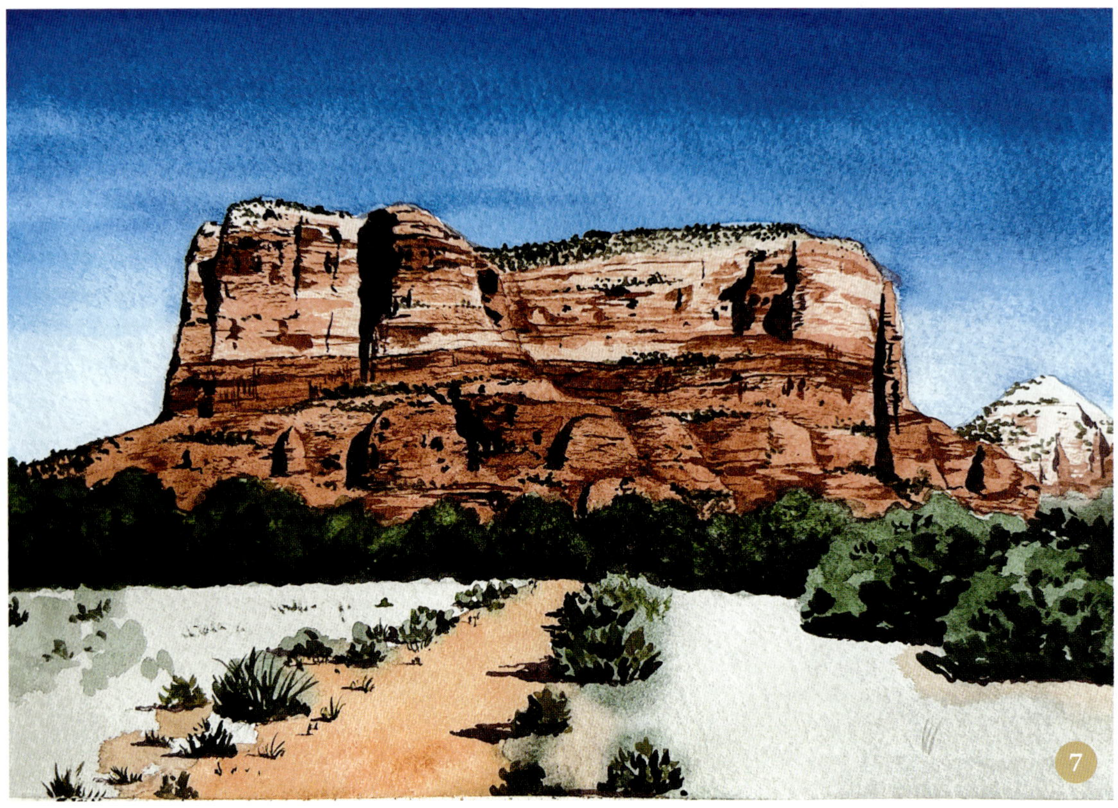

Step 7

Let's define some of the closer trees and shrubs. In the larger trees on the right, use the same Dark Green color from Step 6 and add in some large shadow shapes to the bottom of each tree. Use a detail brush to dot on some leaf texture closer to the tops of the trees.

For the smaller shrubs by the path, I used shorter, grass-like strokes, as well as a dotting motion to add shadow and texture. Feel free to **mix some Yellow Ochre into your Dark Green color to create a sage green color** and use that to add further color and texture. You can also add some small grass clumps or blades on their own. You can see I did this mostly on the left side of the path.

Finally, use the Dark Purple color from Step 5 to cast shadows underneath the shrubs and grasses by the path. Notice the sunlight is coming from the top right, so the shadows should extend out horizontally to the left.

Step 8

Now let's finish up the painting with some grassy texture in the Tan portion of the foreground. I **mixed up a very slightly darker version of the Tan color from Step 2** and used my detail brush to start adding grass.

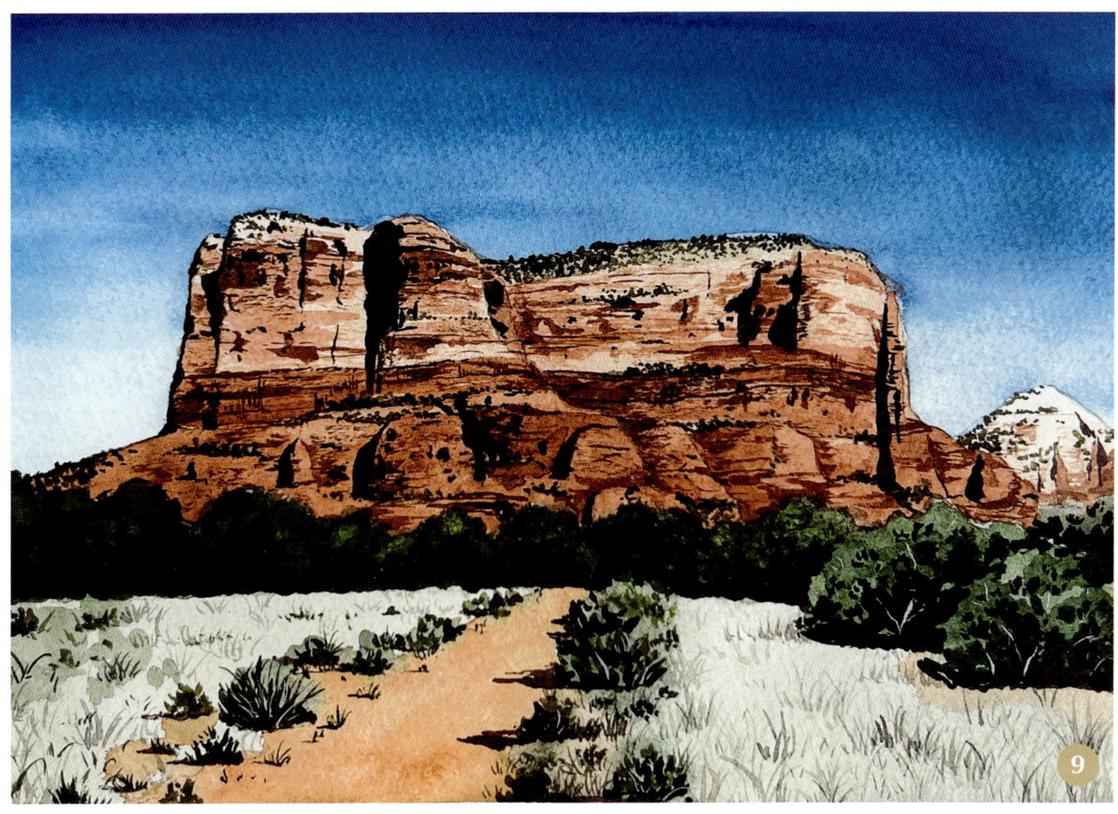

The key to painting grass is to vary your brush strokes—use different lengths, thicknesses and directions to make it look more natural. I also prefer to add grass texture in clumps, rather than individual grass blades evenly spaced around the painting. Notice in the reference photo that there are some areas with darker shades of grass than others; use this to guide where to put these darker grass clumps.

Using the Green from Step 2, you can also add in a few blades of grass or small shrubs throughout the grass section to add some variation.

Step 9 (optional)

I can't resist a little gouache highlight, so I mixed up an opaque light gray color by adding a little Van Dyke Brown and a little Payne's Gray to my white gouache, then used my detail brush to indicate some trunks and branches on the large trees on the right. I also added a few highlights to the shrubs near the path. Restrain yourself here—less is more!

Once you're happy with these details, you're all done! Take off the tape, sign and date your painting and admire your work!

desert flora

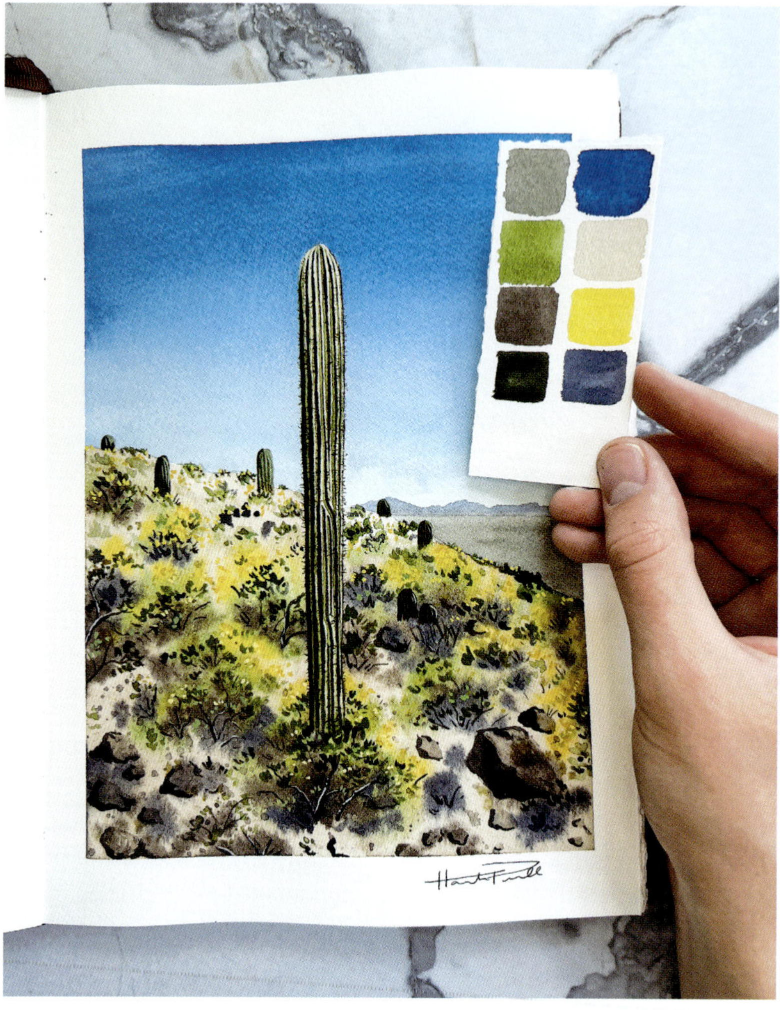

While visiting Arizona in the springtime, I was in awe of the beautiful flowers and vegetation everywhere we went. It wasn't what I expected in the desert and made for some amazing views. This particular reference photo was from a hike on Camelback Mountain, and I think it makes for the perfect desert reference photo. We'll be using some fun wet-on-wet techniques for this project and embracing the chaos of watercolor!

materials

Watercolor paints

- Cadmium Yellow, Yellow Ochre, Burnt Sienna, Sap Green, Ultramarine Blue, Phthalo Blue and Van Dyke Brown
- White gouache (optional)

Watercolor paper of your choice

- I used my cold press Fabriano Artistico sketchbook size 6 x 8.5 inches (15 x 21.5 cm)

Brushes

- one larger brush (I used a ½ inch oval), one medium brush (I used 4 round) and one detail brush (I used a size 0 round)

Orientation

- portrait

Set up your paper as you like and make sure to add a drop or two of water to your colors so they start to soften.

Reference photo

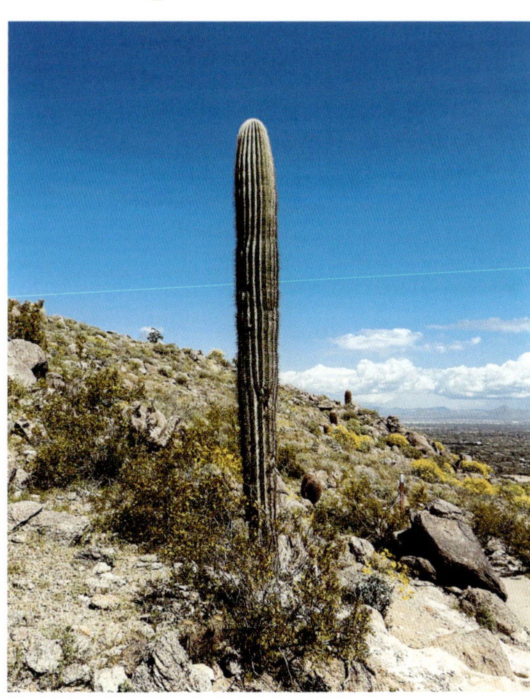

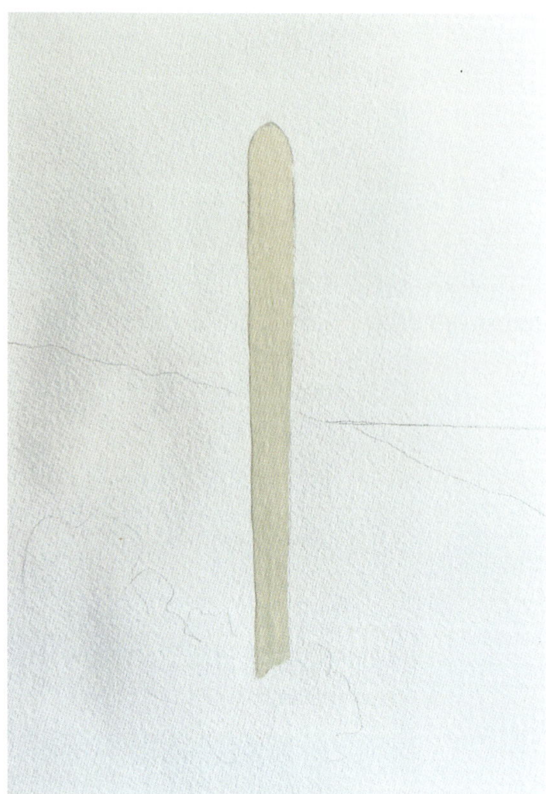

Sketch

Sketch the hill, starting a little over halfway up the left-hand side of the paper and creating a gentle slope to the right. Add a horizon line in the distance beyond the hill, just under halfway up the paper. Sketch out a rounded column shape for the large cactus, which is the main focal point of the piece.

TIP: I covered the cactus with masking tape so that I could easily paint the background around it. To do this, cover your sketch of the cactus with tan masking tape (you should be able to see the sketch through the tape), then use an X-acto knife to lightly cut out the shape of the cactus. Press just hard enough to cut through the tape but not hard enough to cut through the paper. Alternatively, you could use masking fluid if you have it, or simply paint the background around this shape, though this is more tedious.

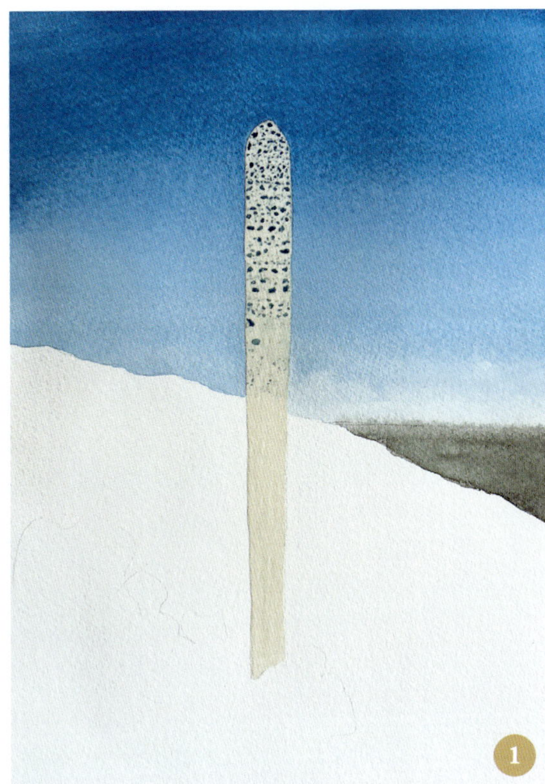

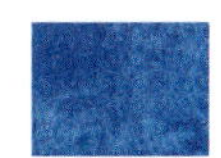

Sky Blue
Ultramarine Blue + Phthalo Blue

Gray
Ultramarine Blue + Van Dyke Brown + Burnt Sienna + Sap Green + water

Step 1

As usual, let's paint the background first. This consists of a clear blue sky and the gray land behind the hillside. To start, paint a simple clear blue sky that fades toward the horizon line, painting around the shape of the hill. I'll summarize it briefly for you here, but for more detailed instructions, see The Grandest Canyon project earlier in this chapter (see page 57).

Using a large brush loaded with your Sky Blue color, start at the top of the page and use horizontal strokes to work your way down the sky section. Once you've reached halfway to the horizon line, mix some water into your Sky Blue color and continue with the horizontal strokes.

When you've painted to just above your horizon line, clean off your brush completely and use clean water to fill in the rest of the area to the horizon line, going back over this section with horizontal strokes as needed to get a smoother blend. Let this dry a little, then use the Gray color to fill in the distant land below the horizon line with a flat wash.

Once the sky is completely dry, **add a little more Ultramarine Blue to this Gray color** and paint in a distant mountain range at the horizon line. Blend out the bottom of the mountain range with a clean, damp brush, so that it fades into the land. Let this fully dry before moving on.

Tan
Van Dyke Brown + Yellow Ochre + plenty of water

Brown
Van Dyke Brown + little Ultramarine Blue

Sage Green
Sap Green + Yellow Ochre

Yellow
Cadmium Yellow

Blue
Ultramarine Blue + little Van Dyke Brown

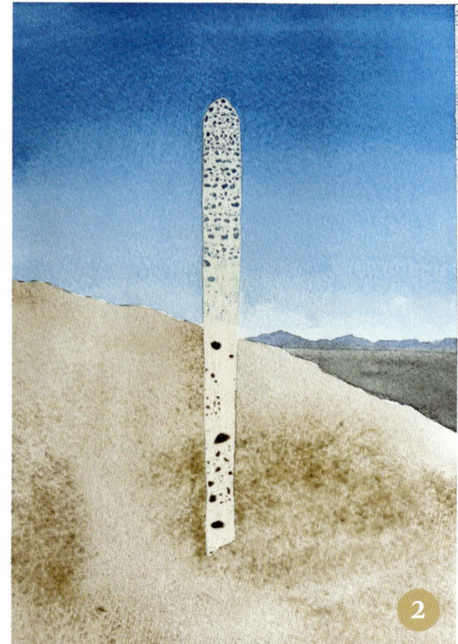

Step 2

Now it's time for the fun part. To imitate the brush in the foreground, we'll use a loose, wet-on-wet technique as our base layer. Mix the colors swatched above.

> **PAUSE:** Please read through the following instructions before you start so you can work quickly without stopping to read.

Use your large brush to cover the entire hill section in the Tan color. Quickly switch to your Brown color. Use dotting and short sweeping motions to create the dark shadows of the shrubs on the hill. Use the reference photo as inspiration for the size and locations of the shrubs.

While that's still wet, add your Sage Green color on top of each of your Brown spots. Feel free to add some individual Green dots as well. Everything should be spreading out and blending together—don't panic!

Next, pick up your Yellow color. Add this in with the Green and on its own for wherever you want clusters of yellow wildflowers.

Finally, add a little depth to the shadows with the Blue. I like layering it with the Brown and Green colors, or adding some small dots in places that haven't been filled in yet.

Last, use a dry brush to lift any pools of paint on your paper or add subtle highlights.

Now this is when you might be wondering how the heck this mess of colors turns into a desert scene. Sometimes we have to make a mess in order to make something beautiful, so trust me and yourself and get ready to dig your way out of the Ugly Stage! Let this fully dry before moving on.

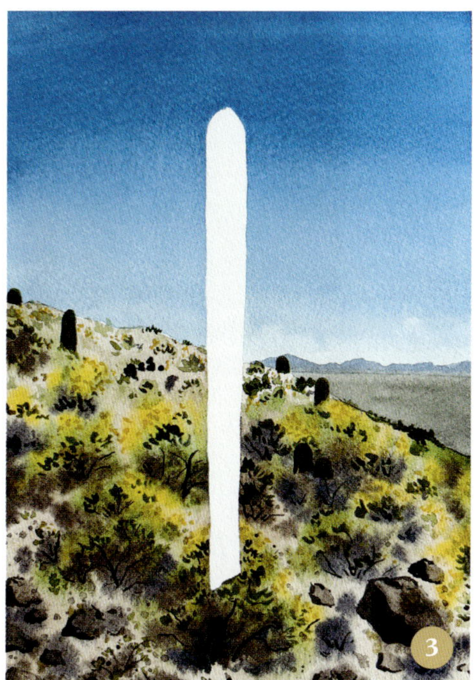

Step 3

Now, it's time to make something out of these blobs of color. This is where a little bit of improvising comes in because your colors have mixed and flowed together in a unique way. The trick here is to pick out certain shapes, colors, etc., and turn them into something meaningful. For example, if I have a large splotch of brown on the paper, I could add some dark shadows to make it look like a large rock. If I have a shape that looks like it could be a shrub, I can add some branches and limbs and some extra leaf texture at the top. It's a bit like one of those inkblot tests; see the shapes and turn them into something meaningful.

For this step, we'll use the same colors from Step 2, minus the Tan color. I also switched to my detail brush for more control. Make sure to use the reference photo as you work on this step. Here are some ideas for you:

- Pick out some shrubs in your landscape. Use the Brown color to add some stems and branches in the shadows and use your Green to add some dots for leaves. You could also add some extra bright yellow flowers over the existing yellow spots using super-saturated Cadmium Yellow.
- Find some (or create some) rocks. Note that in the reference photo the light is coming from the right side, so the shadows will exist on the left sides of the rocks. Create some rounded or jagged shadows with your Brown and/or Blue colors, then fill in the tops of the rocks with a watered-down Brown shade.
- Add in some smaller cacti with your Green color. These are like narrow tombstone shapes—some taller and some shorter.
- Water down either your Blue or Brown (or both) and flick the paint onto the paper with your brush. This will add some extra texture that looks like pebbles, especially when used in the foreground (at the very bottom of your page). Make sure you protect any areas where you don't want paint splatters with paper towels—you'll have little control with this technique!

NOTE: There is no need to add a ton of detail to every shape here. Once you've added a certain amount of detail, the viewer's brain will fill in the rest. Make sure to keep an eye on your whole painting as you're working to make sure you're not overdoing it on the details.

Light Green
Sap Green + Yellow Ochre + water

Dark Green
Sap Green + Yellow Ochre + Van Dyke Brown + Ultramarine Blue

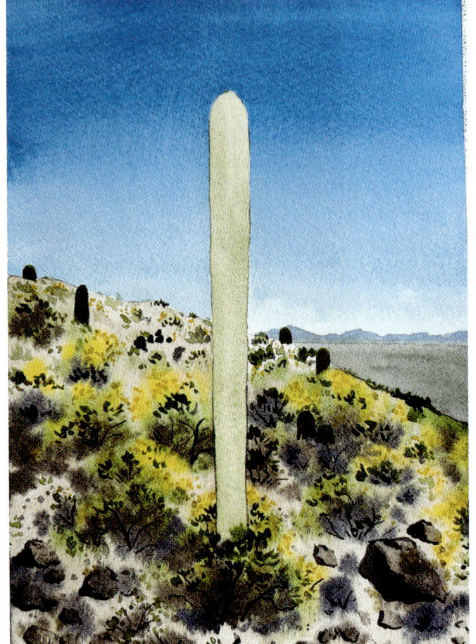

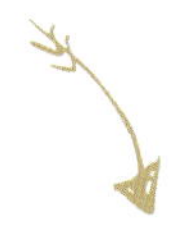

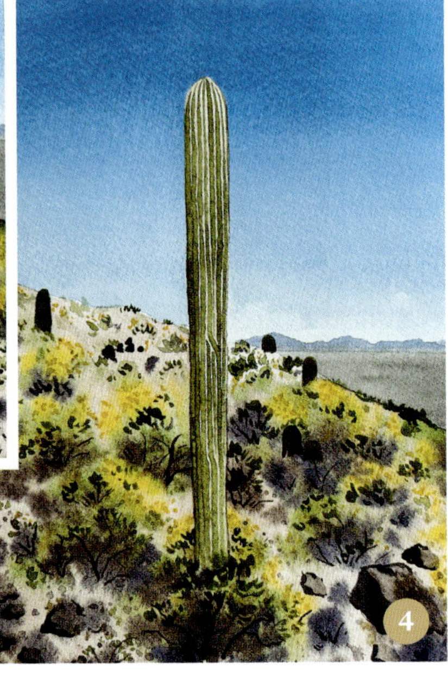

Step 4

Let's paint the main cactus. Remove the masking tape/fluid if you used it and mix up your three green colors: Light Green, Sage Green (from Step 2) and Dark Green. To start, paint in the entire cactus shape with a flat wash of Light Green. Fully dry before moving on.

Next, use the Sage Green from Step 2 and a detail brush to add the vertical ridges to the cactus. Take a look at the reference photo for this and notice that not all the ridges are straight up and down. Some end up going a bit diagonal, and the others follow. Notice that the ridges tend to narrow to a point at the top of the cactus but some remain a bit thicker than others. Imperfections are encouraged here!

Finally, switch to your Dark Green and enhance these ridges by adding shadows. I essentially followed the Medium Green ridges and painted over about half of each ridge with the Dark Green.

Add some small, thin spikes coming from these ridges with the Dark Green, both around the outside of the cactus and between each ridge.

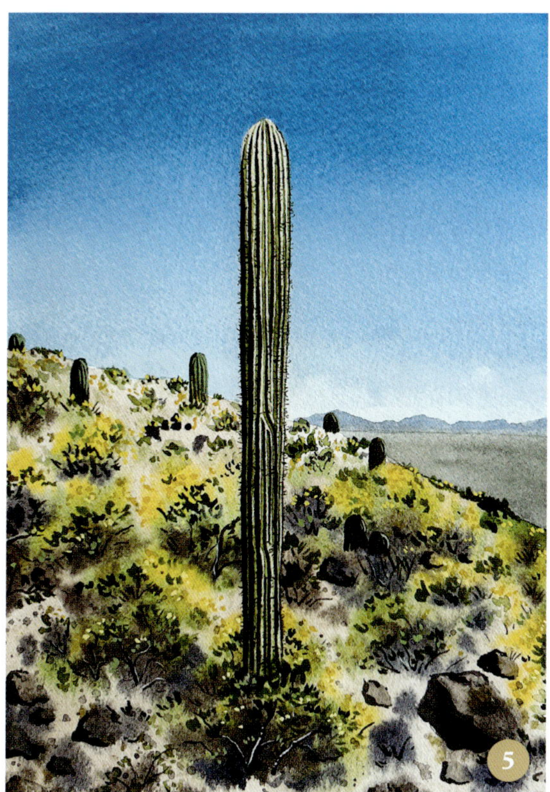

Step 5

Time for some finishing details. If you have a weird spot between the bottom of the main cactus and the shrubbery around it, add some more detail to disguise that seam. For my painting, I just added some more dark green leaves around that area.

You can also use your gouache to add some final sparkling highlights here. This can really pull the painting together and make it pop. Here's what I did:

I mixed a light gray with my white gouache, Van Dyke Brown and Ultramarine Blue, and added this highlight to just a few of the shrub branches.

I mixed up a light green with Sap Green and white gouache to add a few light highlights to the leaves of the shrubs.

Finally, I mixed a light yellow color with Cadmium Yellow and white gouache to add a few individual light yellow flowers to the piece. It's SO tempting to put these everywhere because they're so pretty but try to control yourself and just add a few.

Once you're done adding your highlights, you're all done with this piece. Take off the tape, sign and date your painting and admire your work.

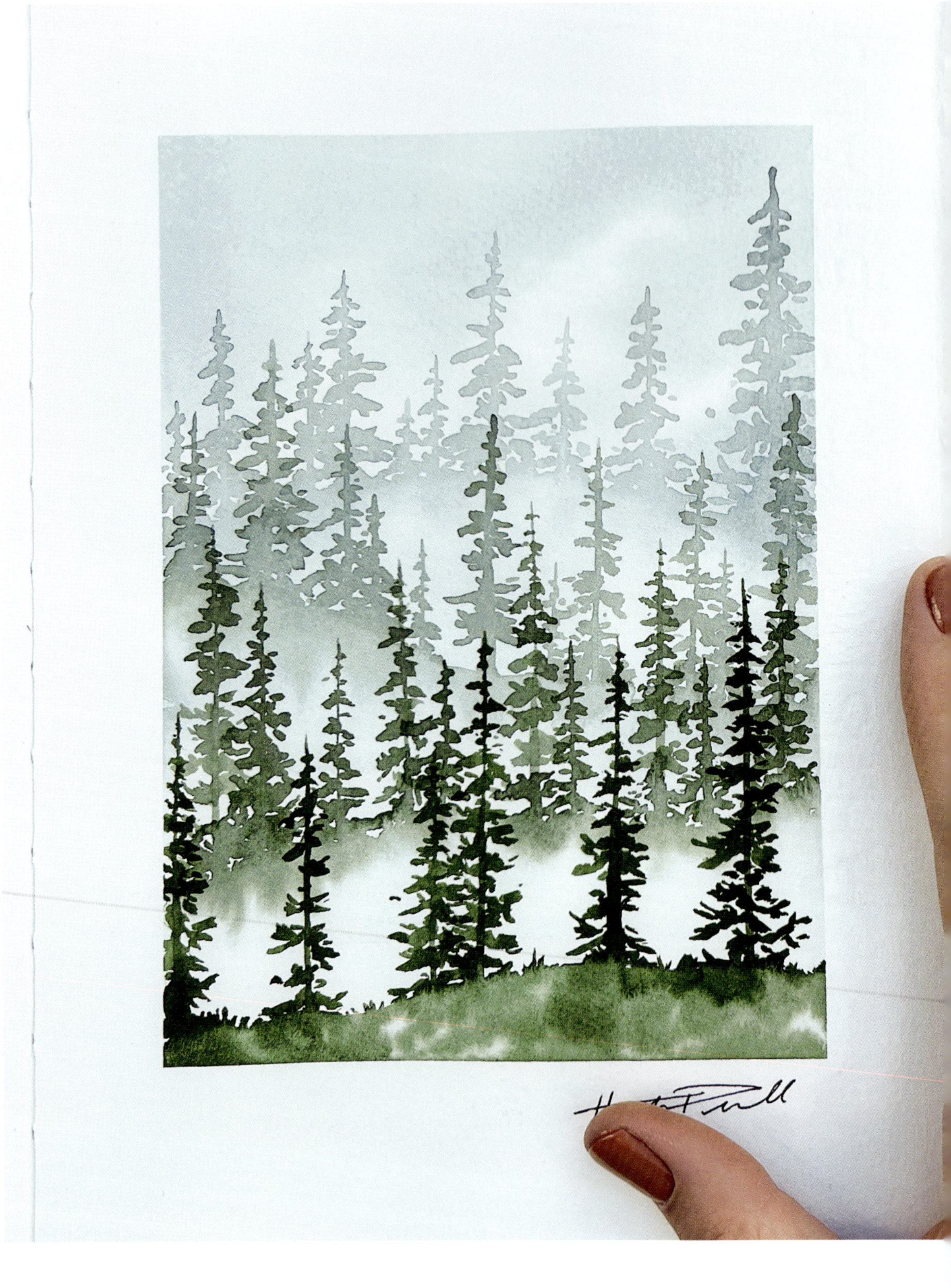

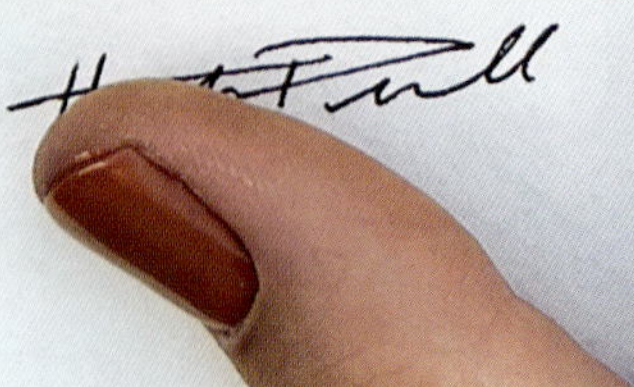

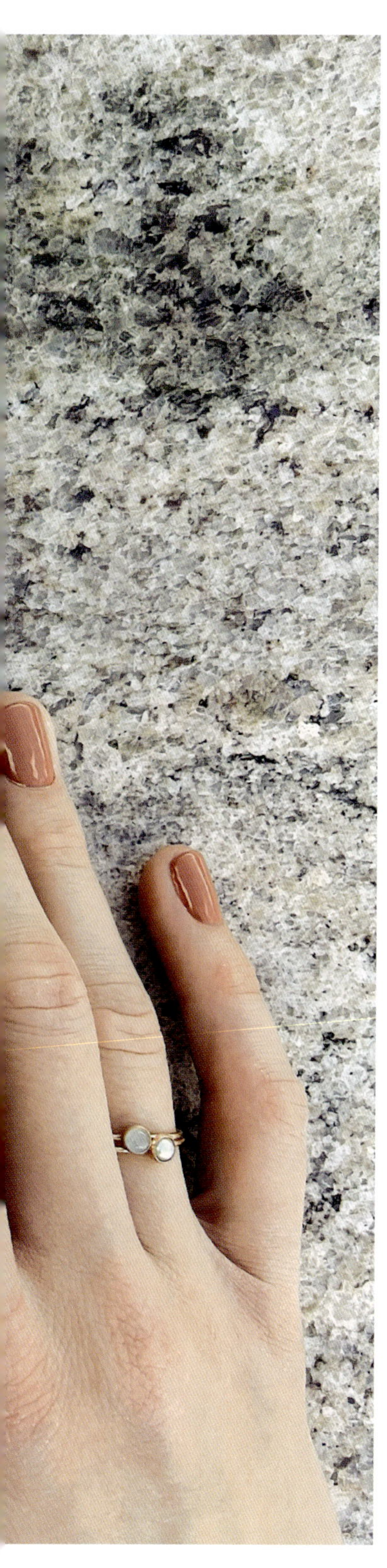

chapter 4
funky forests

Trees are some of my favorite subjects to paint. Each one is unique, and the feeling of capturing the shape and sheer size of a tree in watercolor is pretty cool. I've curated the landscapes in this chapter to heavily feature trees as the focal point, but there are often other elements within those landscapes like water or mountains. When this happens, feel free to refer to those chapters for a little more information and guidance on how to paint those elements. And remember, trees (like anything else in art) require practice, so if you aren't yet confident painting them, all it takes is repetition, and you'll find it comes easier and easier!

one tree at a time

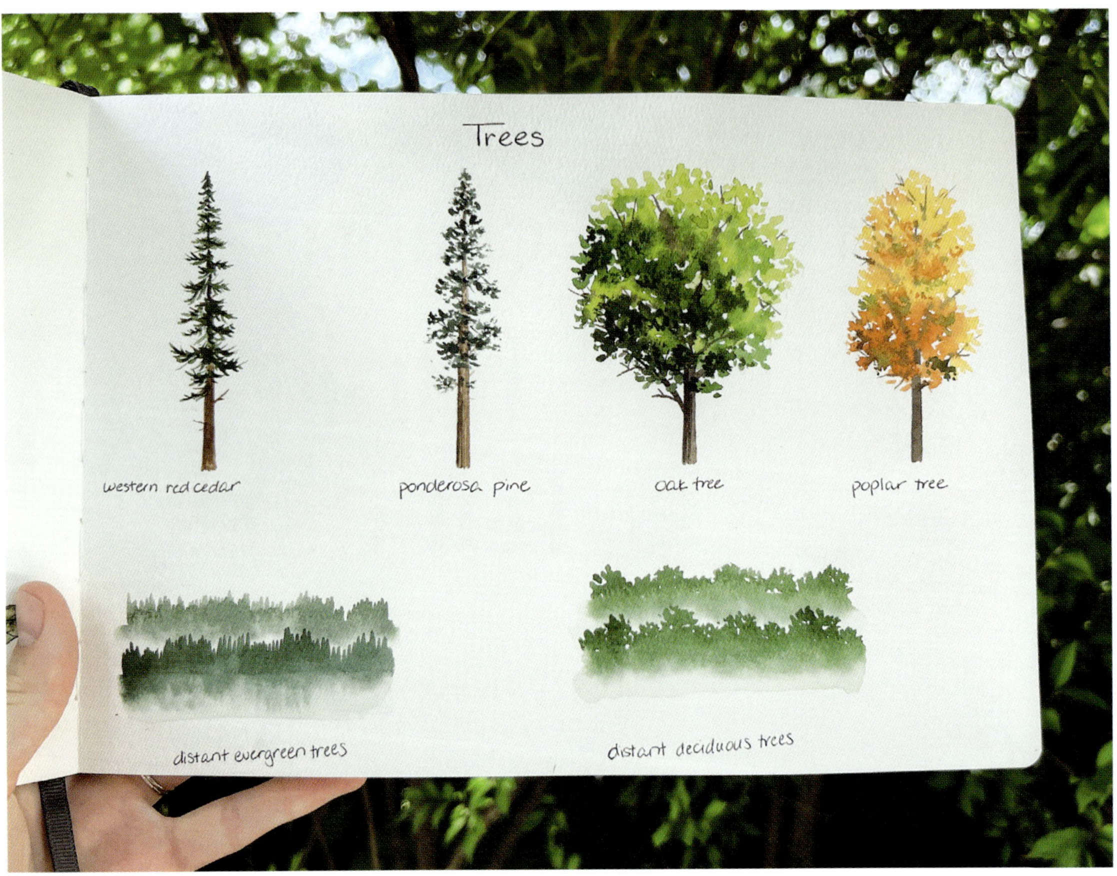

To begin this chapter, let's start by painting a few distinct types of trees. This will help you practice with the different techniques and species of trees. I picked out four trees for you to try out in this project, but feel free to research and practice your own favorite types of trees! I learned a lot about painting trees from the incomparable Bob Ross; though he paints in oil, the technique is much the same. Feel free to check out one of his videos for a little more advice on the subject and for a relaxing half hour of entertainment!

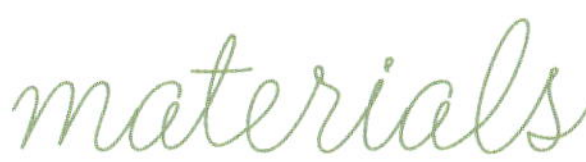

materials

Watercolor paints

- Yellow Ochre, Burnt Sienna, Sap Green, Ultramarine Blue, Van Dyke Brown and Payne's Gray

Watercolor paper of your choice

- I used my cold press Fabriano Artistico sketchbook size 6 x 8 inches (15 x 21.5 cm)

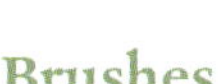

Brushes

- one medium brush (I used a size 4 round) and one detail brush (I used a size 0 round). If you want to paint larger trees, use larger brushes!

Orientation

- landscape

Set up your paper as you like and make sure to add a drop or two of water to your colors so they start to soften.

Evergreen Trees

To create realistic evergreen trees, we will focus on making a narrow triangle silhouette, while adding snaggy and irregular branches and leaving some trunk exposed.

Western Red Cedar

We will start with my favorite tree, the Western Red Cedar, which is very common in the Pacific Northwest.

Sketch

Draw a vertical column which gets slightly wider at the bottom and tapers to a single line at the top.

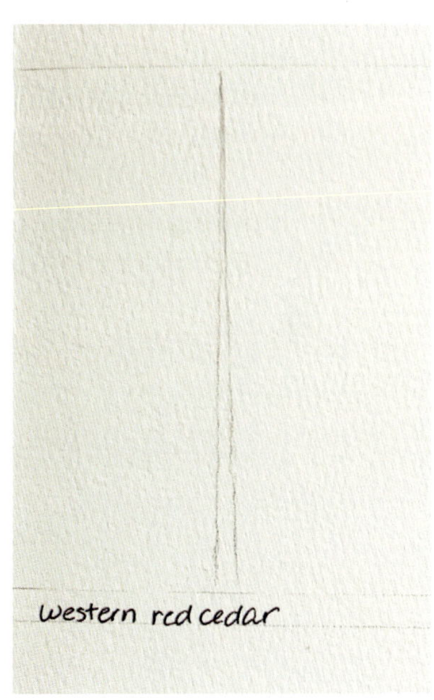

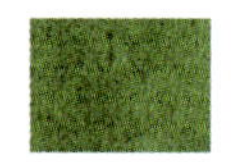

Green
Sap Green + Van Dyke Brown

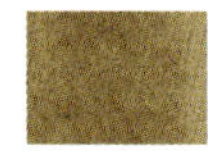

Brown
Burnt Sienna + Van Dyke Brown + little Ultramarine Blue

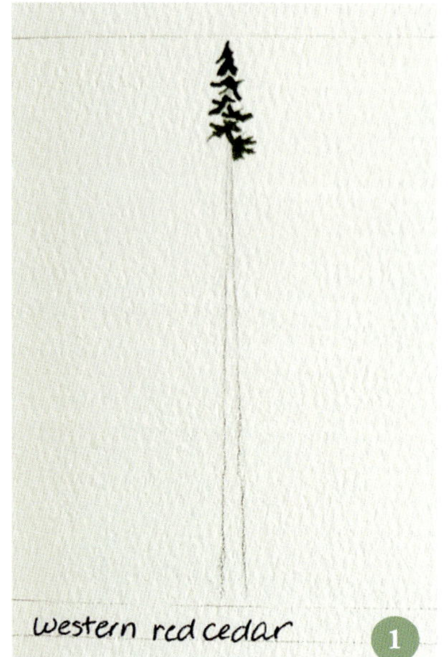

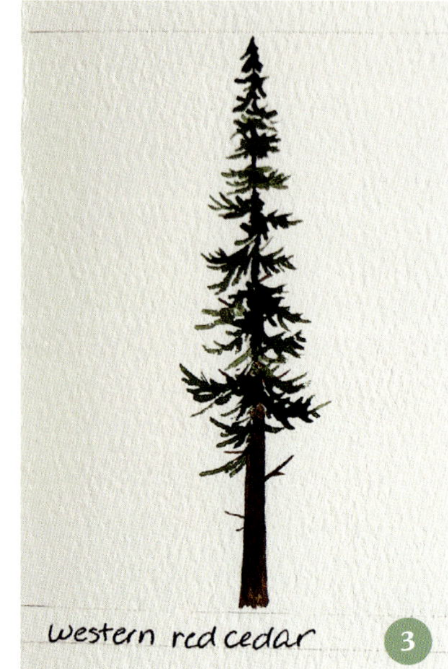

Step 1

Mix up an earthy Green color and a Brown color. Use a medium brush and start adding Green branches with "swooping" motions at the top of the tree, starting small and making them slightly larger as you work your way down the tree. Cedar tree branches form shallow U-shapes, with smaller twigs stemming from those larger branches. Leave some space where the pencil-drawn trunk is still showing. Add branches to about three-quarters of the tree and then fade them out toward the bottom of the tree.

Let this dry before moving on.

Step 2

Paint in the trunk using the Brown color. Leave some areas where the branches of the tree are blocking the trunk from view!

Step 3

Finally, you can switch back to the Green color to layer a little bit more texture on top of the branches. This step is optional, but it adds a nice level of detail to the tree.

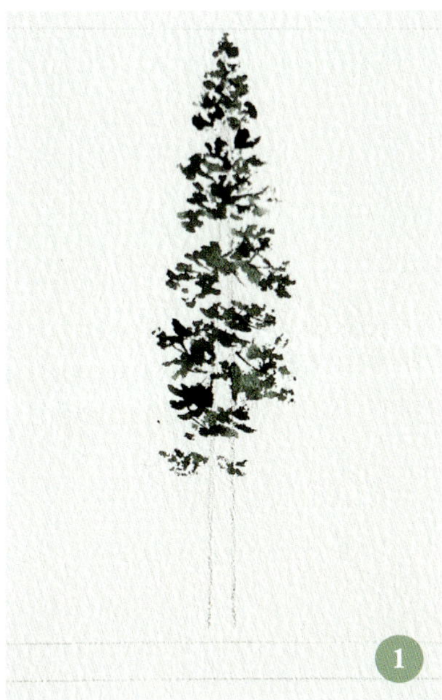

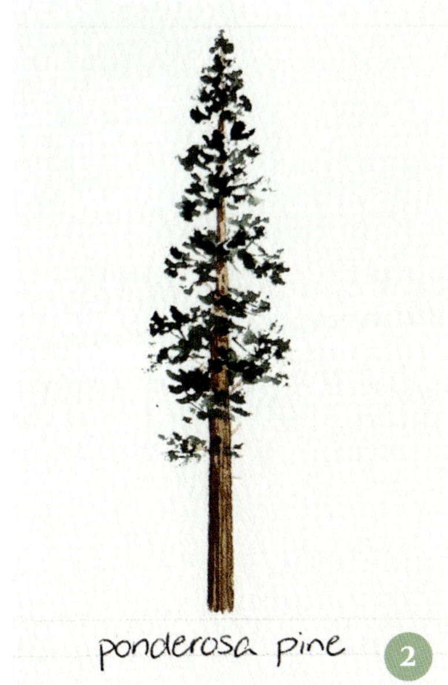

Ponderosa Pine

Next, we will paint a Ponderosa Pine tree. Use the same colors and sketch a trunk in the same way as with the Cedar tree.

Step 1

This time, angle your brush so it is nearly parallel to your paper. Use the side of your brush and the Green color to create small, rough dots and dashes. Form these into branches, which should get longer as you work your way down the tree to form a narrow cone shape. Again, leave some of the trunk exposed and fade out the branches once you've filled in three-quarters of the tree or so. Once you're done, let it dry.

Step 2

Add in the trunk with the Brown color. You can add an extra layer of Brown to one side of the trunk to form a shadow.

Step 3

Go back over the branches with the Green in the same way as in Step 1 to add extra texture.

Light Green
Yellow Ochre + Sap Green + little Burnt Sienna + water

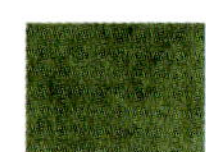

Dark Green
Sap Green + Van Dyke Brown + Ultramarine Blue

Medium Green
Sap Green + little Ultramarine Blue

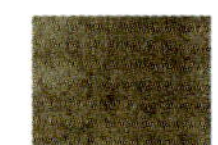

Dark Brown
Van Dyke Brown + little Ultramarine Blue

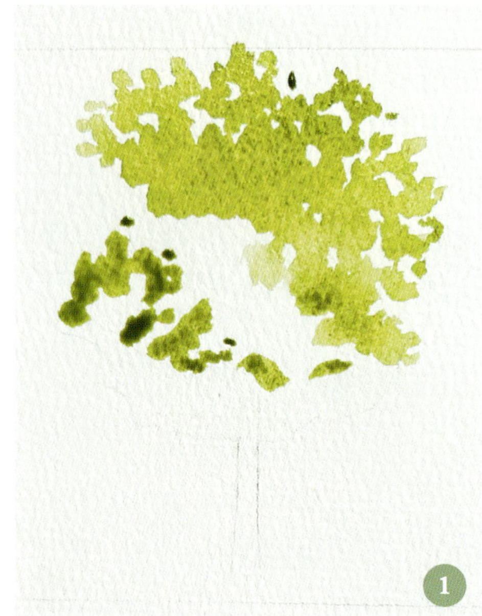

Deciduous Trees

Deciduous trees are so much fun to paint with watercolor! We will use different shades of green (or reds and oranges in autumn) to create the form of the tree and allow those colors to blend together in a natural way.

Oak Tree

For our deciduous trees, we will start with an Oak tree, which has the classic rounded shape.

Sketch

Start by sketching out a large, loose circle—the edges should be wiggly and uneven. Then sketch in a trunk at the bottom of the tree. Lightly erase the circle you sketched so that you can still see it, but it won't show through the final painting.

PAUSE: Please read through Steps 1-4 before you start so you can work quickly without stopping to read.

Step 1

Mix up the four colors swatched above before starting. Use a medium brush (I used my 4 round) and the Light Green to start painting the top right side of the tree, as well as some other smaller spots where the light might hit throughout the tree.

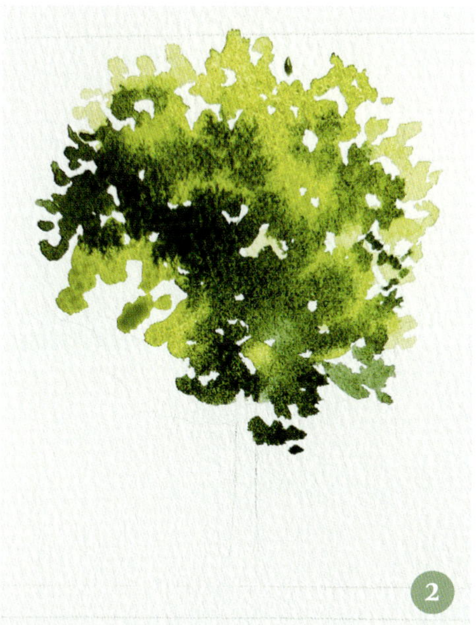

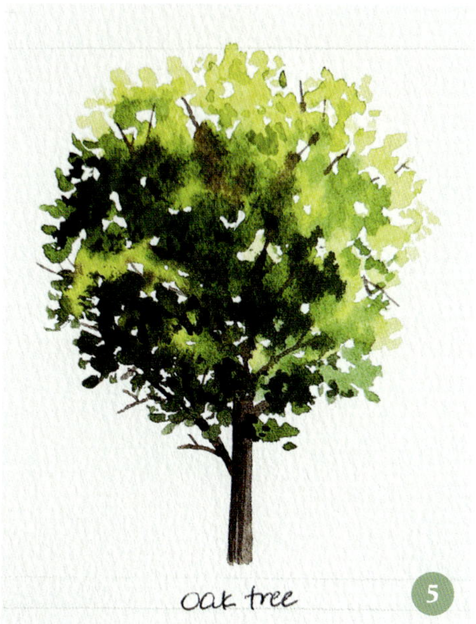

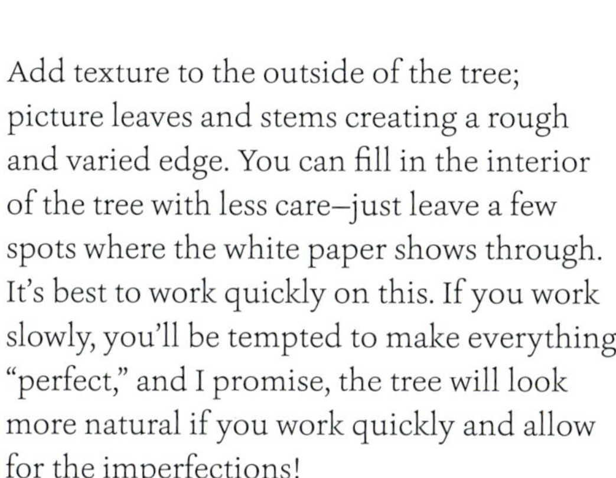

Add texture to the outside of the tree; picture leaves and stems creating a rough and varied edge. You can fill in the interior of the tree with less care—just leave a few spots where the white paper shows through. It's best to work quickly on this. If you work slowly, you'll be tempted to make everything "perfect," and I promise, the tree will look more natural if you work quickly and allow for the imperfections!

Step 2

Quickly switch to the Medium Green color. Fill in the middle section of the tree, working your way to the bottom left side. Allow it to mix with the Light Green color; you can even add some dots of Medium Green to the Light Green sections. Continue forming the edge of the tree with the texture I mentioned in Step 1.

Step 3

Switch to the Dark Green and fill in any remaining parts of the tree. Feel free to layer dots of this color on top of the other sections of the tree to add texture and shadows.

Step 4

Paint in the trunk and a few branches throughout the tree with the Dark Brown color. I like to have these branches go through the small spots of white paper left throughout the tree. Don't worry about the Brown mixing with the greens; this makes it look more natural.

Step 5

Once everything is dry, you can take your detail brush and whichever Green you like, and add some clusters of dots over the top of a few sections as leaf texture. Don't overdo this; just a little bit of this texture is enough to suggest leaves on the whole tree.

Yellow
Cadmium Yellow + little Burnt Sienna + water

Burnt Orange
Cadmium Yellow + Burnt Sienna + Van Dyke Brown + little Ultramarine Blue

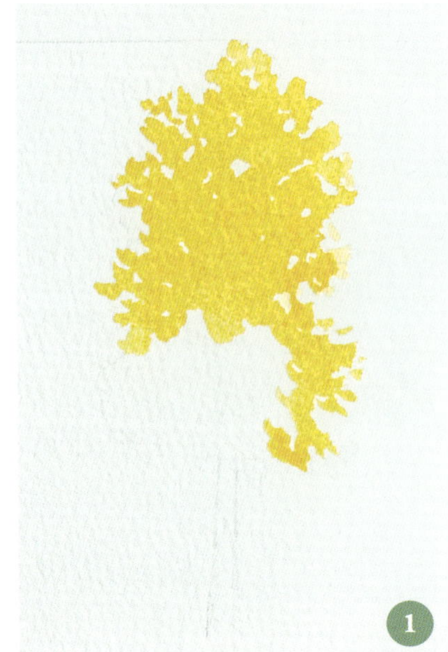

Autumn Poplar

Finally, we will paint a Poplar tree in autumn to practice using those colors. Create a sketch similar to the Oak tree, but keep in mind poplar trees have a more oval shape.

PAUSE: Please read through Steps 1–4 before you start so you can work quickly without stopping to read.

Step 1

For the colors, use the same Dark Green and Brown colors from the Oak tree. In addition, mix the Yellow and Burnt Orange colors noted above. Start with your medium brush (4 round) and the Yellow color and begin filling in the top half of the tree. Make sure to create the textured edge around the outside of the tree to indicate leaves.

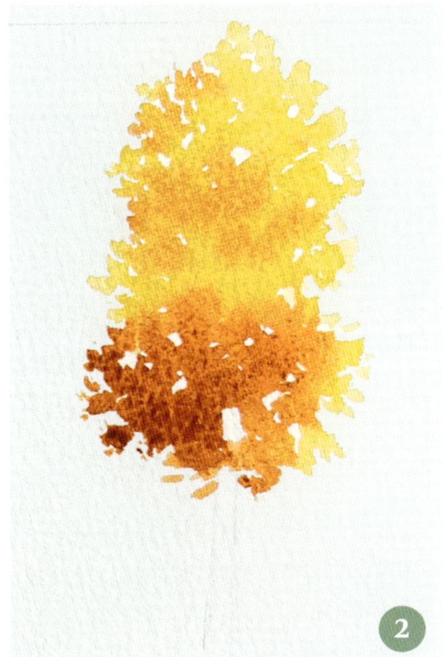

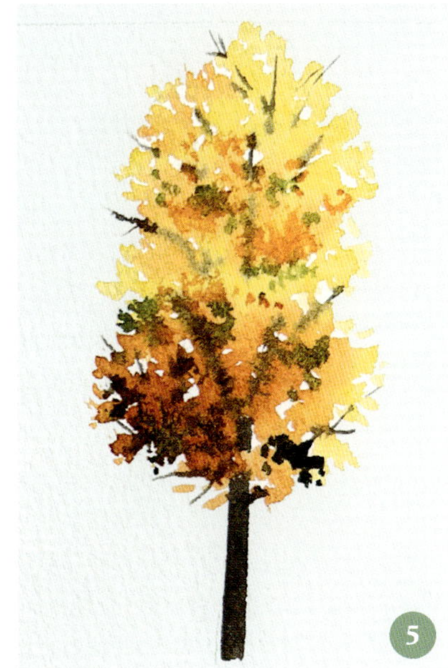

Step 2

Switch to the Burnt Orange color and fill in the other half of the tree. Add dots of this color into the Yellow section as well.

Step 3

Use your smallest detail brush and the Dark Brown paint to fill in the trunk and add some branches throughout the tree. Again, don't worry about the Brown mixing with the other colors of the tree.

Step 4

Lastly, before the tree has completely dried, drop in a few dots of Dark Green around the tree. This adds a little color variation to the tree!

Step 5

Once the tree has dried, you can use any of the four colors to add some clusters of dots over a few spots in the tree.

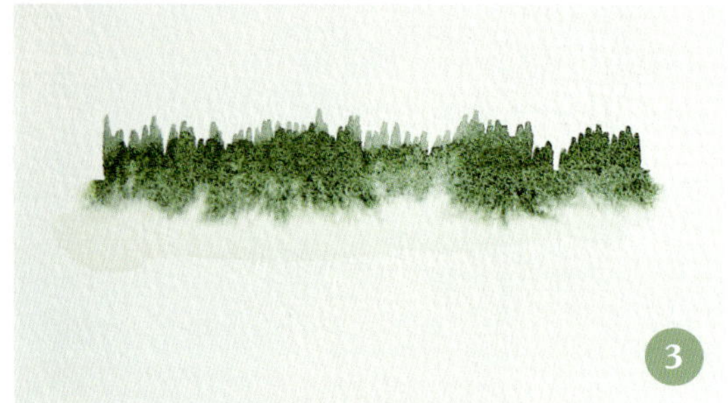

Distant Trees

This is a great time to practice painting distant trees. This technique is perfect for a layered landscape where you have some hills or mountains that are further away, and you just want to imply that they are covered in trees.

Distant Evergreens

Evergreen forests in the distance lose all the detail in their branches and end up looking like very narrow tops of triangles. We will imitate that shape by using the point of our paint brush and a downward brush stroke.

Step 1

Use a medium brush (I used a 4 round) and paint a horizontal stripe of clear water on your paper.

Step 2

Pick up some of the Green color from the Cedar tree section on page 85, and start laying down some short vertical strokes (about ½ inch or 1.25 cm long), ending in the stripe of water. Try to use a light touch with these—you'll get thinner and more delicate trees this way!

Step 3

Be sure to change up the height of each of the individual trees and elevation of the landscape a bit—you don't want it to look like a fence! Add some shorter trees, some taller trees or create a few hills and valleys as you work your way across. You should notice the green color spreading and mixing into the clear water as you go. **Work quickly and add more clean water to the horizontal stripe if it dries.**

Step 4

Let this first layer dry, then you can add another layer directly underneath. Place your next stripe of water just a little below where the first one was and add the trees on top just as before. This should create a misty effect between the two layers and give the illusion of distance!

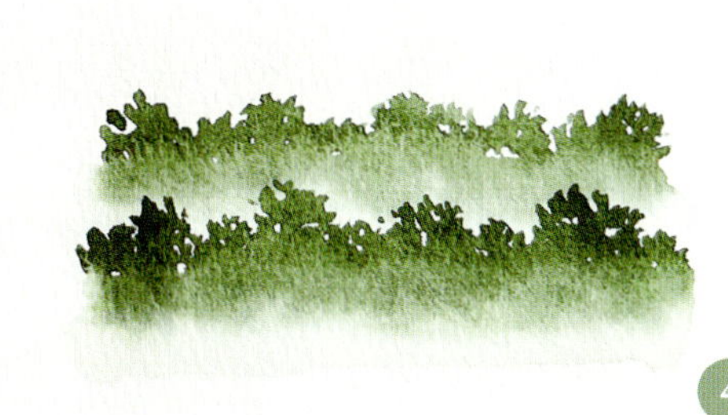

Distant Deciduous Trees

Now, we will do exactly the same technique but with rounded and leafy deciduous trees.

Step 1

Lay down another horizontal stripe of water on your paper.

Step 2

Using the Medium Green from the Oak section on page 88 and a dotting motion with your brush, start painting some rounded shapes for the trees just above the horizontal stripe of water. Try to create some texture around the edges of the trees that might look like leaves.

Step 3

Work your way across the section of paper, allowing the Green paint to blend in with the stripe of water on the paper. Make sure you are using a variety of different shapes for your trees–some bigger, some smaller, some wider and some skinnier.

Step 4

Once you've added trees along the entire horizontal stripe of water, let that layer dry. Then, you can add another layer just below it in the same manner.

NOTE: When painting distant trees like this in a complete landscape painting, make sure you're paying attention to the color of each layer. More distant layers will look more blue or gray and much lighter and less detailed, while closer layers will look darker, greener and more detailed!

glorious sunset

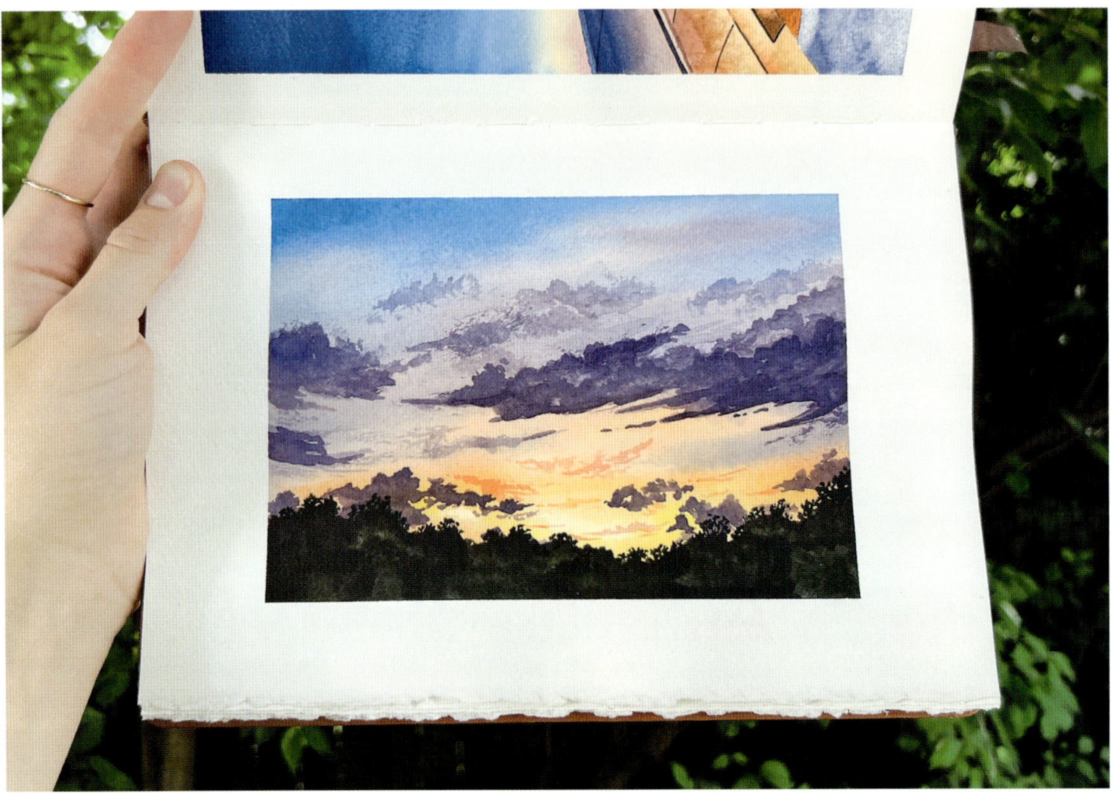

Sunsets are some of the most fun and free subjects to paint in watercolor. I love using bright colors and watching them melt together on the page. In this project, we will go over some basic techniques to use while painting a sunset, but we will also get some great practice painting those distant deciduous trees to "ground" the painting and make it feel complete! I've based this lesson on a sunset I saw from an old apartment of mine. I like to use sunset reference photos to get the general color palette, as well as the shape and direction of any clouds. However, I want you to feel free to deviate from the reference photo as much as you like when painting sunsets. They are very forgiving because they can show up in infinite ways, so use these opportunities to really play with your paints and let them flow together on the page.

materials

Watercolor paints

- Cadmium Yellow, Cadmium Orange, Cadmium Red, Magenta, Ultramarine Blue, Phthalo Blue, Sap Green, Payne's Gray and Van Dyke Brown

Watercolor paper of your choice

- I used my cold press Fabriano Artistico sketchbook size 5 x 7 inches (12.7 x 17.78 cm)

Brushes

- one larger brush (I used a ½ inch oval), one medium brush (I used a 4 round) and one detail brush (I used a 0 round)

Orientation

- landscape

Set up your paper as you like and make sure to add a drop or two of water to your colors so they start to soften.

Reference photo

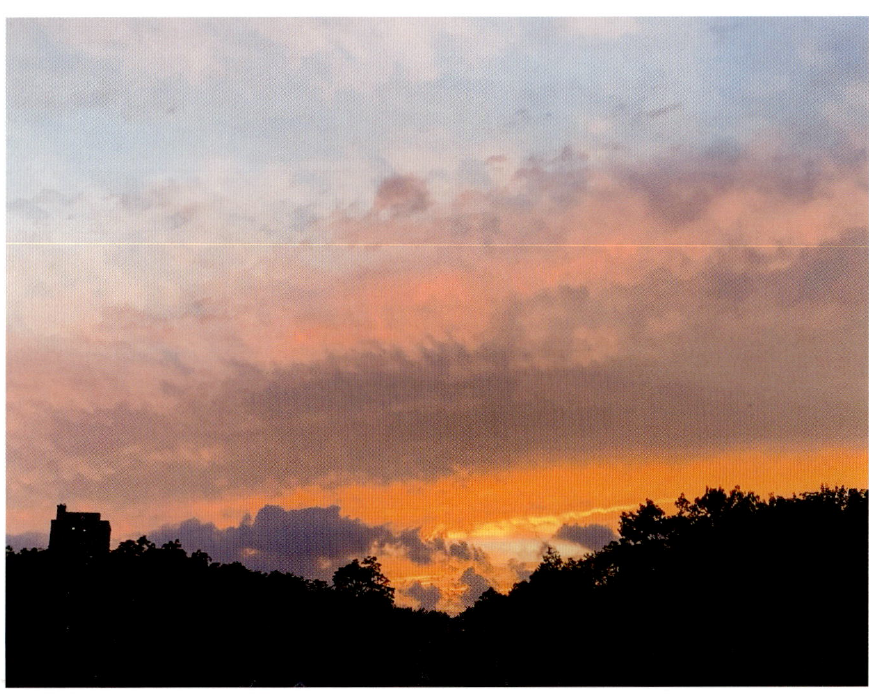

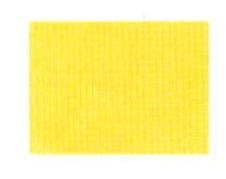

Yellow
Cadmium Yellow

Orange
Cadmium Orange + little Cadmium Red

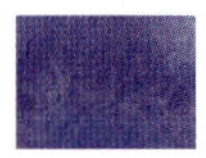

Purple
Ultramarine Blue + Magenta + little Van Dyke Brown

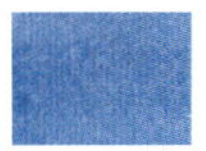

Blue
Ultramarine Blue + Phthalo Blue

Step 1

Mix the main sunset colors swatched above, making sure they are fairly saturated (add less water) to get a vibrant sunset.

PAUSE: Please read through Steps 2–6 before you start so you can work quickly without stopping to read.

Step 2

Use your large brush and cover the entire paper with water. Then, use a sweeping motion with your brush to place your Yellow paint in the low center of the paper.

Step 3

Next, pick up your Orange color and place this color around the Yellow on both sides. No need to blend much—the water on the paper will do that for you!

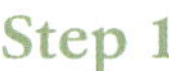

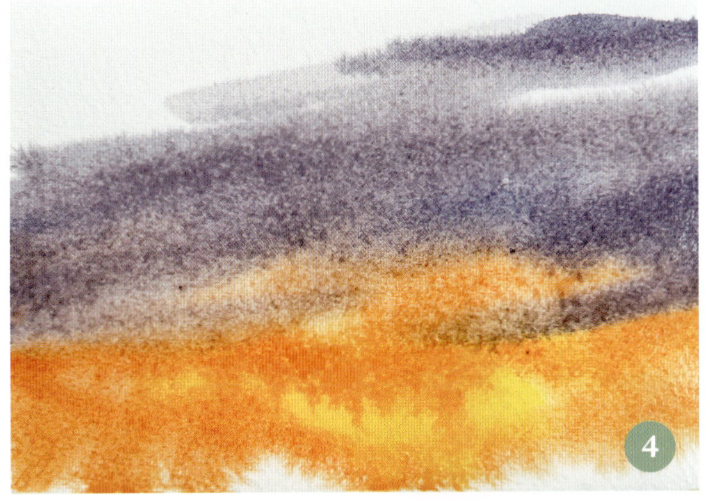

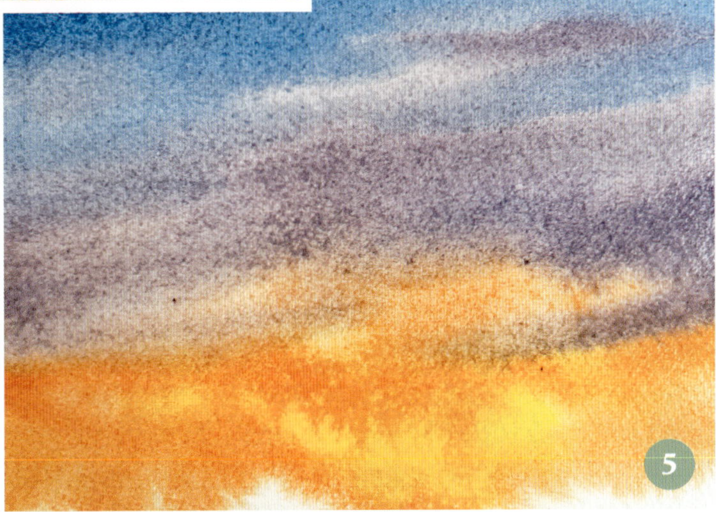

Step 4

Now pick up the Purple color and cover a little over half of whatever area is left above the Orange color. Make sure you're using long, sweeping brush strokes to show movement in the sky!

Step 5

Last, use the Blue to cover any areas that haven't been covered.

I left mine as is, but you can blend these colors together a bit if you feel like you need to. Either use a clean, damp brush to blend some of the colors together or pick up and tilt your paper in different directions to softly blend the colors together.

Step 6

Before this dries, use a completely dry brush to pick up some of the paint in the Yellow section to create bright highlights. You may have to go over it a few times to create the highlight—just keep drying off your brush with your paper towel and picking up the paint.

Let this fully dry before moving on.

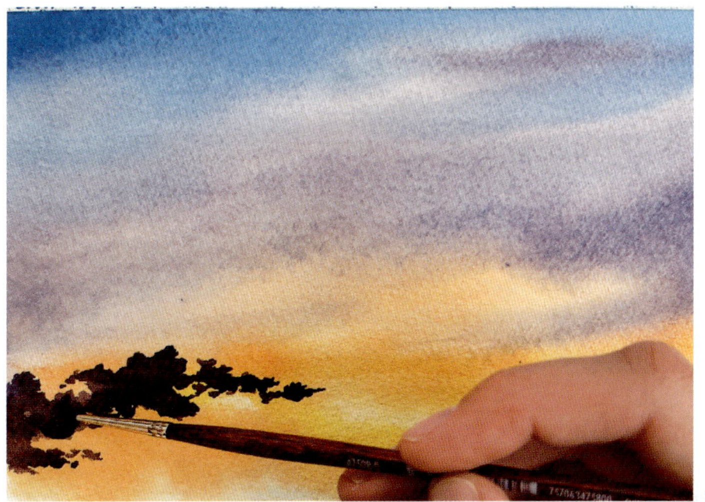

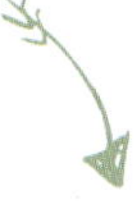

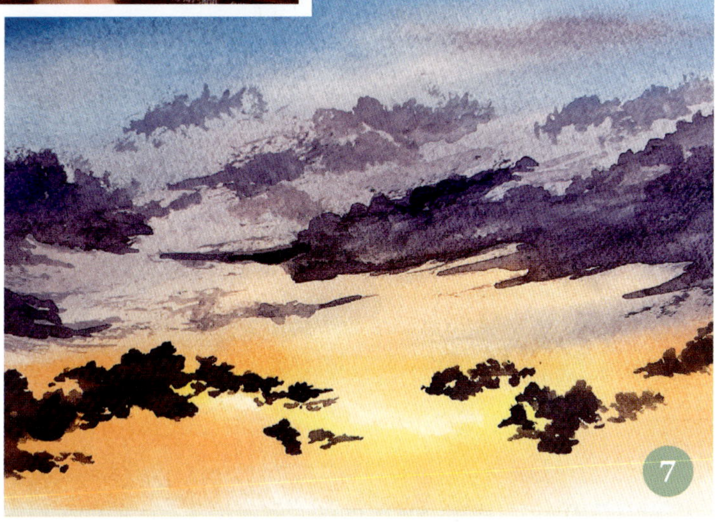

Step 7

Next, we will create some clouds in the foreground. Use a smaller brush and pick up the same Purple color from Step 1. Use circular motions and sweeping brush strokes to create fluffy clouds throughout the painting. Make sure you add some small clouds and some larger clouds and vary the shapes you're using to make it look natural. You can also use a dry brushing texture to add some wispy clouds (see page 16) or water down the Purple color to create lighter clouds.

Feel free to use a clean, damp brush and blend out any marks you make while they are still wet; this can give you a really soft shape to your clouds!

Dark Green
Sap Green + Ultramarine Blue + Van Dyke Brown + Payne's Gray

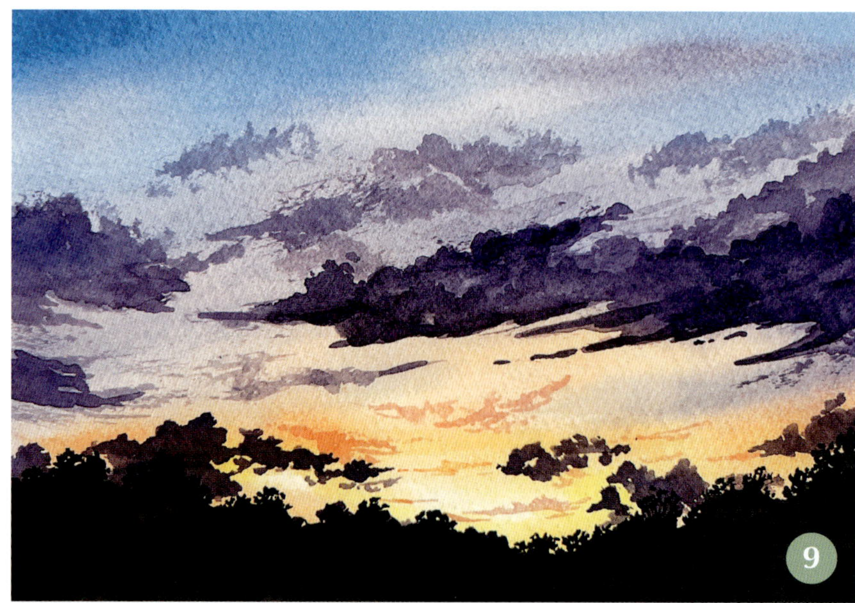

Step 8

Add a few lighter clouds closer to the horizon using skinny, streaky brush strokes to make them appear far away. I used **watered down Cadmium Orange and Magenta** interchangeably for this step.

Step 9

Lastly, let's add in some trees. When creating a painting where the sky is the main focus, it's always good to add a bit of land at the bottom of the painting to ground (pun definitely intended) the painting. Mix up the very Dark Green that is swatched above. Use a smaller brush and a dotting motion to form some general rounded circle shapes at the bottom of the painting. Don't make a straight line of trees though. Make some trees larger and some smaller and change up the overall elevation of the land (see page 93 for more detail on painting distant deciduous trees).

Step 10

Use your detail brush to add some extra leaves and texture to the outside edges of these trees. Take a look at the trees in the reference photo for a better idea of what this looks like. You don't need to do this to every single tree—just pick out a few and add a bit of detail.

Once you're happy with your trees, you're all done! Take off the tape, sign and date your painting and admire your work!

misty forest

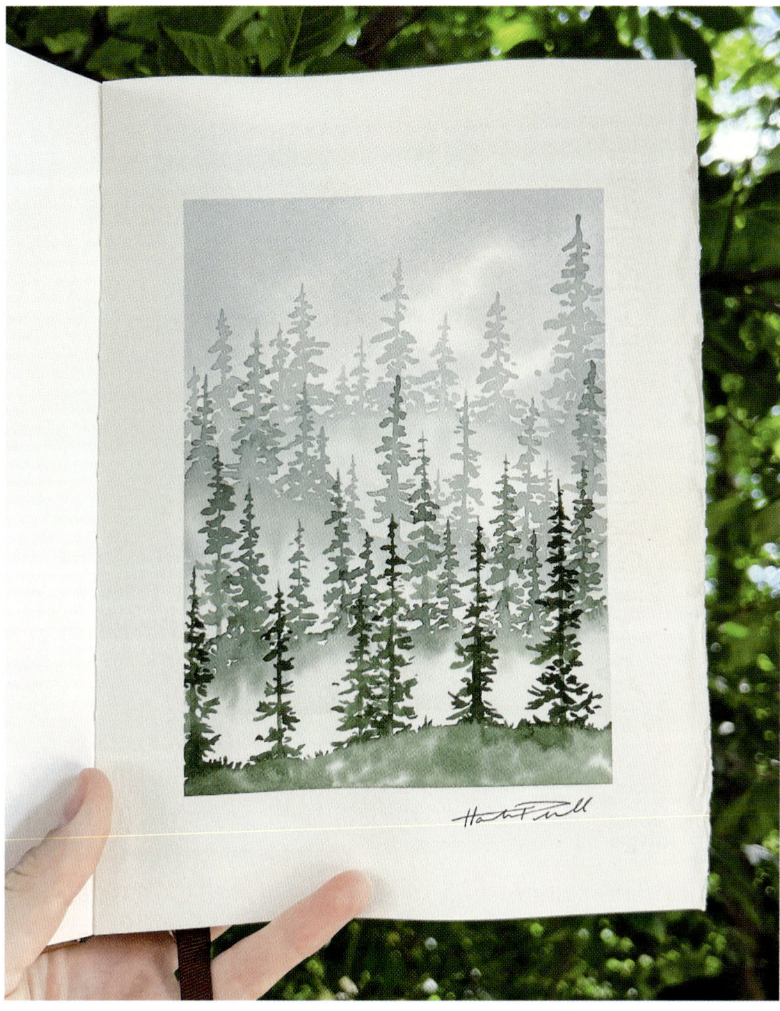

To get more comfortable painting trees and to practice showing distance, we're going to create a misty forest painting. It's a pretty simple technique once you get the hang of it, and the end effect is super cool! This does require some wait time in between layers, so make sure you've got your hairdryer or your patience ready. I did not use a specific reference photo for this since I've painted trees many times, so you are welcome to wing it like me or find some reference photos on the internet to help you on this one.

materials

Watercolor paints

- Payne's Gray and Sap Green

Watercolor paper of your choice

- I used my cold press Fabriano Artistico sketchbook size 5 x 7 inches (12.7 x 17.78 cm)

Brushes

- one larger brush (I used a ½ inch oval) and one smaller brush (I used a size 4 round)

Orientation

- portrait

NOTE: For this project, I used a size 4 round brush for my smaller brush, because it holds enough paint while still being small enough to make the fine details needed for the tree branches. You could also use a size 3 or 2 round, but I wouldn't suggest using a true detail brush.

Set up your paper as you like and make sure to add a drop or two of water to your colors so they start to soften.

Step 1

Since this is a misty forest scene, we're going to paint in a light gray, slightly moody background. Mix a Light Gray color first. Then, using a large brush, cover the entire paper with clean water. Pick up your Light Gray paint and put down some random swooping shapes and brushstrokes starting at the top of the paper. Leave some blank areas and stick to the top two-thirds of the page.

Tilt your paper in different directions to get a soft blend between the Gray paint and the white areas of the paper, or gently blend the paint with a clean, damp brush. Lastly, use a completely dry brush and a tapping motion to pick up excess water/paint from the paper and add soft cloud shapes.

Let this fully dry before moving on.

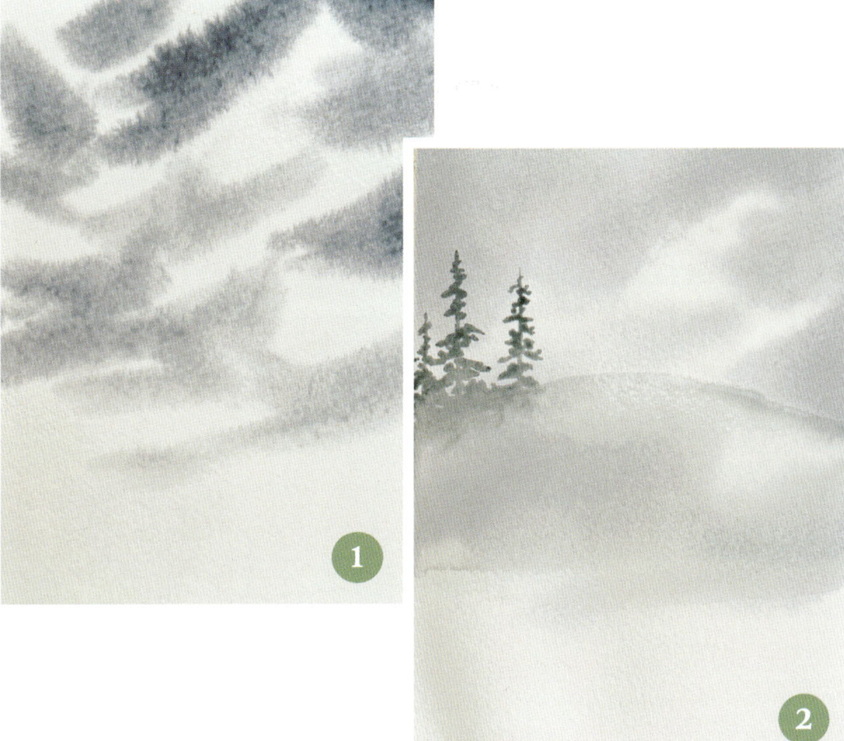

Light Gray
Payne's Gray + water

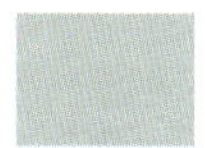

Gray-Green
Payne's Gray + little Sap Green + water

Step 2

Once the sky is fully dry, we can move on to the first layer of trees. Mix a Gray-Green color, adding lots of water to desaturate it.

Use a large brush to put a stripe of clean water a little over halfway up the paper. The stripe should not be a straight horizontal line–pretend you're painting a hill or valley with the water. Then use your smaller brush to start painting trees above this stripe of water using your Gray-Green color. As the paint meets the water, it will spread out and fade, which gives the painting a misty effect. You can paint trees all the way across the paper or paint them in clusters with gaps between; just try to make sure they are unique in height and pattern.

Resist the temptation to make them all "perfect" or make them the same way each time. They will look so much more natural with little imperfections and unique shapes.

I like to follow this general pattern when painting evergreen trees: Paint a vertical line for the trunk and then start at the top and work in a zigzag motion adding branches that get slightly longer each time. Leave some spaces where the trunk is bare and vary the branch shapes and sizes as you work.

If the stripe of water starts to dry before you're done, add more water!

Let this fully dry before moving on.

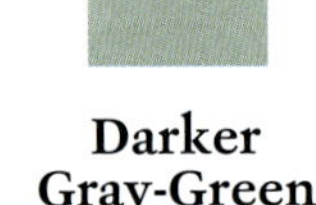

Darker Gray-Green

Payne's Gray + Sap Green + water

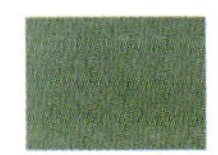

Deep Gray-Green

Payne's Gray + Sap Green + less water

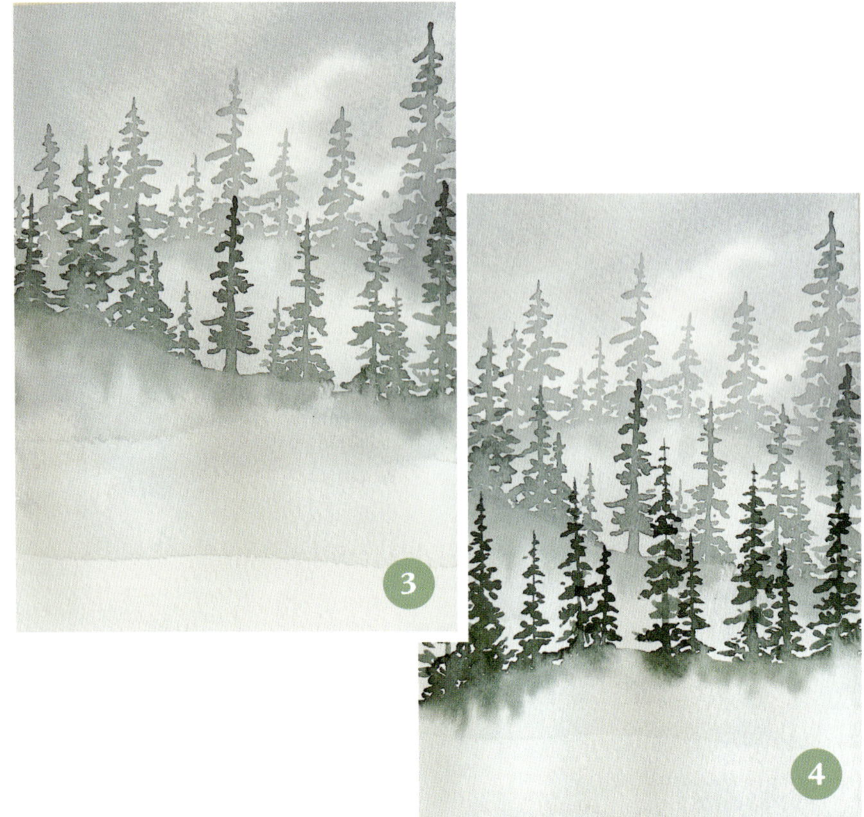

Step 3

Mix a slightly darker version of this Gray-Green color; it should be a noticeable but subtle change. With the new color, repeat Step 2 a little lower on the paper. Change the direction and angle of the stripe of water and then paint in your trees. They should at times overlap the trees from layer one.

Let this fully dry before moving on.

Step 4

You've probably caught on to the pattern by now, you smart artist you. Mix your third gray-green color (Deep Gray-Green), adding more paint and less water and an even higher percentage of green paint. Add another stripe of water below the second layer and start painting in your trees. These should be more detailed than the previous layer, and they can overlap the other layers.

Let this fully dry before moving on.

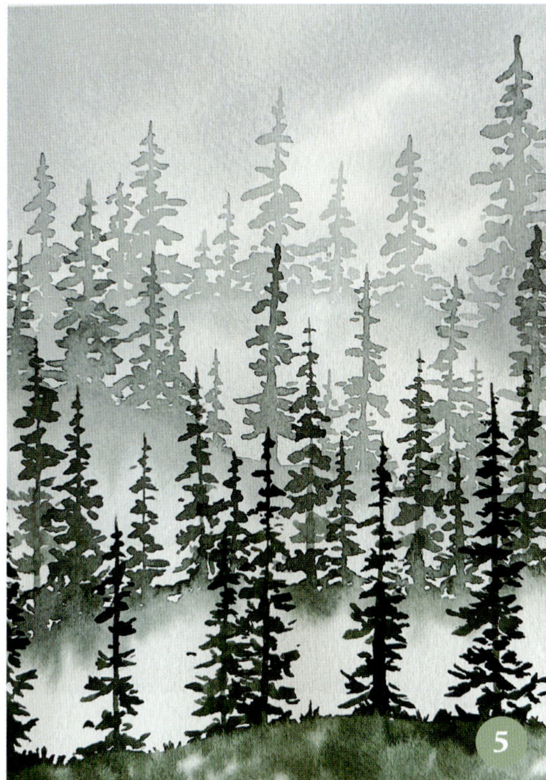

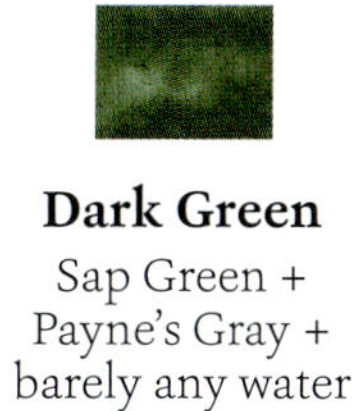

Dark Green

Sap Green + Payne's Gray + barely any water

Step 5

For the last layer, mix your most saturated color yet—mostly green and just enough water that the paint can flow on the paper. The stripe of water should be basically at the bottom of the paper at this point, and I shaped it like some uneven ground for the trees to stand on. Add in your trees, and for this layer, add the silhouettes of little rocks or grass around the base of these trees if you'd like.

And that's it! Let it dry, take off the tape, sign and date your painting and admire your work!

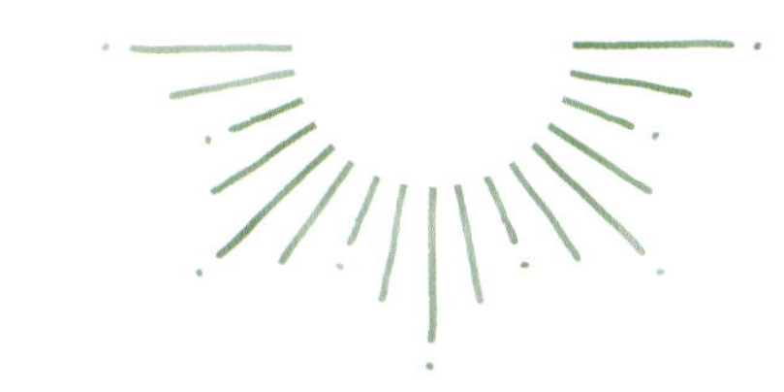

autumn reflections

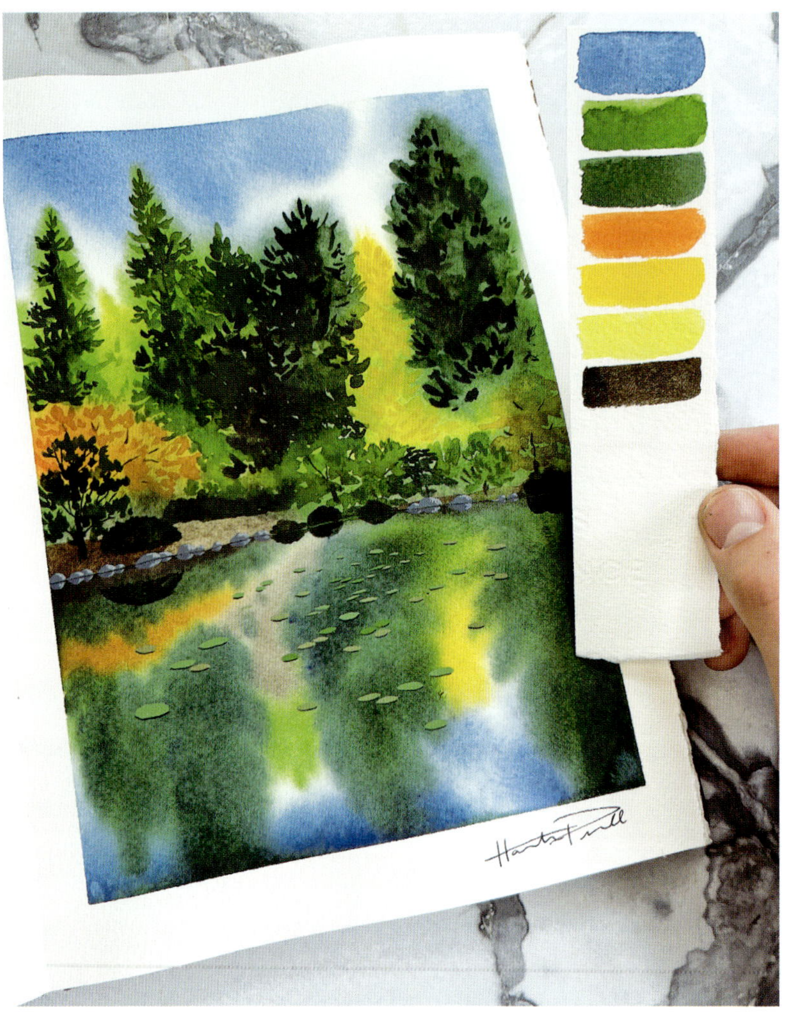

This reference photo comes from my lovely mother, from an afternoon she spent in a local public garden one autumn day. I love the vibrant trees and the beautiful reflection, and I figured it would be the perfect fall forest project. Our focus for this painting will be creating different kinds of trees, as well as an accurate but artistic reflection, so that you feel confident creating your own reflections in the future.

materials

Watercolor paints

- Ultramarine Blue, Phthalo Blue, Sap Green, Lemon Yellow, Cadmium Yellow, Cadmium Red, Van Dyke Brown and Payne's Gray
- White gouache

Watercolor paper of your choice

- I used my cold press Fabriano Artistico sketchbook size 6 x 8.5 inches (15 x 21.5 cm)

Brushes

- one larger brush (I used a ½ inch oval), one medium brush (I used a size 4 round) and one detail brush (I used a size 0 round)

Orientation

- portrait

Set up your paper as you like and make sure to add a drop or two of water to your colors so they start to soften.

Reference photo

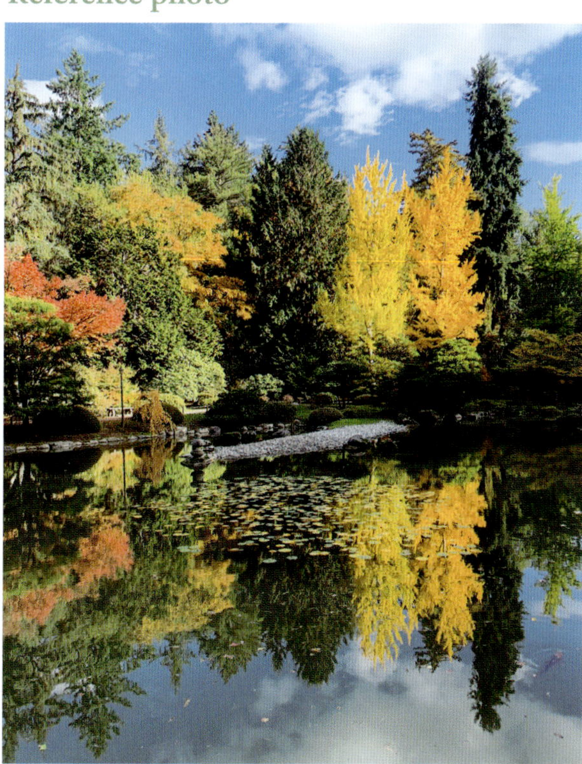

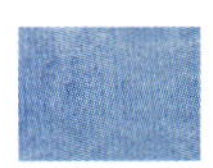
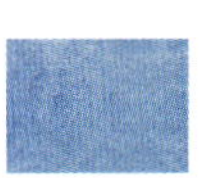

Sky Blue
Phthalo Blue + Ultramarine Blue

Light Yellow
Lemon Yellow

Yellow
Cadmium Yellow

Orange
Cadmium Yellow + Cadmium Red

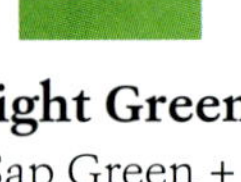

Light Green
Sap Green + Cadmium Yellow

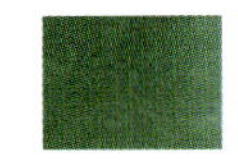

Dark Green
Sap Green + Ultramarine Blue

Brown
Van Dyke Brown + little Ultramarine Blue

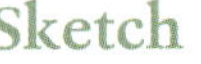

Sketch

Start by sketching out the horizon line (where the water meets the land) a little under halfway up the page and sketch the little hills just above the horizon line.

Step 1

We'll be tackling this piece in halves, starting with the top half. Since we're painting everything at once, you'll need to prepare all of the colors first (see the swatches above). Add enough water so the paint flows well but keep the colors pretty saturated.

PAUSE: Please read through the following instructions before you start, so you can work quickly without stopping to read.

Use a large brush for this step and start by filling in everything above the horizon line with clean water from your cup.

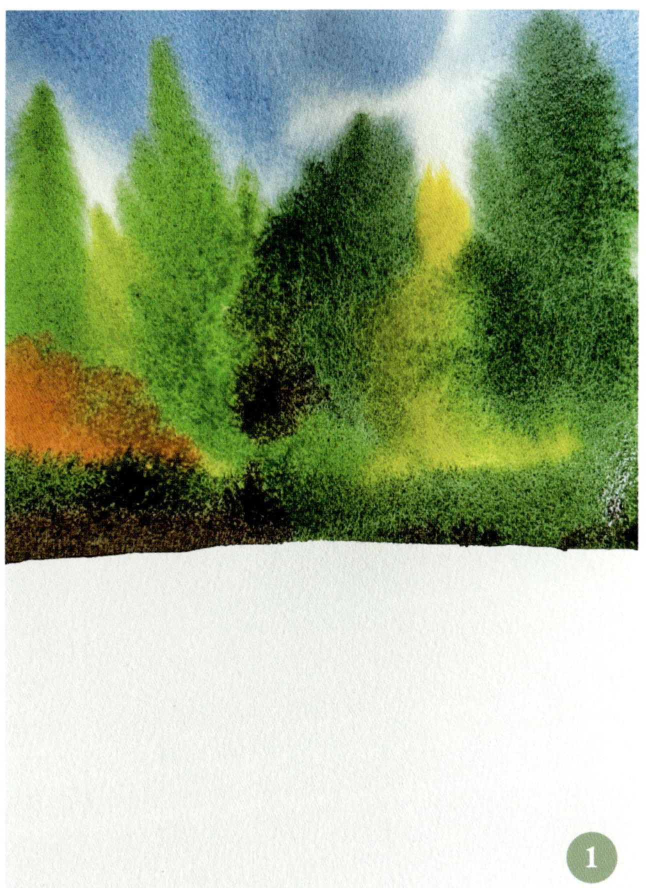

Pick up your Sky Blue color and put a few dots and sweeping paint strokes at the top of the page, leaving a few white spaces. Keep this to the very top of the page.

Pick up your Light Yellow color and paint in an oval tree shape on the right side of the page—around where the yellow tree is in the reference photo. Switch to your darker Yellow and drop in some dots in that tree shape.

Pick up your Orange color and create a smaller, rounded tree shape just above the horizon line on the left.

Use your Light Green and paint in a couple of loose, tall tree shapes behind and in between the Yellow and Orange shapes. Transition to the Dark Green and paint in a couple more. I did this by painting stacked V shapes, starting with a small V and each one getting larger.

Use your Dark Green and Brown colors to fill in any blank areas right above the horizon line or in between the trees.

This will look messy, and that's okay! Resist the urge to mess with it and just let it dry!

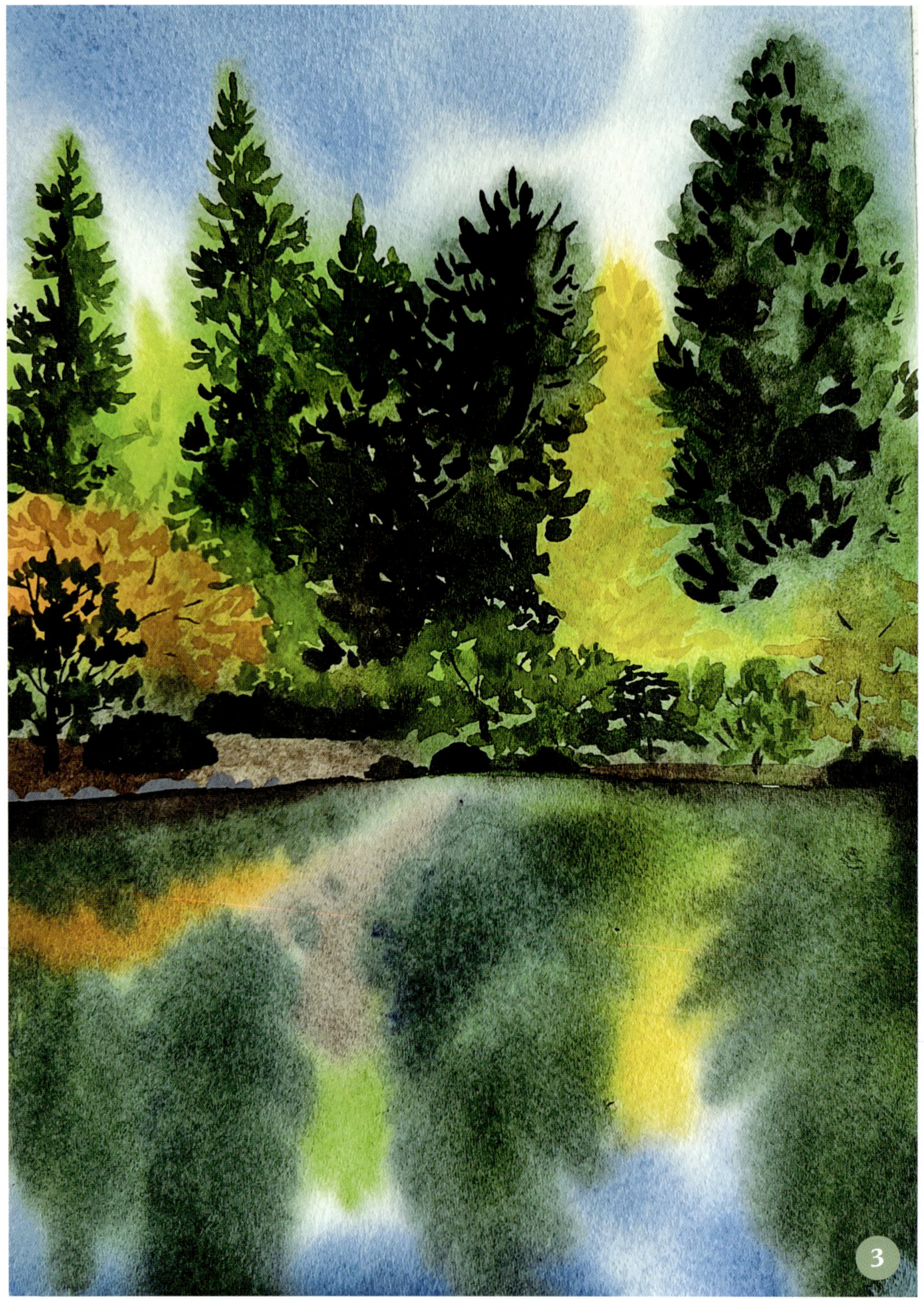
3

Step 2

Next, let's add some detail to this top half using the same colors as in Step 1. For example, use Dark Green to add some general leaf and branch details to the dark green tree shapes you painted in Step 1. Use the Light Yellow or darker Yellow to add leaf details on top of the yellow tree. Continue this way until you've added some general details to everything in this top section.

You can also add some small, rounded bushes with Dark Green right where the land meets the water.

Step 3

Next, let's paint in the reflection. You'll need exactly the same colors as in Step 1, except this time you're going to **add a *little* Payne's Gray to each color** to darken it and dull it down.

I find it helpful to turn my paper around 180 degrees so that I'm painting the reflection right side up. Complete this section exactly the same way as the top section, putting down a layer of water first, adding in the sky and the trees. Do your best to create a mirror image here; imagine you're folding the paper in half along the horizon line and recreate all of the main shapes from the top section onto the bottom section. For example, put a yellow tree directly underneath the yellow tree in the top half, a large dark green tree opposite one in the top half, etc.

Let this dry completely.

Step 4

Next, let's create a more detailed mirror image reflection of a few elements. This step takes some brain power, especially when it's new to you. Do your best; this is what will really bring this painting to life!

First, if you created any small bushes or trees that are right at the water's edge, paint the exact same thing reflected in the water. You'll notice I did this for those little dark green, rounded bushes. Don't worry about any ripples or distortion here. The reflection is so close to the horizon line and the water is so calm that it's basically a mirror.

NOTE: If the element you're reflecting is very close to the horizon line, the reflection will also be close to the horizon line. If the element is a little higher up on the page (see the large round bush on the left side of my painting as an example) the reflection will be the same distance below the horizon line.

To create the rocks at the horizon line, mix white gouache with Payne's Gray to create a light gray. Then use a detail brush to paint little rounded rock shapes at the waterline. Use a lighter gray version of this color (add more white gouache) to dot on a highlight on each of the rocks. For the reflection, use a slightly darker gray (add more Payne's Gray), turn your paper around 180 degrees and reflect each rock shape into the water. Try to leave a little sliver of paper showing through between the rocks and their reflection. And don't forget to add the corresponding highlight to the reflection!

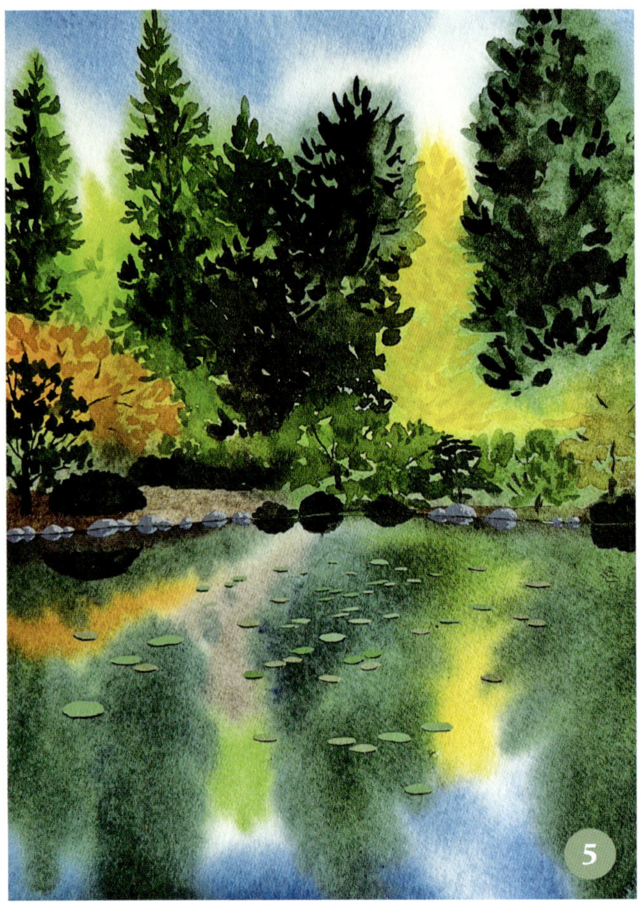

Step 5

Lastly, let's add some lily pads floating on this pond. This is another element that will sell this reflection as realistic to the viewer. Mix up an opaque light green by mixing sap green with white gouache, and mix a light brown by mixing Van Dyke Brown with white gouache. The key to lily pads is perspective; the ones further away from us (closer to the horizon line) are basically little dashes. The ones closer to us (toward the bottom of the page) are larger and more of an oval shape. Using your detail brush, add some with the light green and some with the light brown, randomly throughout the pond section.

Once you're happy with the number of lily pads, switch back to your Dark Green watercolor and add a thin line on the bottom edge of each of your lily pads. This will create a small shadow and make it look like they're sitting on the water.

Once you're happy with the lily pads, you're all done with this painting! Take off the tape, sign and date your painting and admire your work.

perspective of the worm

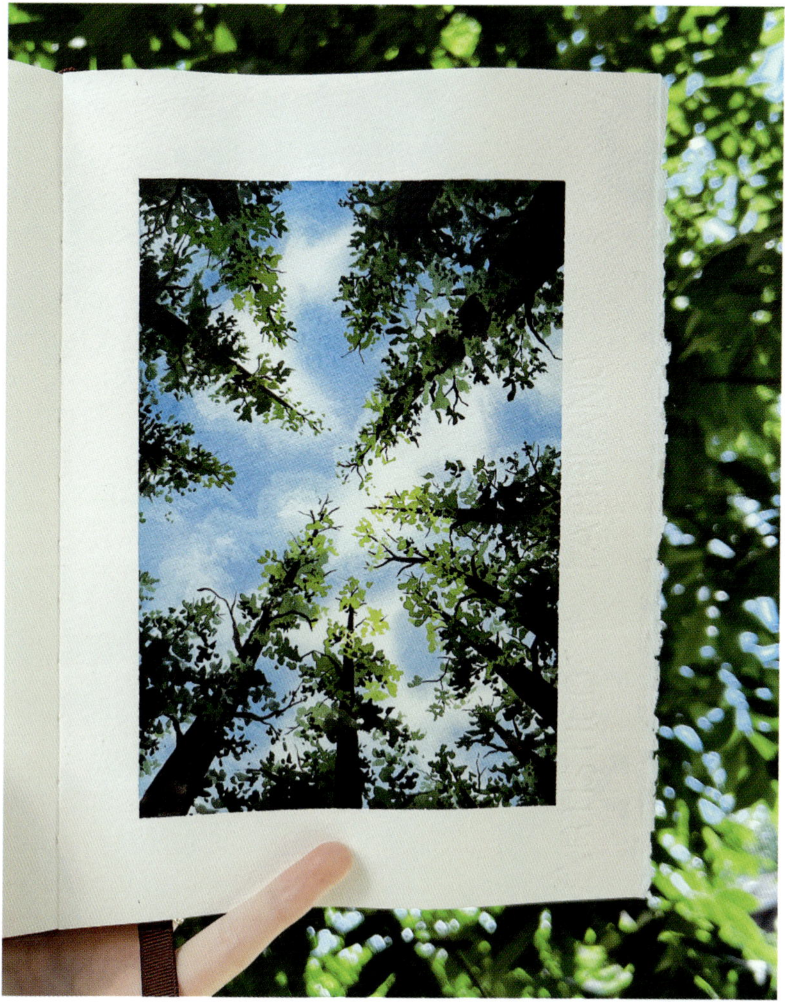

This next project will challenge our perspective skills and give you a new appreciation for the size and scope of trees. We won't be using a reference photo for this one, but if you need some extra support, feel free to find a reference photo on the internet or lay down in a forest near you to see this perspective for yourself!

materials

Watercolor paints

- Ultramarine Blue, Phthalo Blue, Sap Green, Cadmium Yellow and Van Dyke Brown

Watercolor paper of your choice

- I used my cold press Fabriano Artistico sketchbook size 6 x 8 inches (15 x 20 cm)

Brushes

- one larger brush (I used a ½ inch oval), one medium brush (I used a size 4 round) and one detail brush (I used a size 0 round)

Orientation

- portrait and landscape both work. You pick!

Set up your paper as you like and make sure to add a drop or two of water to your colors so they start to soften.

Step 1

We will start with a sunny blue sky background. I will briefly go over the directions for this here, but for more details, please see the instructions in the Rolling Hills project on page 20. First, mix your Sky Blue color.

Use a large brush to put down a layer of clear water over your entire paper. Then drop in some loose, swooping brushstrokes of Sky Blue, leaving some white on the page. Tilt your paper to blend the paint softly, then use a completely dry brush and a tapping motion to lift excess paint and create the impression of clouds.

Continuously dry your brush with a paper towel as you work and make sure to complete this before the paint dries!

Let this fully dry before moving on.

Step 2

Next, we will start adding in our trees. We will begin with the leaves of the trees, so mix a Light Green, Medium Green and Dark Green using the color recipes on the right before you start.

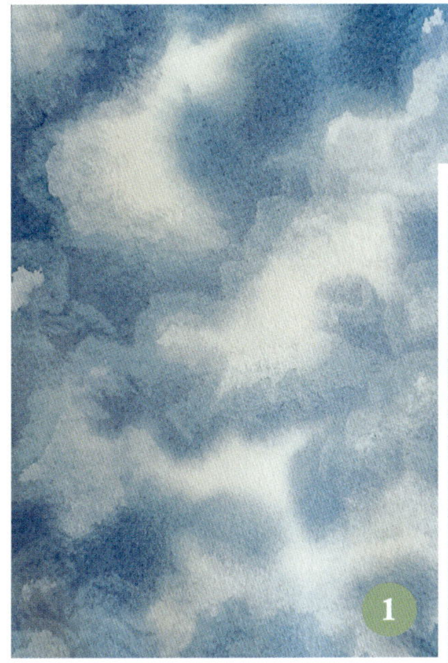

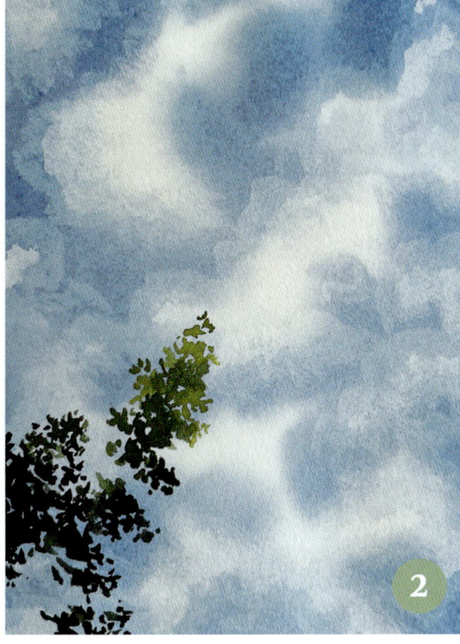

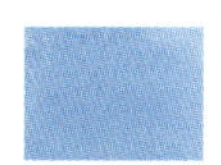

Sky Blue
Ultramarine Blue + Phthalo Blue

Light Green
Cadmium Yellow + Sap Green

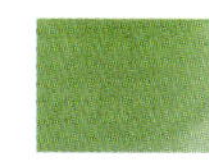

Medium Green
Sap Green + little Ultramarine Blue

Dark Green
Sap Green + Ultramarine Blue + Van Dyke Brown

Use a smaller brush (I used my 4 round) and begin somewhere near the middle of the page with the Light Green color. Dab on some loose dots, starting at a point and working your way outward, creating random branch shapes that get wider and wider.

Once you've gone about one-third of the way down the tree, switch to your Medium Green and continue working. Those two greens should blend together at spots where they meet. Make sure you're leaving plenty of small blank spots throughout the tree for texture!

Once you've gotten about two-thirds of the way down the tree, switch to your Dark Green and finish the tree to the edge of the page.

A few dos and don'ts on these trees:

- DO work quickly and loosely. This will give you a more natural look at the end.
- DO work in a loose triangle shape. The top of the tree should be narrow and the bottom of the tree should be quite wide.
- DO create different-sized trees. Some can be shorter or taller, wider or skinnier!
- DON'T keep your trees separate all the time. It's okay for them to overlap and blend together!

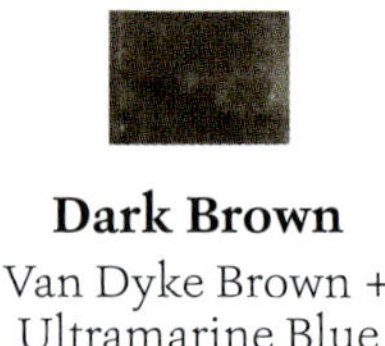

Dark Brown
Van Dyke Brown +
Ultramarine Blue

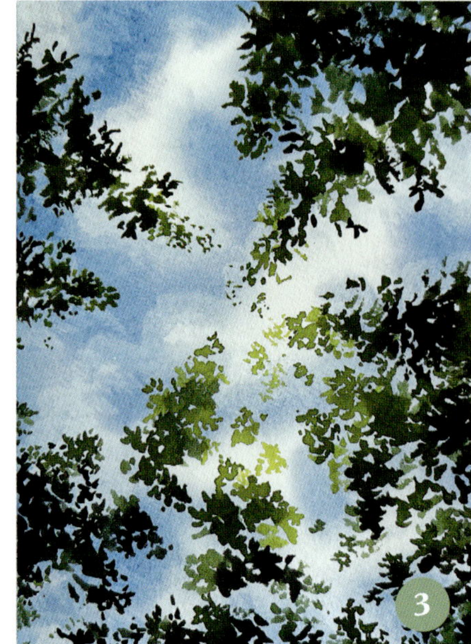

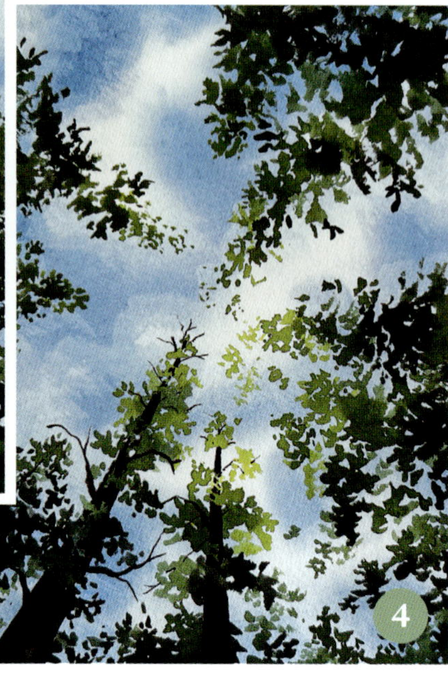

Step 3

Work your way around the page using the techniques from Step 2. Each of your trees should start somewhere near the center of the page and radiate toward an edge like spokes on a wheel.

Let this fully dry before moving on.

Step 4

Once you've created the leaves of your trees, it's time to add the trunks and branches using a Dark Brown color.

Using a detail brush, add in the tree trunks. These trunks should start out very skinny at the top and get much wider as you work your way to the edge of the page.

You can see in the progress photo some areas where the trunk looks like it's behind the leaves. To indicate this, at certain points on each tree, choose a section of leaves that will be in front of your trunk. Don't paint the trunk here—just fill in any small open spots in the leaves with the brown paint. Then continue painting the trunk as normal.

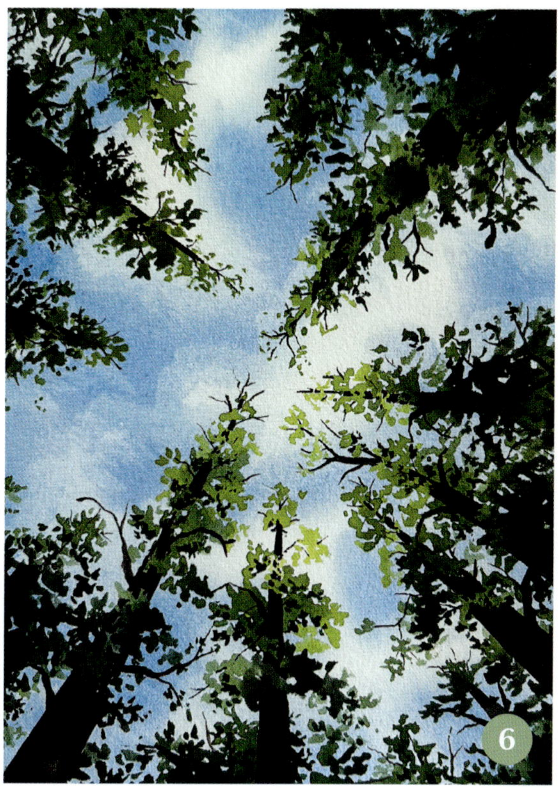

Step 5

After you've added in the trunk, make sure to add in a few wiggly branches. Feel free to add some branches in front of the leaves, as well as some peeking out from behind clusters of leaves. These branches should be thicker and longer near the bottom of the tree and thinner and shorter near the top. They can radiate outward in any direction from the trunk.

Step 6

Once the basic shapes of the trees and trunks are in, you can add a few final details. I used a detail brush and the Medium and Dark Greens to stipple on some extra texture to the leaves in certain areas that looked flat. No need to do this everywhere—just a few places will elevate the detail level of the whole piece. You can do this to the outside edges of each tree, as well, if you want more "leafy" detail there.

This is also where I evaluated my piece as a whole and decided to add one more tree in a spot that looked too bare to me. Take a look at your piece, and if you find a spot that could use another tree, feel free to add it!

Once you're happy with your trees, you're all done with this painting! Take off the tape, sign and date your painting and admire your work.

orcas island sunset

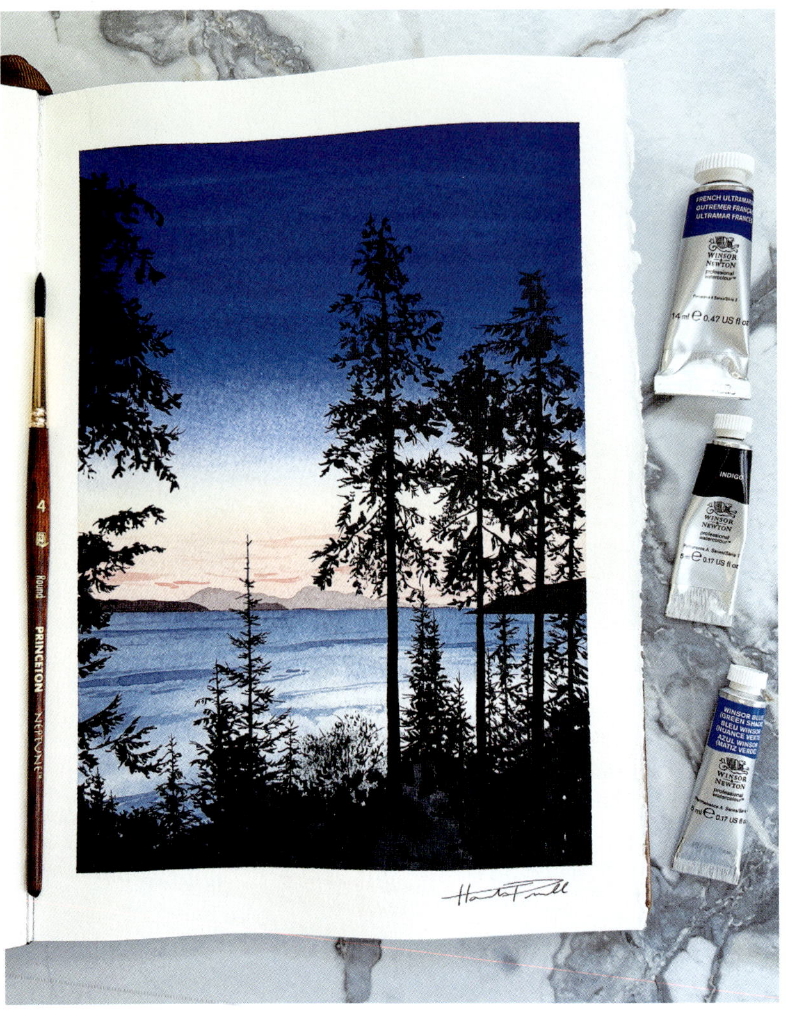

This next project will challenge our tree-making skills, all while creating a fun and peaceful sunset landscape. This reference photo was taken on Orcas Island, which is one of the San Juan Islands in northwestern Washington State. It's an absolutely gorgeous place (especially in the summer) with late sunsets, ocean and island views and temperate forests. This piece will help you continue to practice painting detailed trees, but you'll also get experience painting a sunset gradient and an ocean reflection.

materials

Watercolor paints

- Cadmium Yellow, Cadmium Orange, Alizarin Crimson, Magenta, Ultramarine Blue, Van Dyke Brown and Payne's Gray

Watercolor paper of your choice

- I used my cold press Fabriano Artistico sketchbook size 6 x 8 inches (15 x 20 cm)

Brushes

- one larger brush (I used a ½ inch oval), one medium brush (I used a size 4 round) and one detail brush (I used a size 0 round)

Orientation

- portrait

Set up your paper as you like and make sure to add a drop or two of water to your colors so they start to soften.

Reference photo

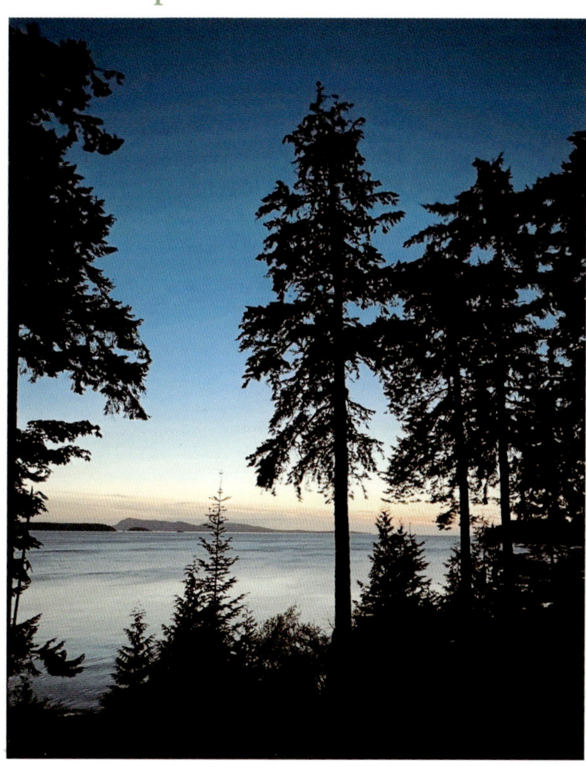

Sketch

Sketch the horizon line about one-third of the way up the paper. I used a piece of tape to mark the horizon line to help me get a completely straight horizon line.

Step 1

As usual, we will start this painting by creating the sky, this time using a gradient technique (see page 15). Mix up a Blue, Yellow and a Pink color. Water down the Yellow and Pink colors but keep the Blue color fairly saturated.

PAUSE: Please read through the following instructions before you start, so you can work quickly without stopping to read.

Start at the top of the page and use horizontal brushstrokes to fill it in with Blue. Once you've covered about one-third of the sky section, add some water to your Blue color and work until you've covered about two-thirds of the sky section. Then, clean off your brush completely and add a thin stripe of clear water underneath the Blue section to blend out that edge.

Next, clean your brush and add a stripe of Yellow right below the Blue section, blending it with the stripe of water you just painted. Finally, use the Pink color to fill in the rest of the sky section to the horizon line.

Lavender
Alizarin Crimson + Payne's Gray + more water

Dark Purple
Alizarin Crimson + Payne's Gray + less water

You can use a clean, damp brush and horizontal stripes working your way back up the paper to blend everything out (though I recommend only doing this once; after that, you'll introduce more texture to the sky).

Let this fully dry before moving on.

Step 2 (optional)

Once the sky section has totally dried, assess how it looks. If you want a more vibrant sky, repeat Step 1 like I did for my painting. If you're happy with it as is, move on to Step 3.

Step 3

Now, we will add some of the distant land and islands on the horizon line. Create two purple colors for this step using the color recipes above.

Using a smaller brush and the Lavender, add an island or two in the distance. Use the reference photo to inspire you here, but feel free to add whatever land or islands you feel like adding!

Let that dry, then switch to the Dark Purple and add a couple additional distant islands. Feel free to overlap the lighter Lavender islands.

Once you're done with this, you can remove the tape at the horizon if you used it.

Blue-Gray
Ultramarine Blue + little Alizarin Crimson + little Payne's Gray + water

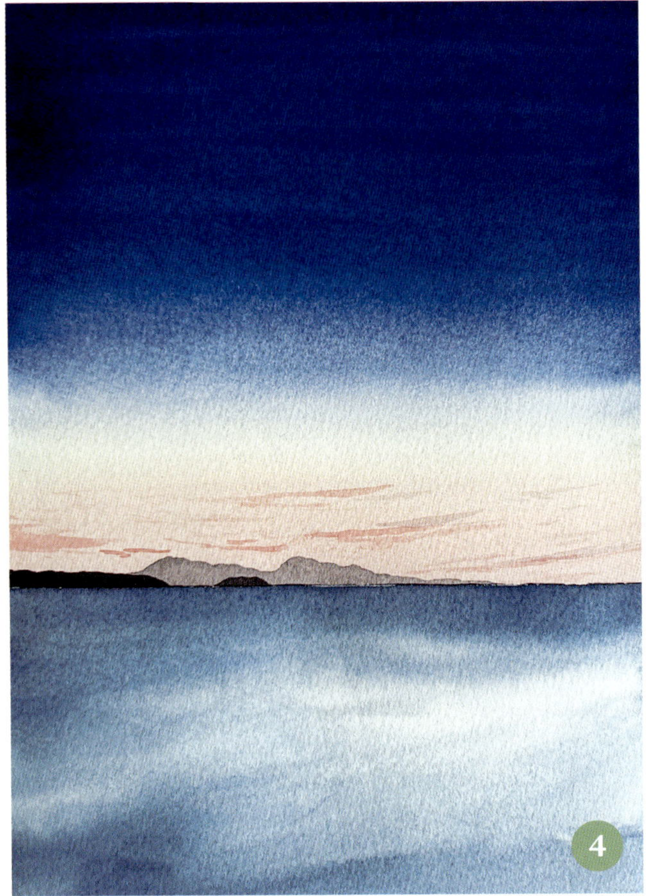

Step 4

Now let's fill in the ocean section. You'll need a Blue-Gray color for this section, but make sure to water it down a bit so it's not too dark!

Notice in the reference photo that there are some sections of the water that are darker gray and some that are quite light. To imitate this, we'll be putting down some Blue-Gray in the sections we want darker, then quickly blending with water.

Use a large brush and the Blue-Gray paint you just mixed and put some large, sweeping horizontal brush strokes directly under the horizon line, as well as some closer to the bottom of the paper. Then quickly switch to a clean, wet brush to fill in the rest of the paper on this section. Use your brush to blend everything together smoothly.

You can also use a completely dry brush to lift some of the color for more highlights and texture. I did this around the center of the water section.

Let this fully dry before moving on.

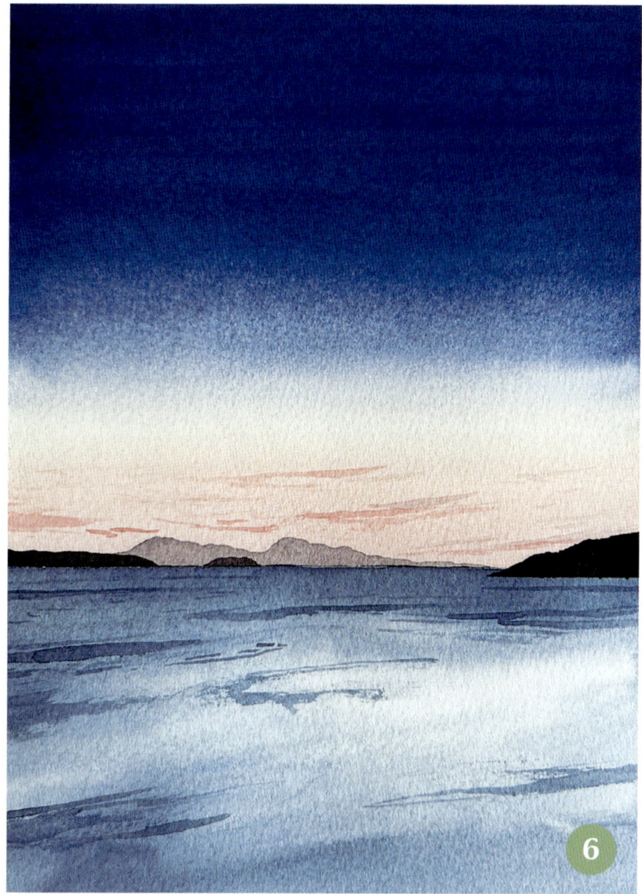

Step 5

Use your small detail brush and the same Blue-Gray color from Step 4 and start adding some sweeping brush strokes to the ocean. Notice in the reference photo these textures are at a slight angle (upwards from left to right). I used a dry brushing texture here (see page 16) and then used the point of my brush to add some swirling and sweeping lines around the paper. Don't try to be too perfect here; little imperfections are good and make it look more natural!

Step 6

Using a very Dark Purple (the same color as in Step 3 with less water) add one or two more pieces of land in the distance, just below the horizon line. Dropping these down slightly below the horizon line makes them appear even closer. Feel free to use a piece of tape again to get a straight line at the bottom.

Black
Payne's Gray + Van Dyke Brown

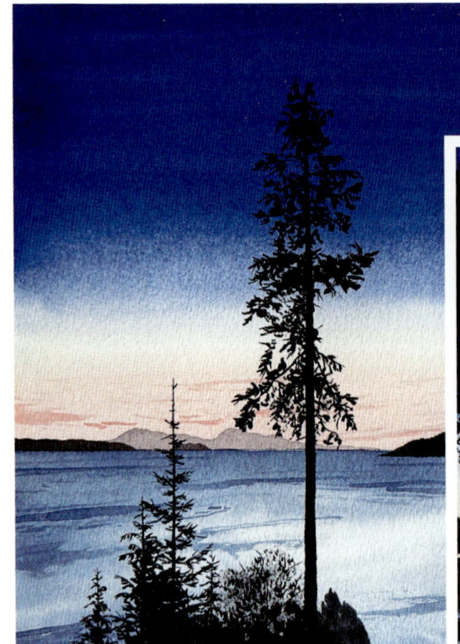

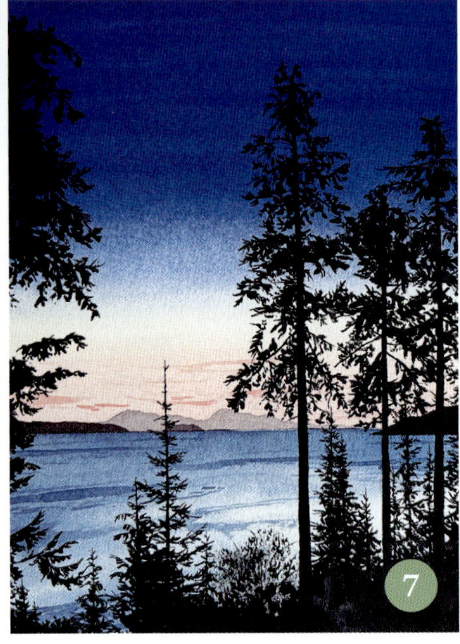

Step 7

Now for the last but most important step of this painting, we will add the trees in the foreground. Use a very dark color for this step.

Using a detail brush, I started with some of the smaller trees to get my bearings, then I painted in the centermost large tree. My general technique for painting these trees is to paint in the trunk first, then work from top to bottom, adding in branches. The branches start out quite small but increase in size and thickness as I work toward the bottom of the tree. A few other things to note while painting in these trees:

- Scraggly is good! Make lots of random marks and work quickly while painting in these trees—it will make them look more natural!
- Keep your trunks under control. They are thinner than you think and don't get very wide at the base. You can always make them thicker later, but you can't make them thinner. They are also not perfectly straight or smooth, so resist the temptation to "fix" them as you'll end up making them too wide.

With that in mind, go forth and create trees! Take your time here; this is the main focal point of the painting, so it's worth it to put extra effort into this step. Once you're happy with your trees, you're all done! Take off the tape, sign and date your painting and admire your work.

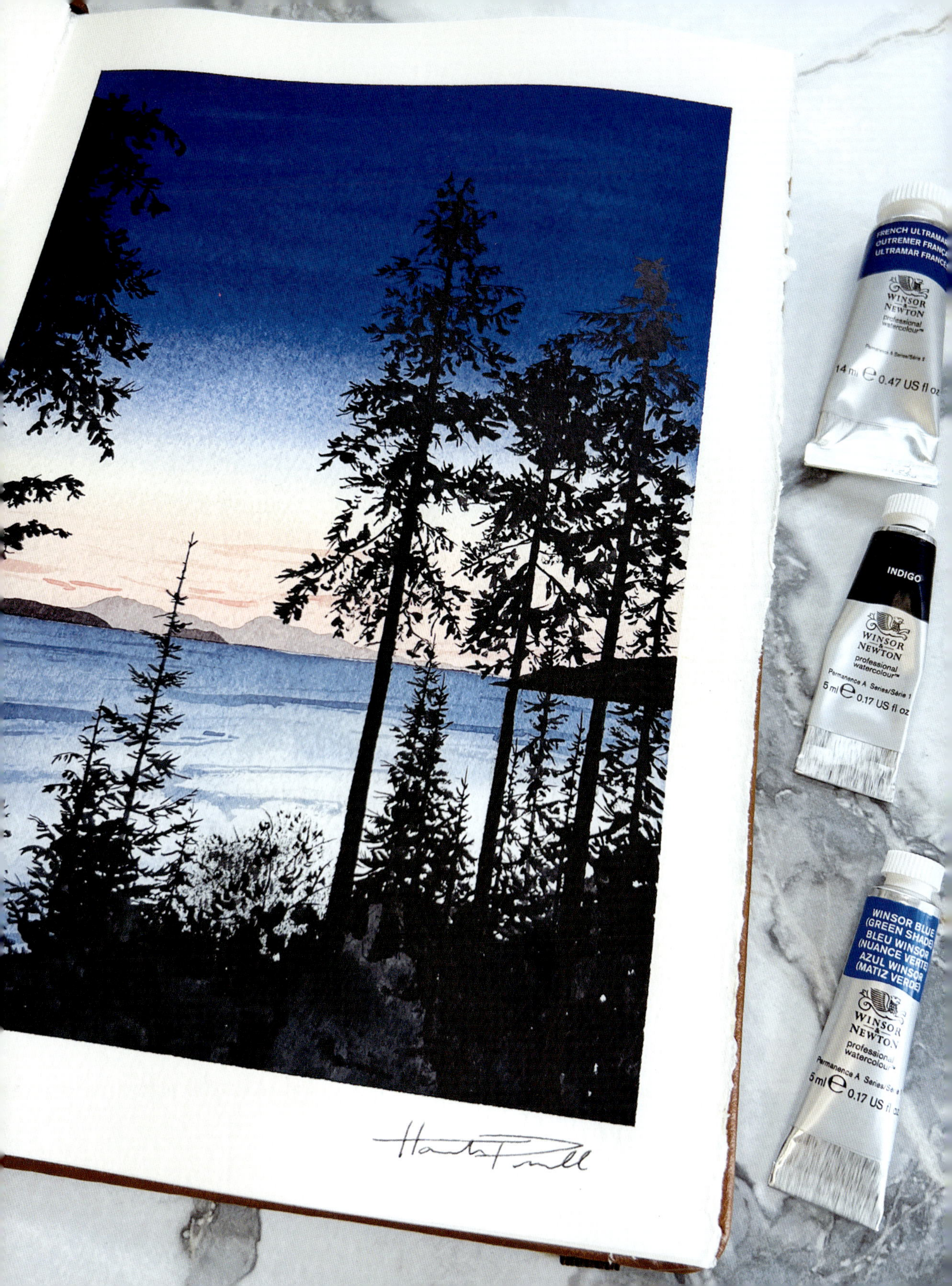
WINSOR & NEWTON
professional watercolour
14 ml ℮ 0.47 US fl oz
INDIGO
WINSOR & NEWTON
professional watercolour
Permanence A Series/Série 1
5 ml ℮ 0.17 US fl oz
WINSOR BLUE
BLEU WINSOR
AZUL WINSOR
(MATIZ VERDE)
WINSOR & NEWTON
professional watercolour
5 ml ℮ 0.17 US fl oz

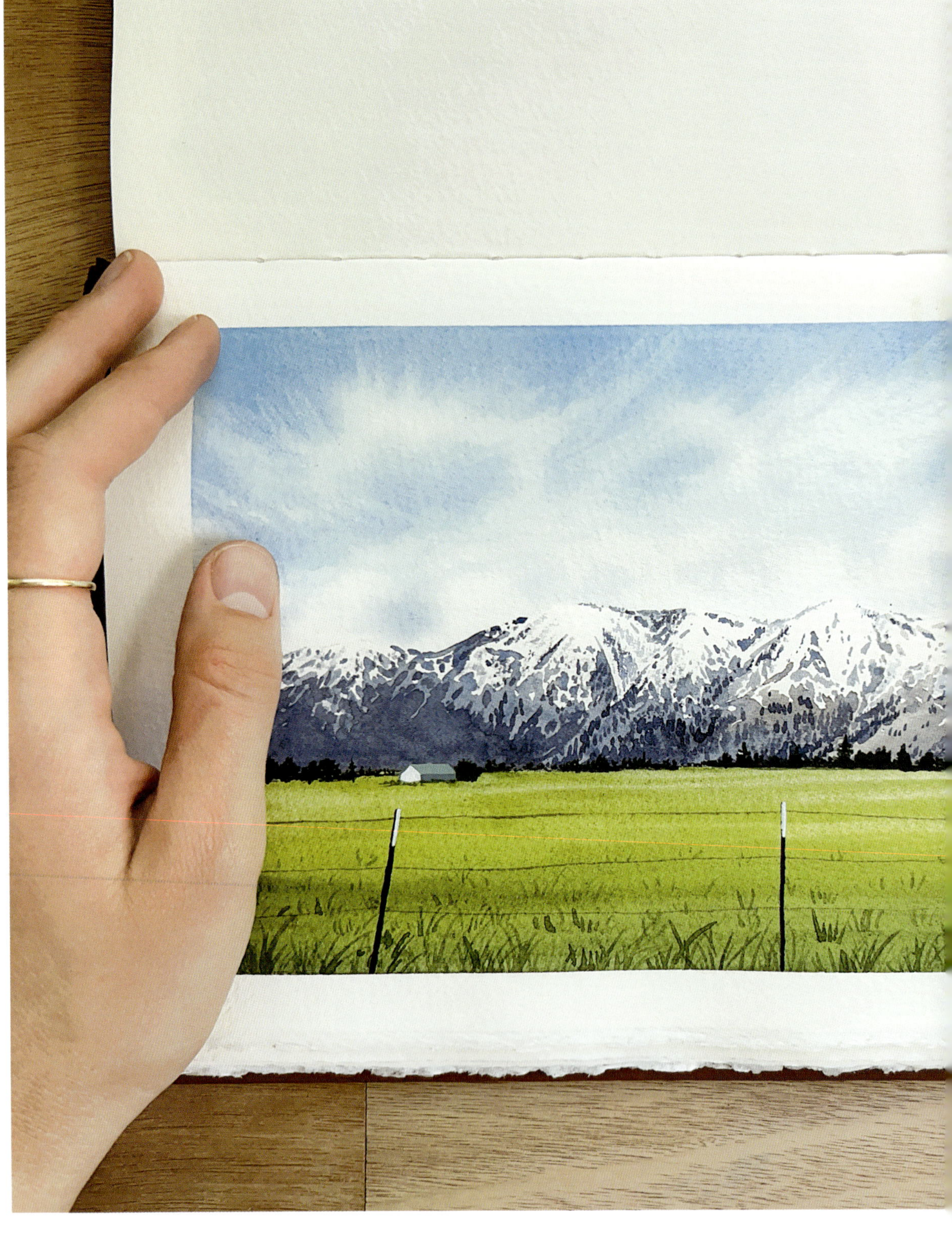

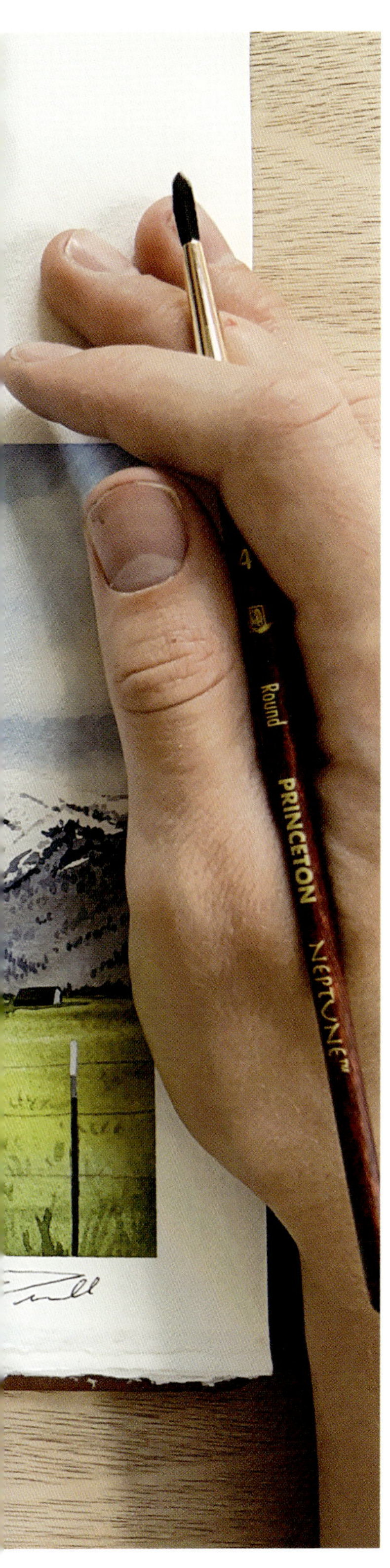

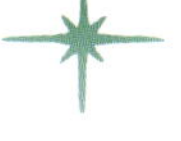

chapter 5 mountains majesty

Mountains make wonderful subjects for watercolor painting. The scale is so fun to capture, there are so many different color options and they are a great background element in any landscape. I grew up in western Washington, surrounded by two mountain ranges, and I loved seeing them in the distance on clear days. I've painted mountains from the time I was a child, and they continue to inspire me today. I hope my appreciation for mountain landscapes will shine through this chapter, and I hope it leaves you inspired as well.

create your own mountains

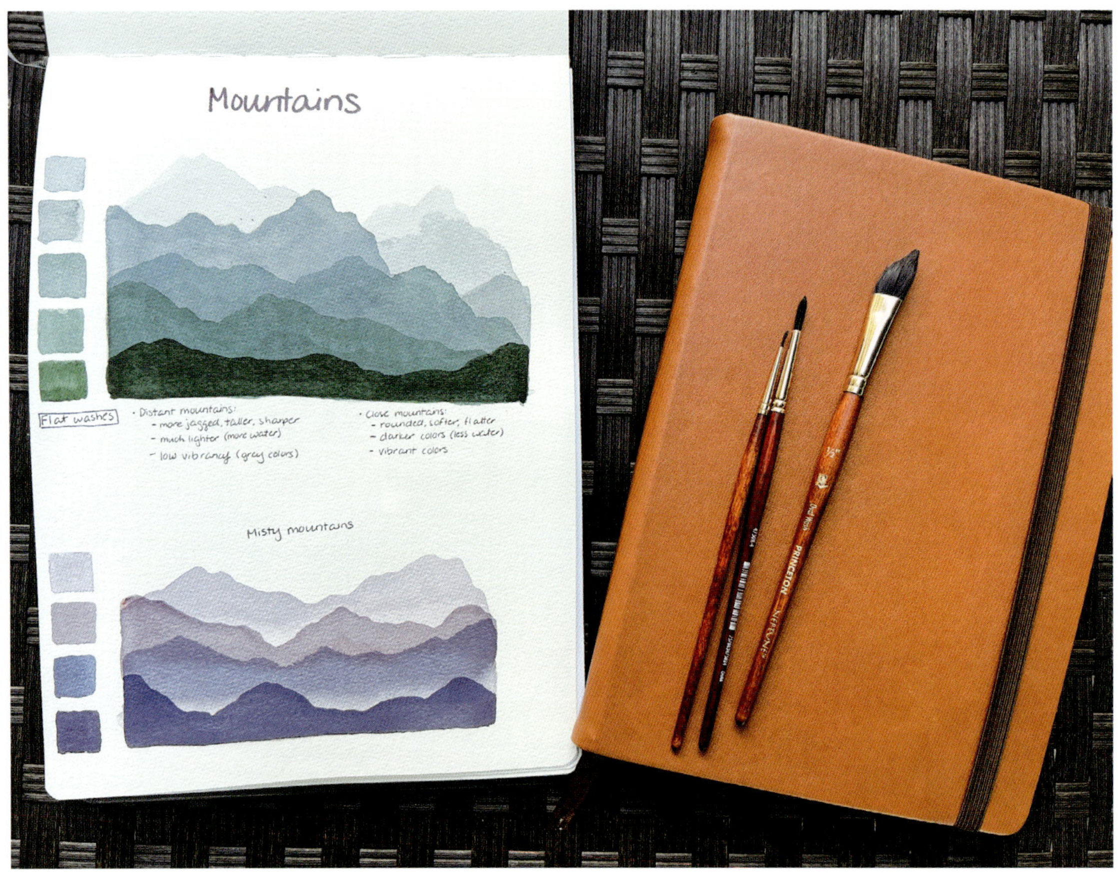

There are a few keys to creating a realistic-looking range of mountains, and once you have those details down, you can create as many mountains as you want! Let's practice those keys first before diving into more complicated mountain scenes. Keep in mind that these are just general guidelines and aren't always true. Always pay attention to your reference photo to make sure these rules still apply and make adjustments when they don't.

When painting mountains, keep the following three keys in mind:

- **Shape**: Distant mountains are usually more jagged, taller and have steeper peaks. There are also usually more peaks and more texture. When painting these, avoid making generic triangle shapes, and instead wiggle your brush randomly to create a unique mountain range. Closer mountains are generally more rounded and smoother and have less extreme elevation changes. You can also overlap a previous layer or make some of the later layers taller than the previous layers in some spots.
- **Value**: Distant mountains are (almost) always lighter in value, so make sure to add lots of water to your paint when creating those distant layers. As you work your way through mountain layers, you should be adding less water and more paint to your color mixtures.
- **Hue:** You can use pretty much any color to paint a mountain range, but distant mountains are almost always grayer and less vibrant than the closer mountains. When mixing the colors for your distant mountain layers, either add some gray paint or add the complementary color (the color opposite the color of your mountains on the color wheel) to neutralize the hue. As you work your way toward the closer mountain layers, start adding more of whatever color your mountain range is and less gray or complementary color.

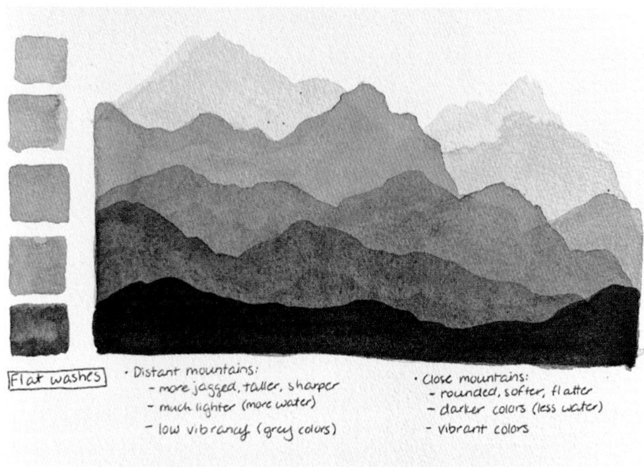

Now let's talk about the two painting techniques I use to paint mountain ranges.

- **Flat washes:** Each layer is a flat wash over the entire mountain area. I generally paint the top edge first, then fill in everything below it with the same color. Once that layer is dry, I will mix my next color and create the next mountain layer just below the first one, again filling in everything below the top edge of that mountain layer. You can see this technique demonstrated in the blue-green mountain range above. Notice I am also following the three keys of shape, value and hue when painting these layers.

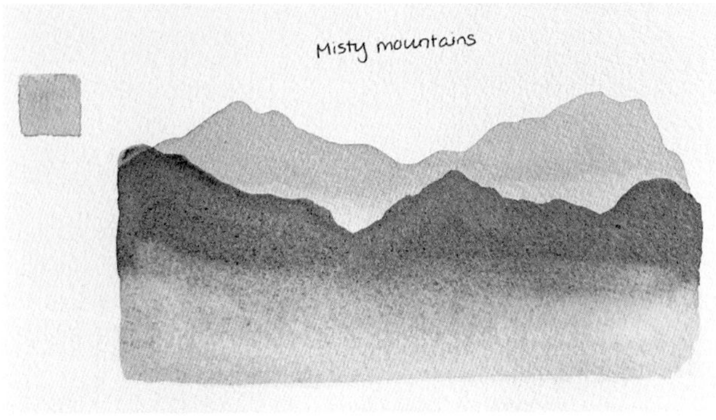

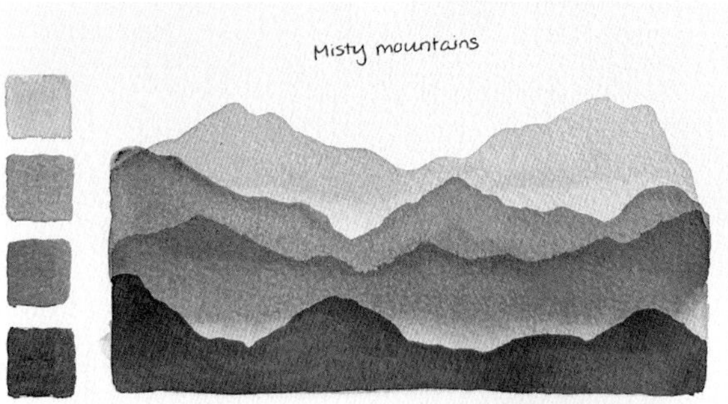

- **Gradient washes:** Each wash is blended with clear water to create a gradient. When I paint these layers, I use the paint I mixed to create the top outline of the mountain layer. I fill in a little bit of the area just below the top edge with the paint color, then I clean off my brush completely and blend out the paint with clean water toward the bottom of the paper. This gradient creates a misty effect at the bottom of each mountain layer. I paint the next layers the same way, painting the top of the layer with color then blending out with water. The final layer can be painted the same way, or it can be a flat wash. Since it's the closest layer, there may not be any mist in front of it. You can see this technique demonstrated in this purple mountain range.

Experiment with these techniques on your own to get the hang of painting mountains. Feel free to pick whatever color you like; mountains can be pretty much any color depending on the light. A few little notes to keep in mind:

- Make sure each layer is **completely** dry before painting in the next one.
- Use a large brush! This will give you uniform washes and help you cover more ground quickly.
- Do your best to create unique shapes for your mountains. The more texture and elevation change they have, the more realistic and interesting they will look!
- Try mixing your next color out of the previous color. This will help give you a cohesive color palette for the whole mountain range.

great smoky mountains

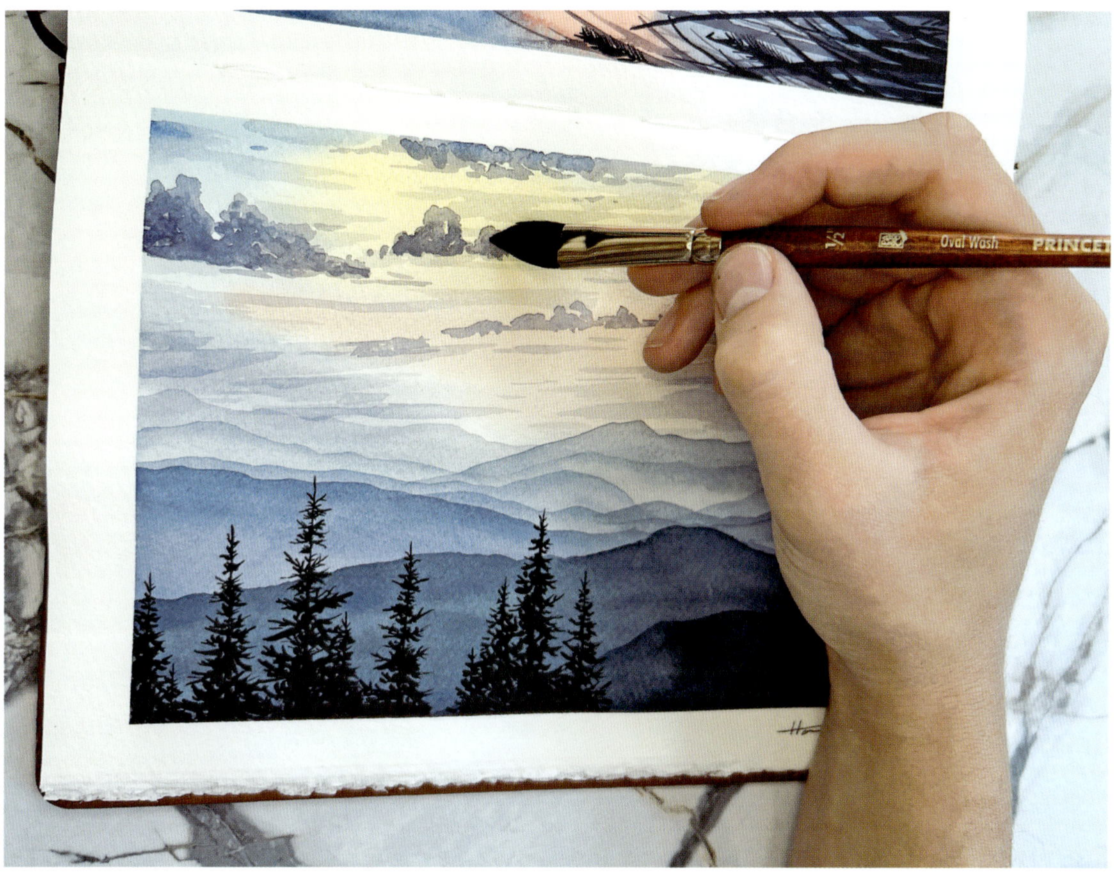

The smoky mountains are perfect for practicing mountain layers, plus this one has a soft pastel sunset to frame it all. Remember: It's SUPER important to fully dry each mountain layer before painting the next one, so make sure you have your hairdryer (or patience) ready. If you get impatient and try to paint another layer before the previous one is dry, you'll end up with bleeds, and you won't get those crisp edges and distinct layers. I hope you enjoy creating a magical mountain scene in this project!

materials

Watercolor paints

- Cadmium Yellow, Cadmium Orange, Magenta, Burnt Sienna, Sap Green, Ultramarine Blue, Phthalo Blue and Van Dyke Brown

Watercolor paper of your choice

- I used my cold press Fabriano Artistico sketchbook size 6 x 8.5 inches (15 x 21.5cm)

Brushes

- one larger brush (I used a ½ inch oval), one medium brush (I used a size 4 round) and one detail brush (I used a size 0 round)

Orientation

- landscape

Set up your paper as you like and make sure to add a drop or two of water to your colors so they start to soften.

Reference photo

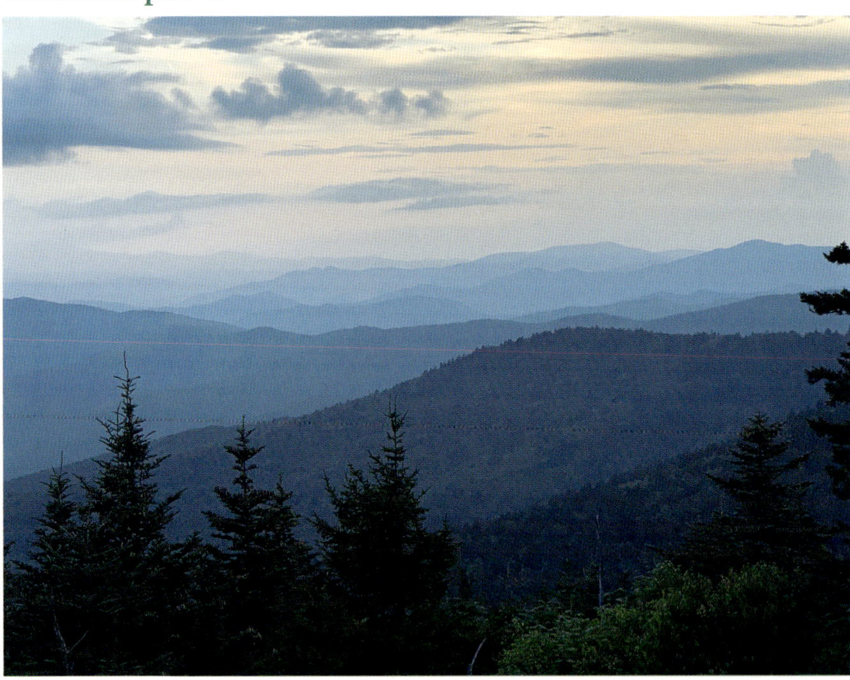

Gray
Ultramarine Blue + little Burnt Sienna + water

Peach
Magenta + Cadmium Orange + water

Yellow
Cadmium Yellow + water

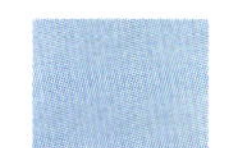

Sky Blue
Ultramarine Blue + Phthalo Blue + water

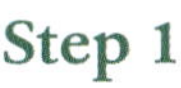

Step 1

We'll work from top to bottom on this painting, starting with the sky. First, mix up the sky colors listed above and make sure to add some water to each of these colors to dilute them.

Use a big brush and cover the top two-thirds of your paper with clean water. Then, start dropping in your colors, using the reference photo as a guide for where they should go. I started with some sweeping horizontal brush strokes with the Gray paint about halfway up the paper.

Add some Peach above the Gray section, then Yellow toward the top of the paper.

Then use the Sky Blue color to fill in the rest of the sky section. Feel free to tilt your paper a little to get these colors to blend or leave it as it is if you're happy.

Let this fully dry before moving on.

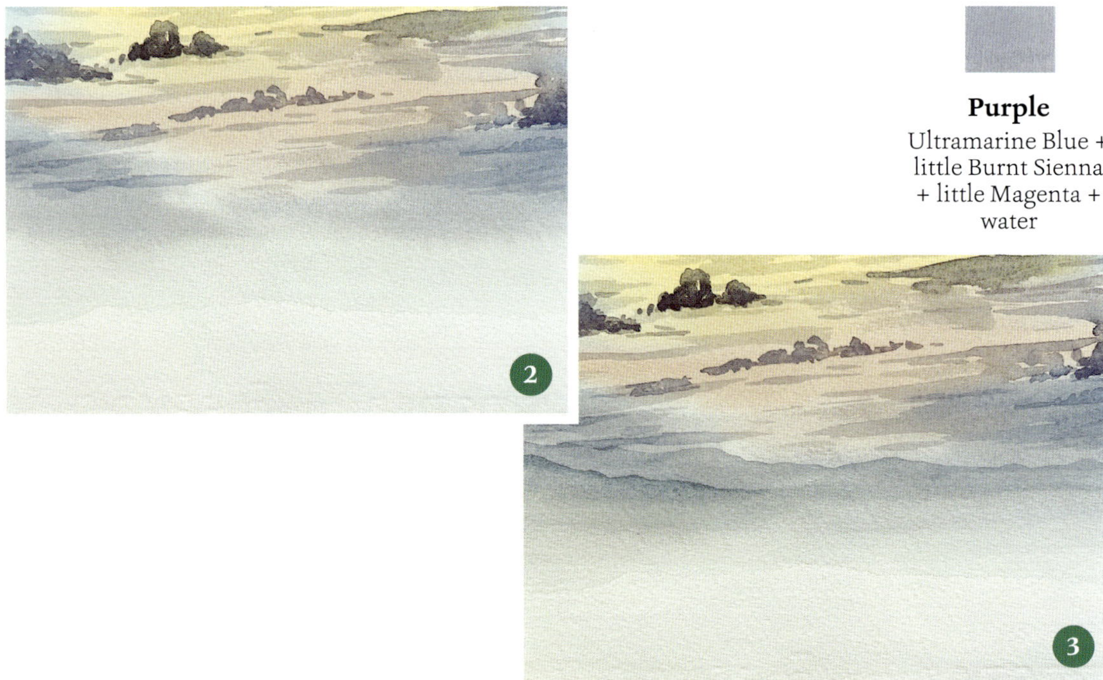

Purple
Ultramarine Blue + little Burnt Sienna + little Magenta + water

Step 2

Once the first layer is dry, use the Gray paint from Step 1 and a smaller brush to add some clouds. You can use a sweeping motion to add wispy clouds or a dotting motion to add fluffy clouds. You can **change the saturation of this color to create different effects**—a more saturated color will make a darker, more intense cloud and watered down paint will make soft, light clouds. Experiment with this a bit on your painting!

Let this fully dry before moving on.

Step 3

Next, we will start on our mountain layers! To start, mix up a light gray-ish Purple color, making sure to **add plenty of water**.

Use a big brush to create your first mountain range about halfway up the paper. Quickly clean off your brush and run your damp brush under the bottom edge of the mountain range to blend it.

Dry this layer fully, then add another layer of mountains just under this one. Use the same color and technique: Paint in the mountain range and then use a clean, damp brush to blend out the bottom. Observe the reference photo for inspiration for these mountain layers.

Add a couple layers in this way, keeping them relatively close together. Feel free to overlap previous layers or have layers that don't go all the way across the page!

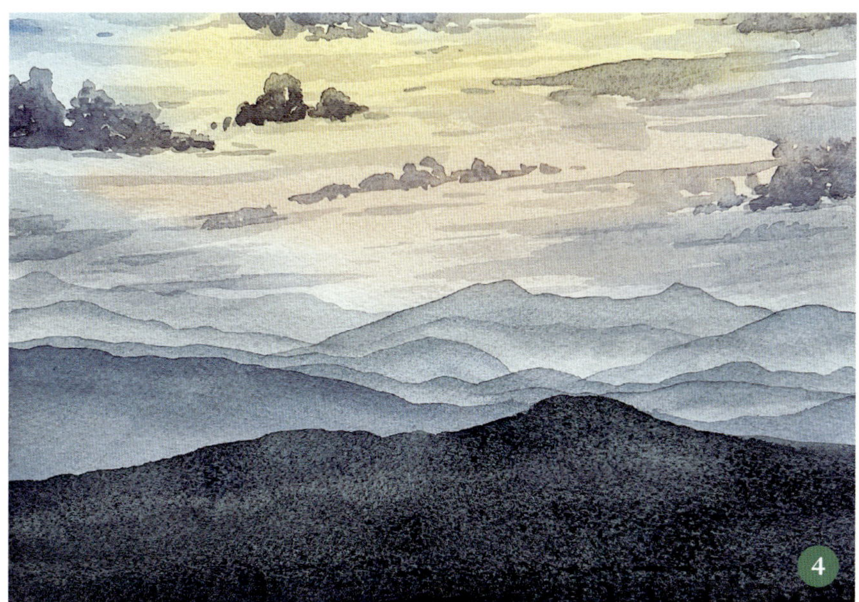

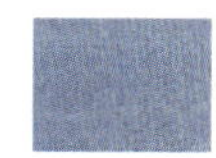

Blue
Ultramarine Blue + little Van Dyke Brown

Dark Blue
Ultramarine Blue + little Van Dyke Brown + little Sap Green

Step 4

As we work our way forward on this painting, we'll need to darken the color and make it more saturated. Mix the Blue color swatched above in the same pan as the old purple color, using whatever leftovers you had to create a cohesive color palette.

Repeat the same technique from Step 3, working your way down the page adding a few more mountain layers. Once you've painted the distant layers, mix up the Dark Blue color shown above and add a flat wash mountain layer all the way across the page.

Let this fully dry before moving on.

Step 5

Add one last mountain layer in the foreground with the Dark Blue color. This layer should start high on the right and dip down to the bottom of the painting near the center of the page.

Let this fully dry before moving on.

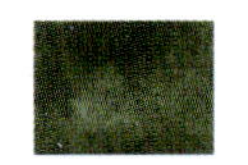

Dark Green

Sap Green +
Ultramarine Blue +
Van Dyke Brown

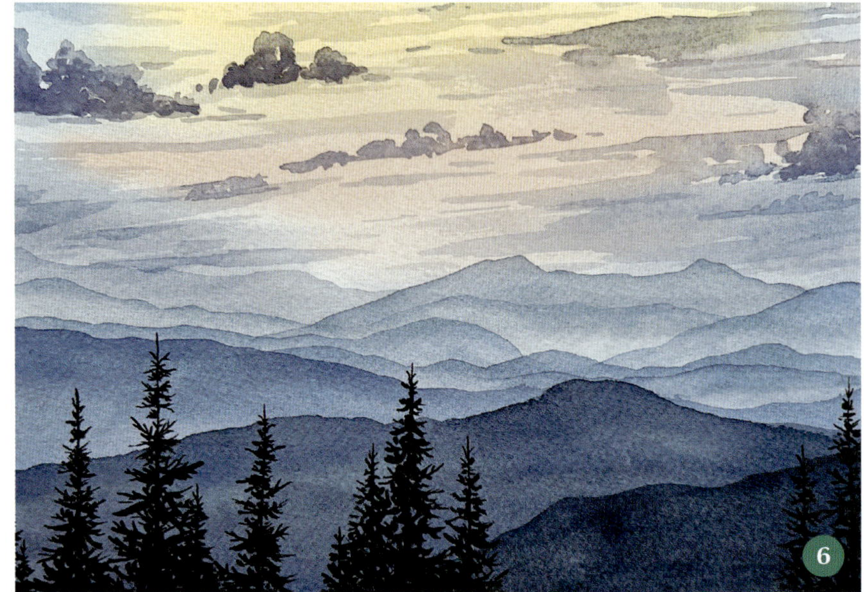

Step 6

The final step of this painting is to add some trees. Mix a very Dark Green, adding just enough water that the paint flows.

Use your detail brush to add some evergreen trees to the bottom of the painting. Use the reference photo for inspiration on the placement and shape of these trees. You can also refer to the Funky Forests chapter, (page 83), if you need any help with painting trees!

Once you're happy with the trees, you're all done with this painting! Take off the tape, sign and date your painting and admire your work.

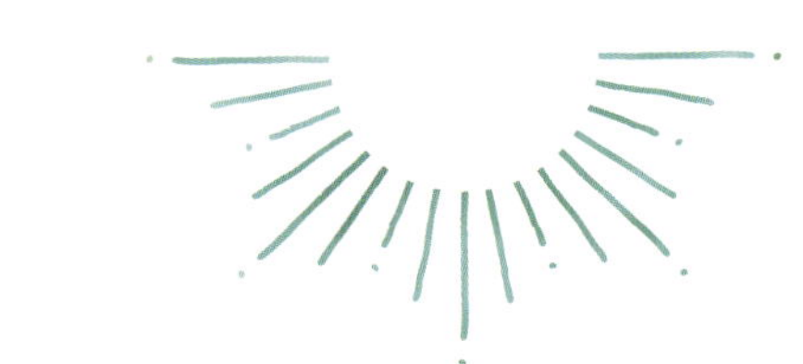

snow in the sierras

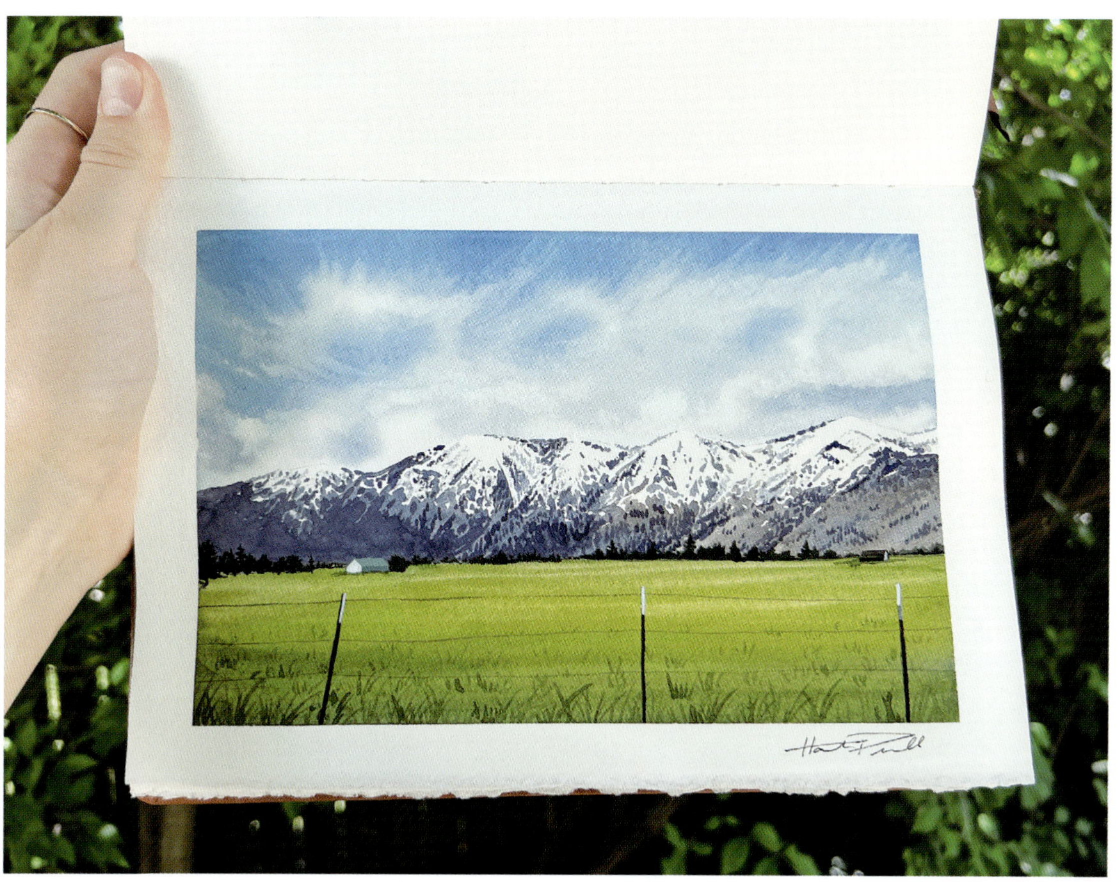

The Sierra Nevada mountains near Lake Tahoe are some of the most beautiful I've seen. I took this picture (page 138) years ago on a trip to visit family there, and I was just in awe of the simple farmland landscapes contrasted with these magnificent mountains. This project will focus specifically on how to paint detailed, snowcapped mountains with watercolor, but you'll also get some practice with painting some simple details in the foreground.

materials

Watercolor paints

- Ultramarine Blue, Phthalo Blue, Burnt Sienna, Cadmium Yellow, Yellow Ochre, Sap Green, Hooker's Green, Van Dyke Brown and Payne's Gray
- White gouache

Watercolor paper of your choice

- I used my cold press Fabriano Artistico sketchbook size 6 x 8.5 inches (15 x 21.5 cm)

Brushes

- one larger brush (I used a ½ inch oval), one medium brush (I used a size 4 round) and one detail brush (I used a size 0 round)

Orientation

- landscape

Set up your paper as you like and make sure to add a drop or two of water to your colors so they start to soften.

Reference photo

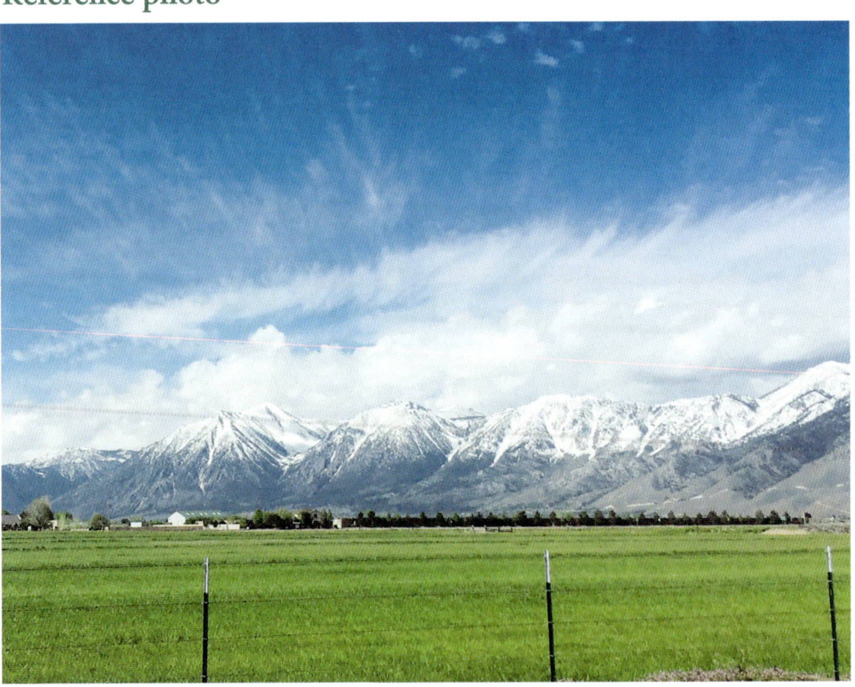

Sketch

Mark the horizon line about one-third of the way from the bottom of the page. Sketch the rough outline of the mountains using the reference photo. Don't stress over getting the mountain contours exactly right—just use the reference photo as a guide for the approximate shape and size!

Blue
Ultramarine Blue +
Phthalo Blue

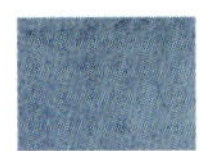

Gray
Ultramarine Blue +
Payne's Gray

Step 1

As usual, we will start this painting by filling in the sky section first. This procedure is similar to that in the Oregon Plains project on page 28, though it differs slightly in the placement of the Gray color. Mix up the Sky Blue and the Gray colors swatched above.

Put down a layer of clear water in the sky section with a large brush, carving out the mountain shapes in the process. Then drop in some random swooping and dotting brush strokes with the Blue color, starting at the top of the page and working your way down toward the mountains as the brush runs out of paint. Then dip into the Gray color and add a few dots and horizontal strokes closer to the mountains to imitate the shadows of the clouds, leaving some white space on the paper.

Once those colors are on the paper, pick up your paper and tilt it to gently blend the colors together with each other and with the white spaces on the page. You can also blend with a damp brush if you want a little bit more control.

Lastly, use a completely dry brush to lift some color off the page and create clouds. Remember, you can only do this while the painting is wet, so don't wait too long. I used long, swooping strokes with my dry brush to imitate those wispy clouds toward the top of the page. Then, I used more of a dotting motion to indicate the fluffier clouds closer to the mountains. Continuously dry off your brush with a paper towel while you're doing this, and once you're happy with your clouds, let this section dry completely.

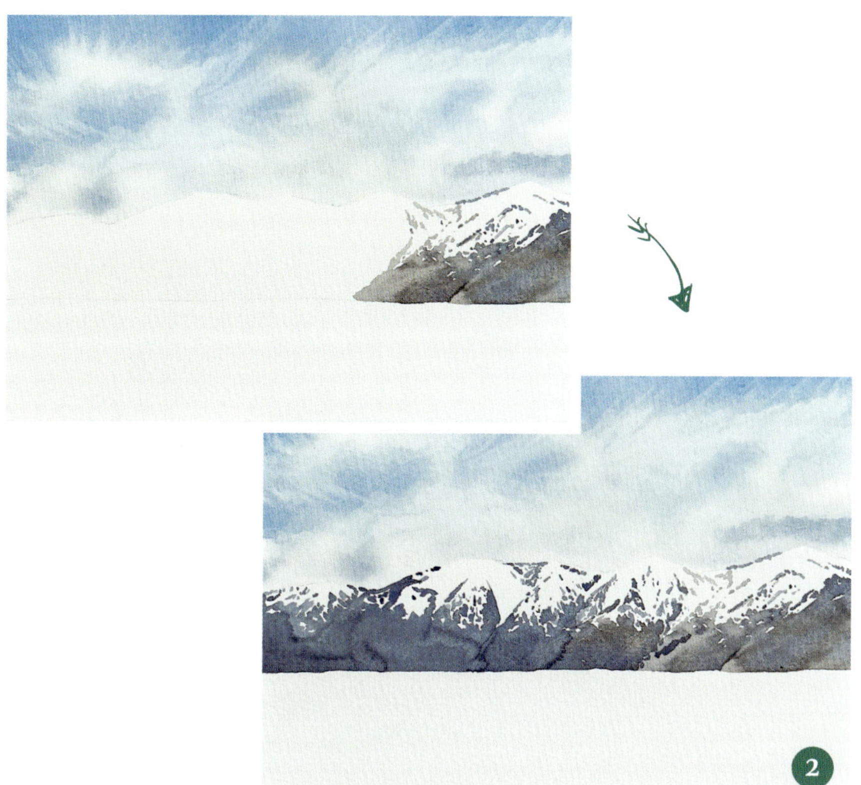

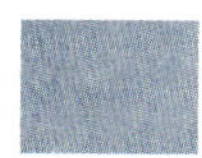

Mountain Gray
Ultramarine Blue + Van Dyke Brown

Mountain Brown
Ultramarine Blue + Van Dyke Brown + Burnt Sienna

Step 2

Now we come to the most demanding part of this painting: the mountains. First, mix the two colors according to the swatches above.

This mountain section will be completed in two layers. In the first layer, we will carve out the general shapes and shadows of the mountain; the second layer will involve adding more details. To start, load your medium brush (I used my 4 round) with the Mountain Gray. Use the reference photo as your guide for color placement. I worked from right to left (though feel free to do the opposite) and filled in one "section" at a time. Feel free to switch to the Mountain Brown and drop that in while the Mountain Gray is still wet or use it to fill in a section or two.

At the tops of the mountains, use a lighter touch with your brush and **slightly water down your colors** to add those smaller contours, shadow shapes and little dots for trees. I'd recommend using both the Gray and Brown colors for this. Make sure to leave plenty of white space at the tops of the mountains as you work so they stay snowy! Toward the bottoms of the mountains, just fill in the area with flat washes. Those sections will be fleshed out more in Step 3.

Don't worry about making this a super smooth wash. I have some blooms here and there. This is fine and will mostly get covered up in the next layer. Let this fully dry before moving on.

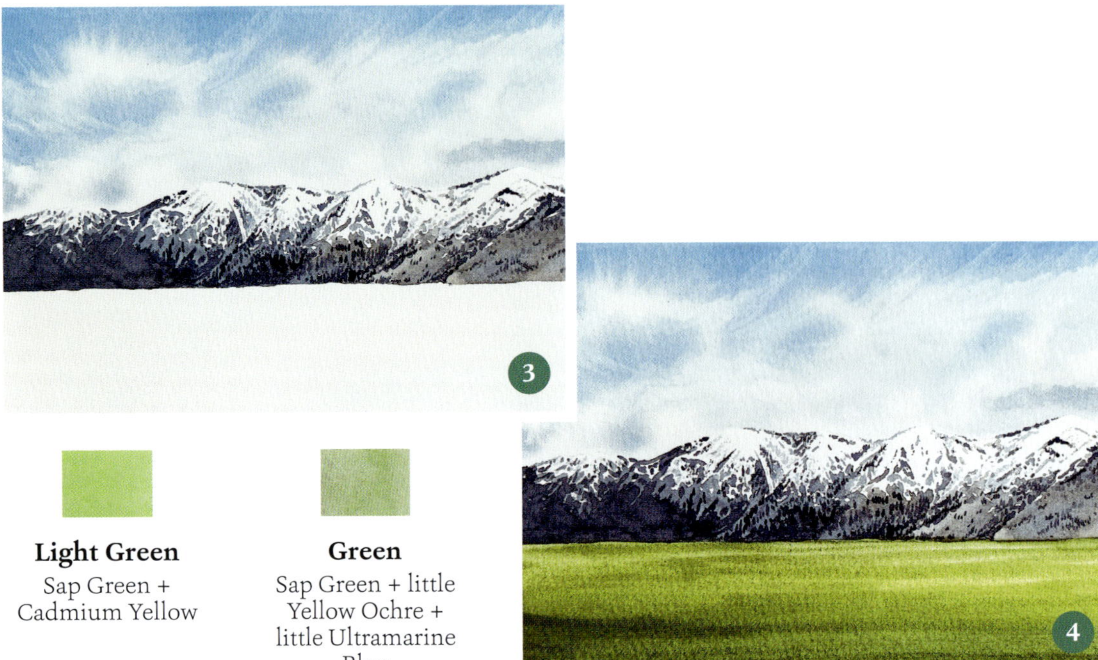

Step 3

Now it's time to add our second layer to the mountains and incorporate some details using a detail brush. At the bottom of the mountains, with the Mountain Gray color from Step 2, use short vertical strokes to indicate clusters of distant trees. This will help show ridges and valleys in this section of the mountains. You can also use this color to completely fill in some sections that need more shadow. The color at the bottom of the mountains should be more saturated. You can also add details with the Mountain Brown, but I preferred to mostly use the Mountain Gray color here.

Toward the tops of the mountains, keep using those short vertical strokes but more sparingly. It's also helpful to water down your color when working on these details.

You can use a dry brushing technique (see page 16) as well; this texture will look like shadows and rock formations.

Step 4

We will finish up this painting by adding in the foreground. First, let's paint that green, grassy field using the colors listed above.

Using a big brush, start with Light Green and use horizontal strokes to fill in the top half of this grassy section and then quickly switch to the Green and fill in the rest. If you do it quickly, those colors should blend together nicely and create some cool textures. For an extra detail, you can use a dry brush and horizontal strokes to create some even lighter spots in the distance (close to the horizon line).

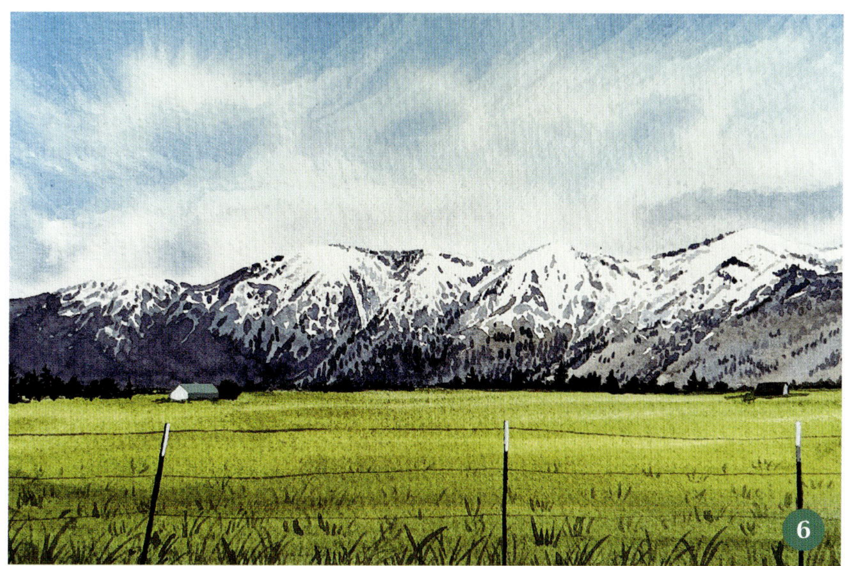

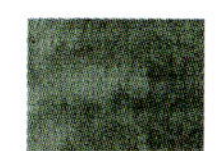

Dark Green
Hooker's Green + Ultramarine Blue + little Van Dyke Brown

Brown
Van Dyke Brown

Dark Gray
Payne's Gray

Step 5

Let's add some finishing touches to this painting to really bring it to life. I started by adding some tiny trees in the distance to disguise that line between the mountains and the field, using the Dark Green color swatched above.

Use your detail brush to dot in the distant trees. Little rounded blobs will look like deciduous trees, and slightly taller triangle shapes will look like distant evergreens.

Next, use a watered-down version of this Dark Green color to add some grassy textures to the very bottom of the painting. To show the distance of the painting, make sure the grass textures decrease in size and frequency as you work your way up the paper toward the horizon line, and don't add any more of this detail once you're about halfway up the grass section.

Step 6

Lastly, let's add some barns or houses in the distance. I used some gouache here, straight white and a teal (white gouache mixed with ultramarine blue and sap green) to paint the barn on the left side of the reference photo. I also used some Brown watercolor to create a smaller barn in the distance on the right side of the page. Use the reference photo for inspiration with this part, but feel free to add in your own barns and structures!

Finally, I added in the fence in the foreground. I used a Dark Gray color and a detail brush to add in the fence posts. Then I watered that color down for the wires connecting the fence posts. For the finishing touch, I used some white gouache to add the white markers at the tops of the fence posts.

Once you're happy with your final details, you're all done with this project! Take off the tape, sign and date your painting and admire your work.

el capitan

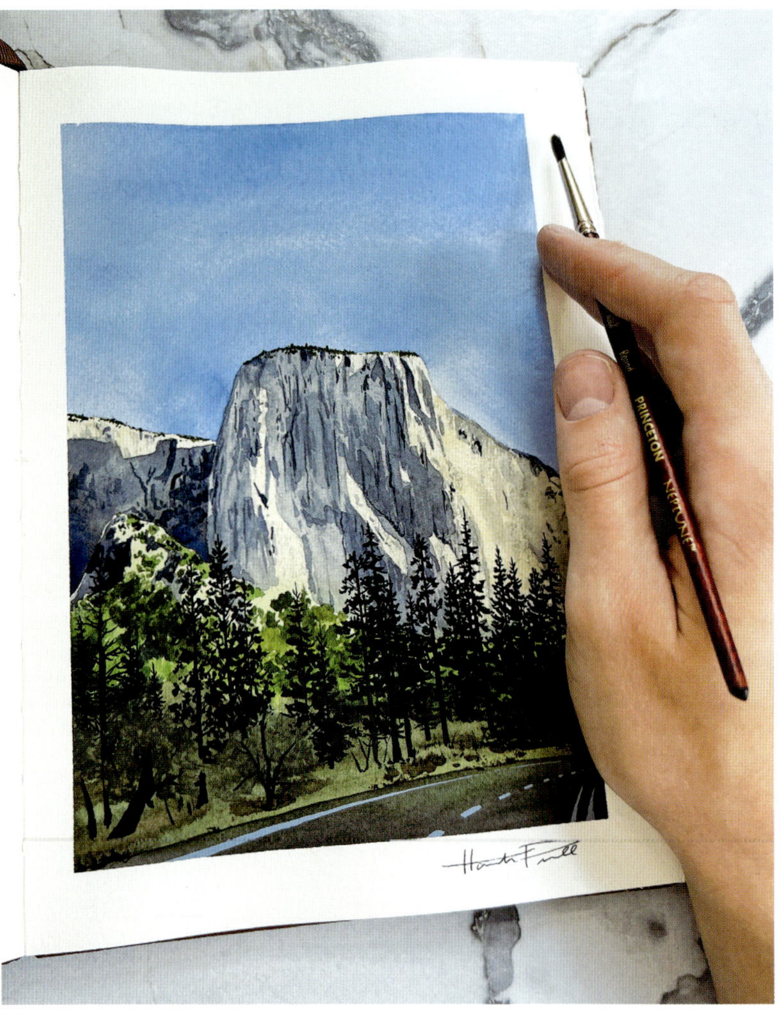

This iconic rock face is famous amongst rock climbers, hikers and outdoors people who visit Yosemite National Park in California. I've personally never been (it's absolutely on my bucket list), but I got this reference photo from my sister while she was visiting the park. This painting requires lots of layering and texture, so stick with it, and I think you'll end up with a result you're happy with!

materials

Watercolor paints

- Burnt Sienna, Yellow Ochre, Sap Green, Ultramarine Blue, Phthalo Blue, Van Dyke Brown and Payne's Gray
- White gouache

Watercolor paper of your choice

- I used my cold press Fabriano Artistico sketchbook size 5.5 x 8.5 inches (approx 14.5 x 21.5 cm)

Brushes

- one larger brush (I used a ½ inch oval), one medium brush (I used a size 4 round) and one detail brush (I used a size 0 round)

Orientation

- portrait

Set up your paper as you like and make sure to add a drop or two of water to your colors so they start to soften.

Reference photo

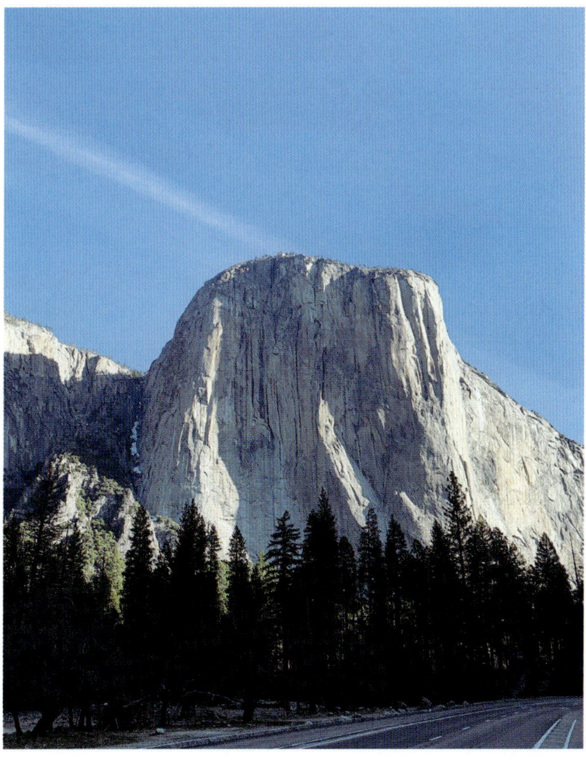

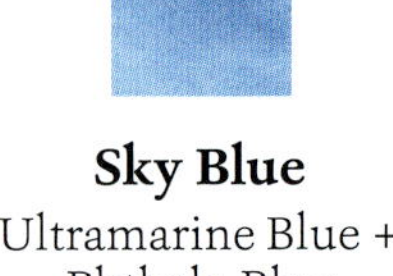

Sky Blue
Ultramarine Blue +
Phthalo Blue

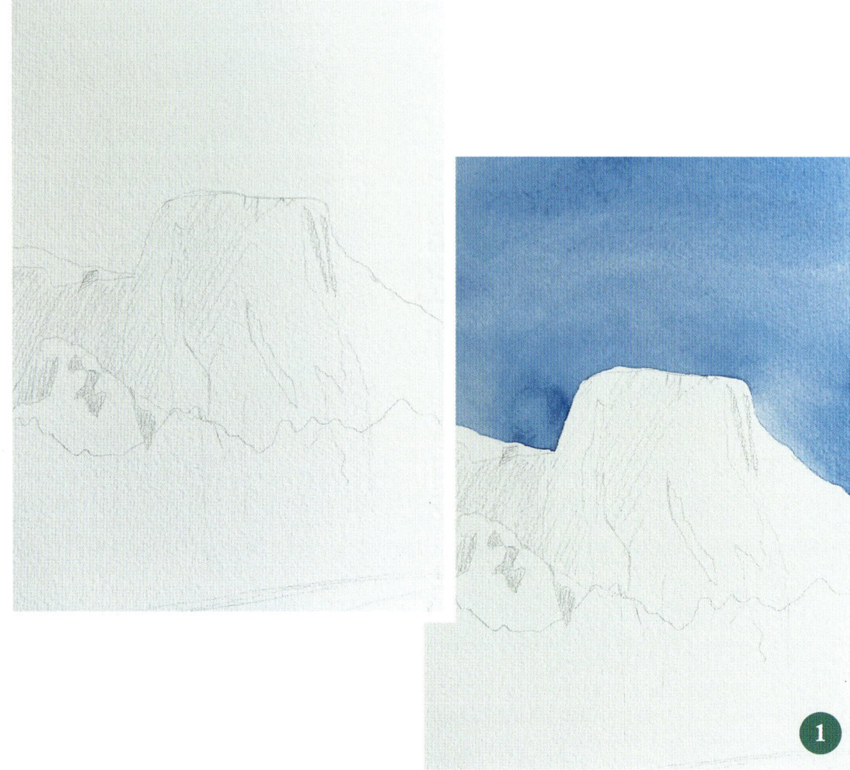

Sketch

Start by sketching the general shape of the mountain. Notice that the flat top is just above halfway up the paper and is pretty centered in the middle. Once you have the top edge, sketch and lightly shade in the major shadow shapes you see. I added a wavy line closer to the bottom to indicate where that line of trees is and a slightly curved line at the bottom for the road. Don't spend too long on your pencil sketch here; it's okay if it doesn't look exactly like the reference photo.

Step 1

Let's start with the sky section. Mix up your Sky Blue color first.

Paint the entire sky section with a flat wash of the Sky Blue color using a large brush. Since the viewer is looking up at El Capitan, we won't see that fading of the blue sky at the horizon line.

Let this fully dry before moving on.

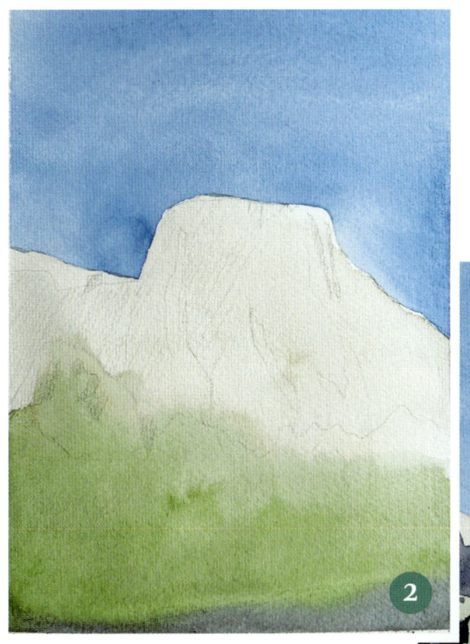

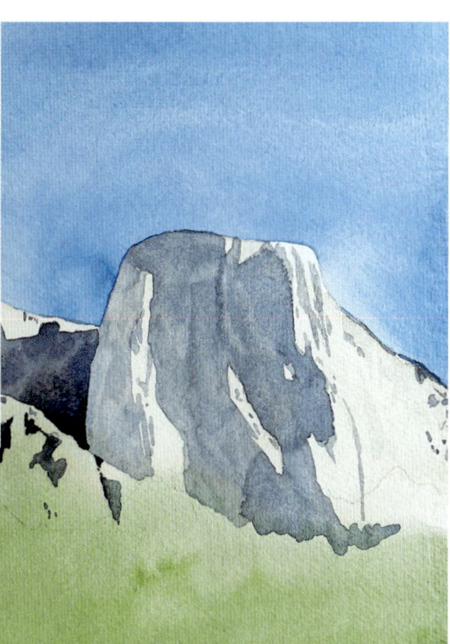

Tan
Yellow Ochre + little Burnt Sienna + little Van Dyke Brown + water

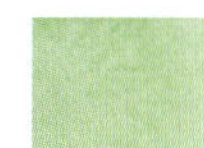

Green
Sap Green + little Yellow Ochre

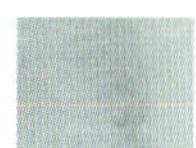

Gray
Ultramarine Blue + Van Dyke Brown + water

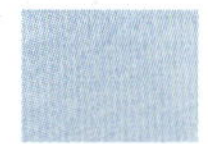

Blue-Gray
Ultramarine Blue + little Van Dyke Brown

Step 2

Next, we'll paint in a general wash of color on the rest of the painting. Mix up the Tan, Green and Gray colors above according to their recipes.

Use a large brush and paint these colors in their general areas. Fill in the mountain with the Tan color, fill in the tree area with the Green and fill in the road at the bottom with the Gray color. No need to wait for each section to dry; we want the colors to blend a bit!

Let this fully dry before moving on.

Step 3

Next, let's start adding the large shadow shapes on the rock face. Mix up **two versions** of the Blue-Gray color swatched above: a strong version (more paint and less water) and a weak version (more water and less paint).

Use a smaller brush (I used my 4 round) and the weaker version of the Blue-Gray color to paint in the major shadow shapes on the rock face. Pay attention to the reference photo here. Make sure to add in some of the smaller shadows as well with some short vertical brush strokes.

(continued)

Brown
Van Dyke Brown + Sap Green

Dark Green
Sap Green + Ultramarine Blue + Van Dyke Brown

Very Dark Green
Payne's Gray + Sap Green

Dark Gray
Payne's Gray

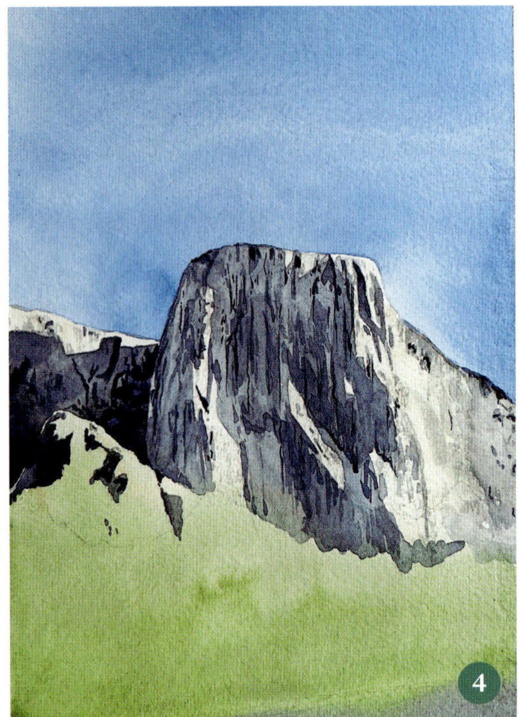

Use the darker version of the Blue-Gray paint to fill in the shadow shapes in the left-hand section of the rock wall, along with the smaller hill in the foreground.

Step 4

Now let's refine the details on the rock face using a detail brush. This is where you should spend the most time and effort as it's the focal point of the painting and the most detailed element.

Add localized washes of the Blue-Gray color from Step 3 to darken up some of the areas within the main shadow shapes and add texture. This is one of those times where messy and random will end up looking the best!

You can also use your dry brushing technique (see page 16) to add texture to both the shadow areas and the areas in the sunlight.

Add some dark gray vertical lines with your saturated Blue-Gray mix from Step 3 to indicate the fissures and cracks that run down the rock face. Don't forget about the areas in the sunlight, especially the section on the right. Use the diluted Blue-Gray mix from Step 3 to add some subtle shadows and texture there, too.

Continue building up texture and shadow, using the reference photo as your guide. Remember, you can always come back to continue working on it later, so if you reach a sticking point, move on to the next step and come back later!

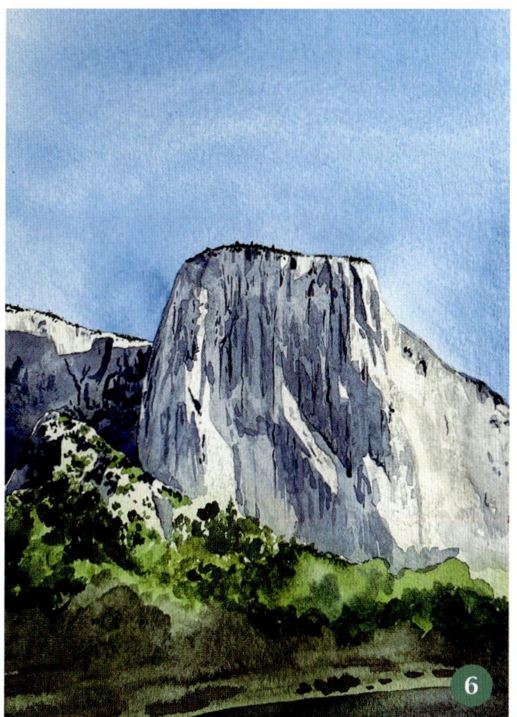

Step 5

Next, let's add some texture to the tree area below the rock formation. Mix up more of the Green color from Step 2, along with the Dark Green and Brown colors swatched on the previous page. Use a detail brush and the Dark Green color to add the tiny trees at the top of the cliff, using a dotting motion with your brush.

Next, switch to a larger brush and start adding tree texture to the hill in the foreground. Tree texture is just slightly larger dots clumped together randomly. Start with the lighter green, and as you work your way toward the road, use bigger dots and brush strokes and switch to the Dark Green and then to the Brown color. **Let this be loose; a lot of this will be covered up by the evergreen trees later.**

Step 6

Use the same Gray color from Step 2 to add another wash of Gray over the road area.

Step 7

Lastly, let's add some trees. Mix up the Very Dark Green swatched on the previous page.

Use a detail brush to start creating the line of evergreen trees along the road. Use the reference photo for inspiration here and feel free to refer back to the One Tree at a Time project on page 84 for extra help on painting trees. My process for these is to first paint a thin vertical line for the trunk, then work in a back-and-forth zigzag pattern adding branches to the tree. The branches should get just slightly longer each time until about the middle of the tree and then they stay the same length. I also added a few sticks and random texture to the ground in front of the trees—just to make everything blend together smoothly.

Space out the trees randomly; make some taller and some shorter and try to change up the shapes for the branches when you can. Variety is key!

For an extra challenge, notice in the reference photo the smaller, round trees closer to the road. To paint these, dilute some of the Gray color from Step 2 with water and use it to sketch out rough circles where these trees are. Then, use the Dark Gray to add in the trunk and a few branches. I just painted a couple of these on the left side of the painting.

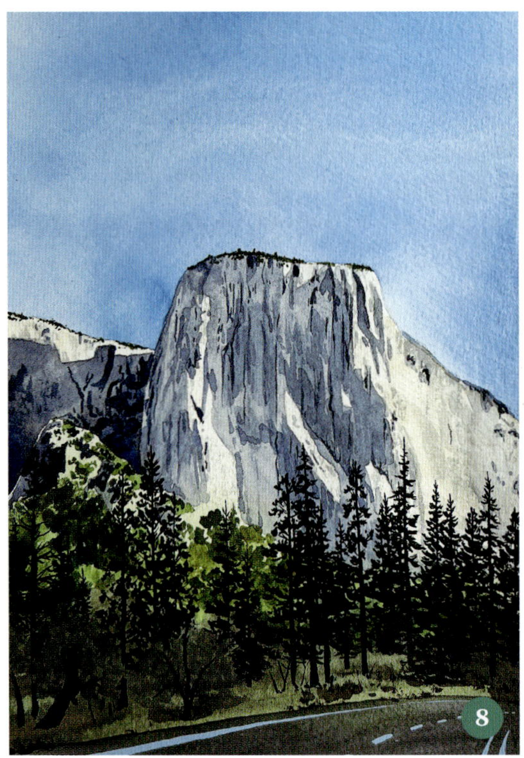

Step 8

Lastly, let's add some lines to the road. Mix white gouache with Payne's Gray to create a medium gray color. Use your detail brush to paint in the solid line on the left side of the road, starting wider on the left and getting thinner as the road continues to the right. Add the center dashed line, as well as the two lines on the right side of the road. Again, make sure these lines start out wider and then get thinner.

Once you're happy with your final details, you're all done with this project! This is a complicated and challenging painting, so if you completed it (regardless of how you feel about the end result) you should be proud! Take off the tape, sign and date your painting and admire your work.

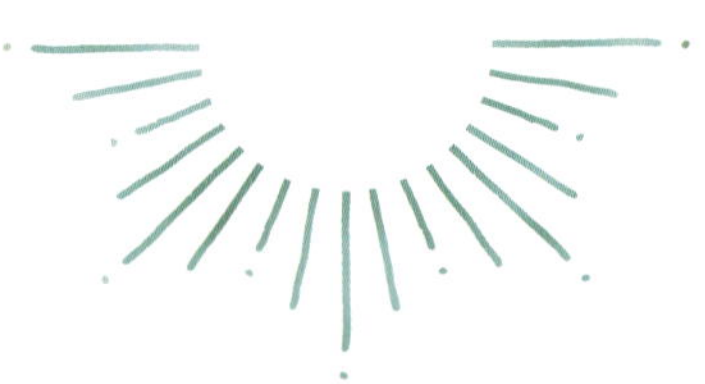

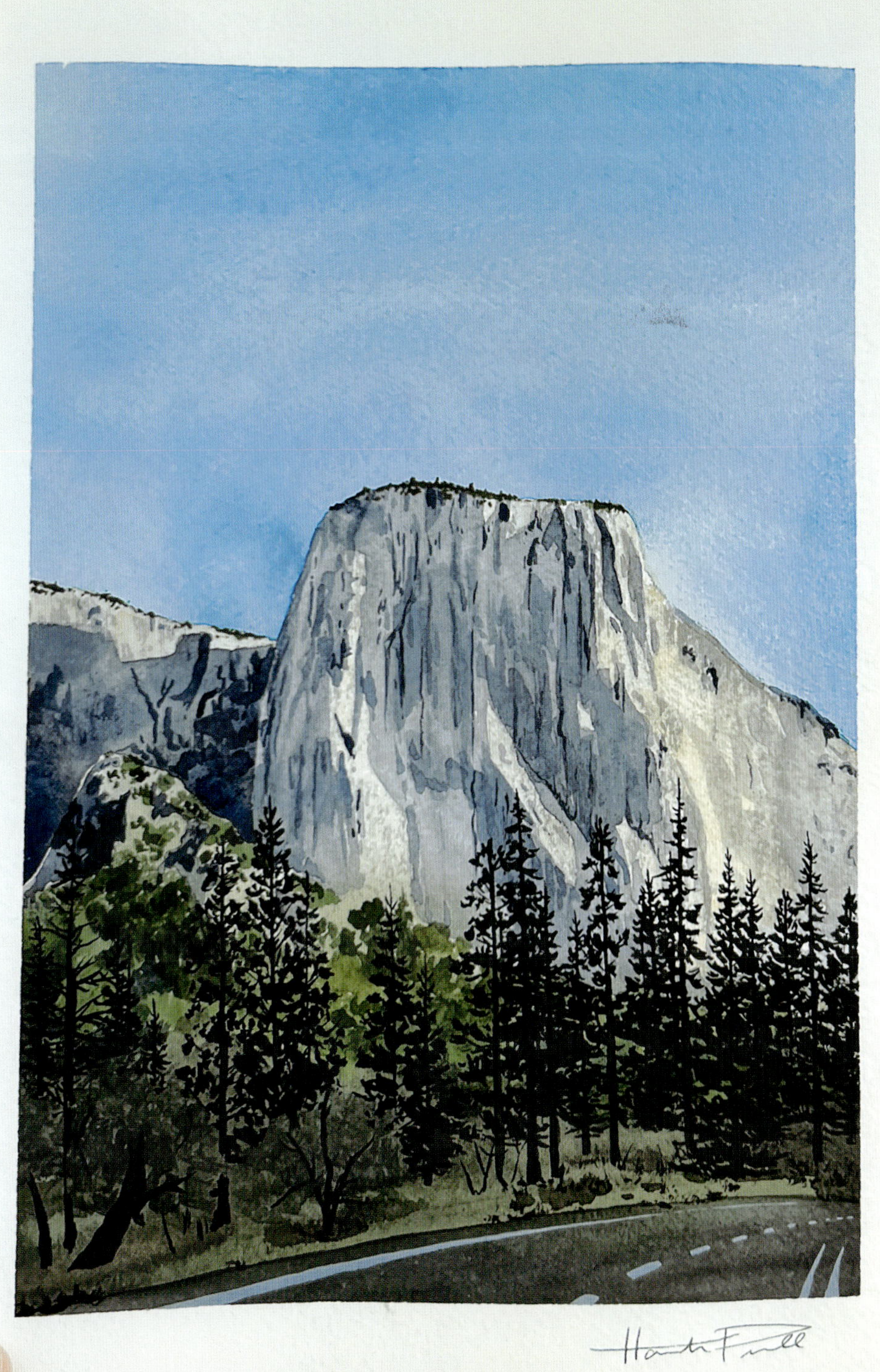

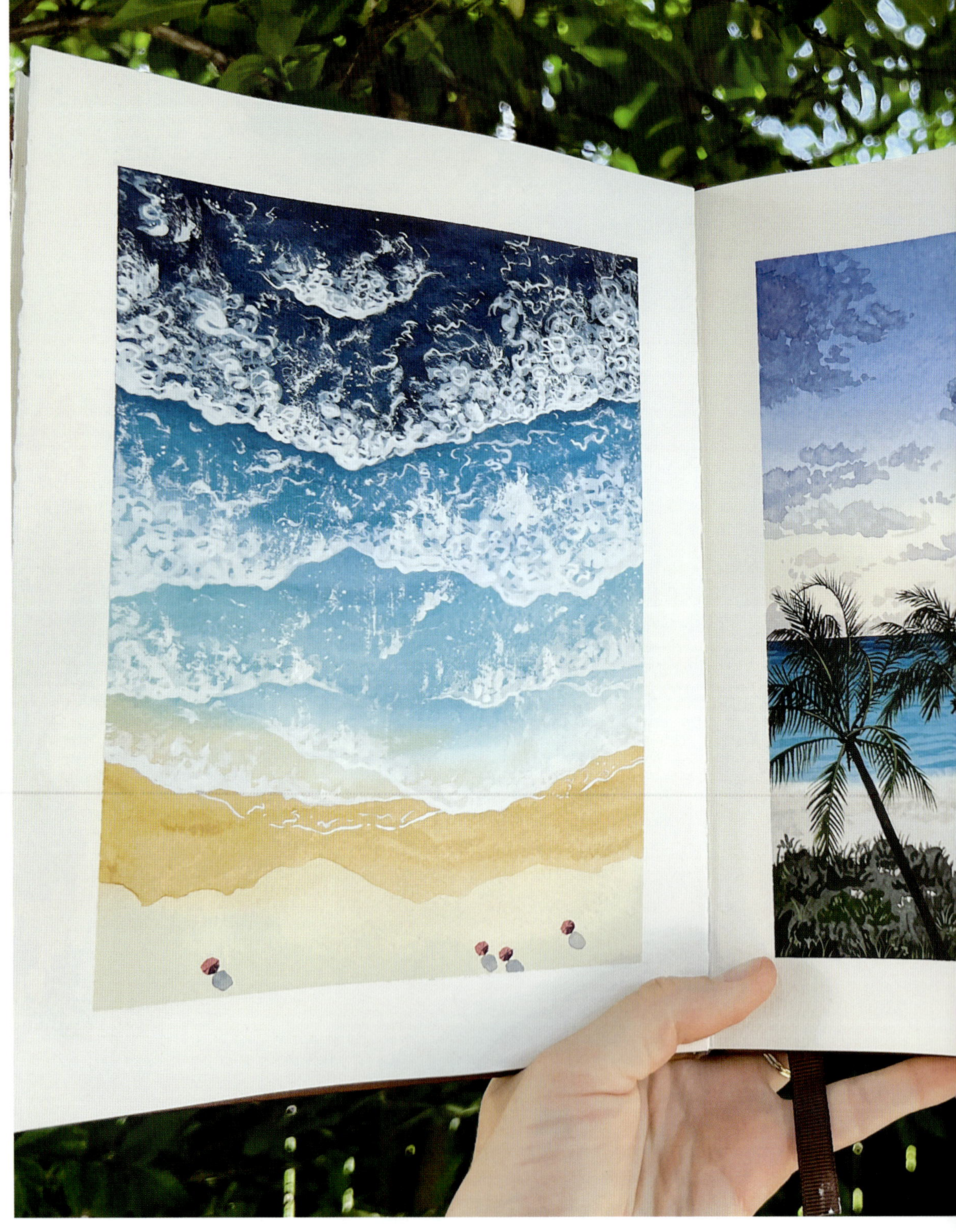

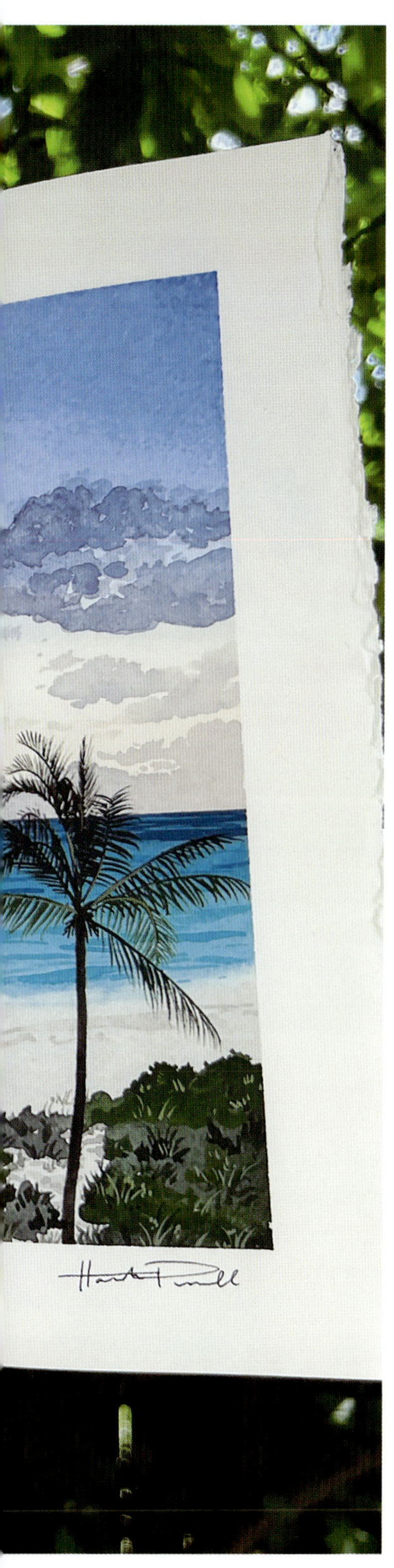

chapter 6
oceans, lakes and beaches

In my opinion, water is one of the most daunting landscape subjects to paint, especially for a beginner artist. It can also be one of the most fun and compelling subjects with practice and the right approach. This chapter will focus on a few techniques that will help you capture the essence of a water scene without needing to paint in every little detail.

There is a distinct advantage to painting water using watercolors. As I'm sure you've noticed, watercolor paints sometimes have a mind of their own. We can use the organic shapes and textures that occur to create an authentic and expressive painting.

one drop at a time

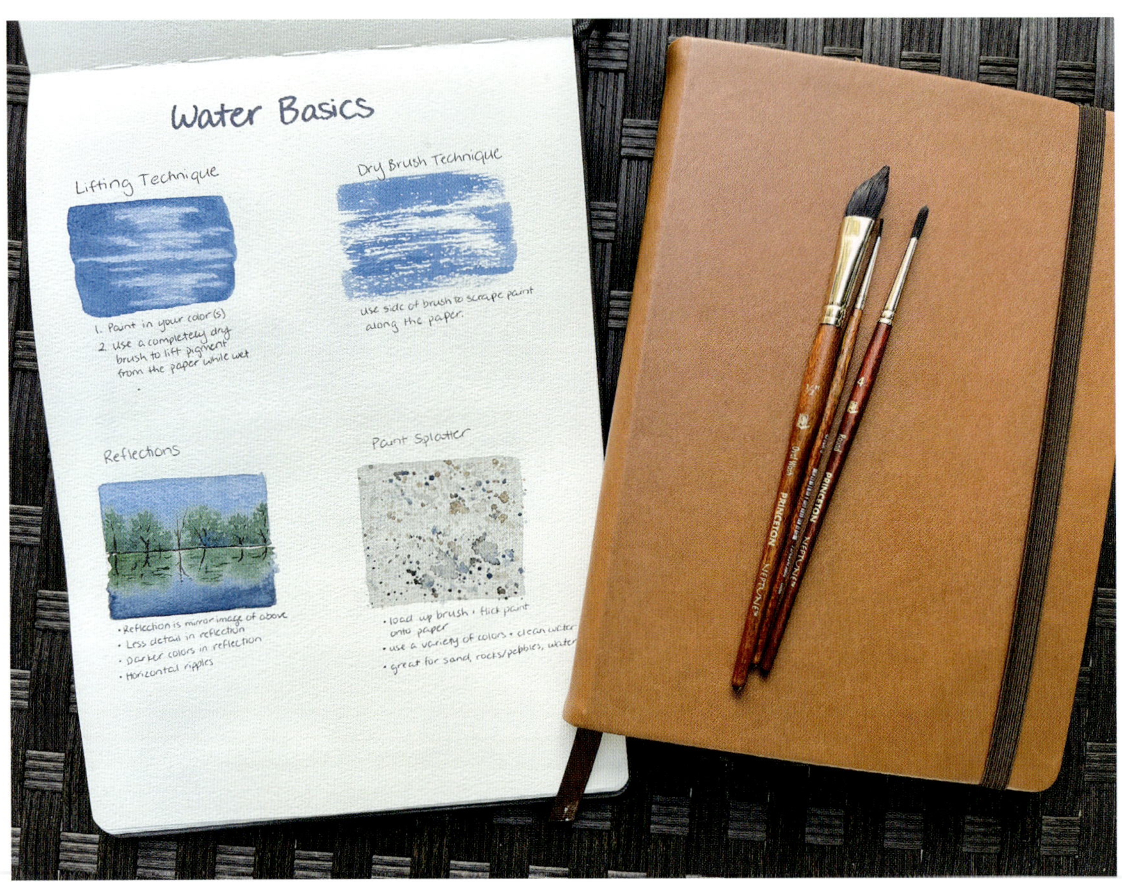

In this first project, we will go over a few easy rules and techniques to keep in mind while painting water. Feel free to practice these in a sketchbook or on a scrap piece of paper so that you get the hang of them before starting on a painting. Or if you're feeling confident, ignore me and skip ahead to a project!

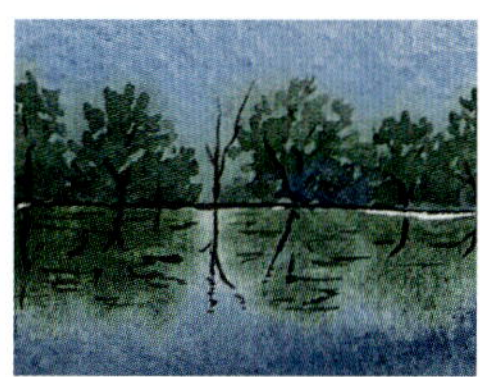

- **Reflections:** The best way to make a water illusion look real is to create an accurate reflection. For the most part, calm water is a mirror-image reflection of what's above, with slightly darker colors and less detail. This can be a bit of a brain teaser but makes sense with practice.

NOTE: Exceptions to this rule include rough water and large ocean scenes because the water is moving a lot more. In those cases, the water reflects the sky colors only.

- **Dry brush:** Use the side of your brush to lightly scrape paint across your paper. The texture of watercolor paper makes the paint break, and you can use this to create water texture and highlights. Be sure to use horizontal strokes for this!

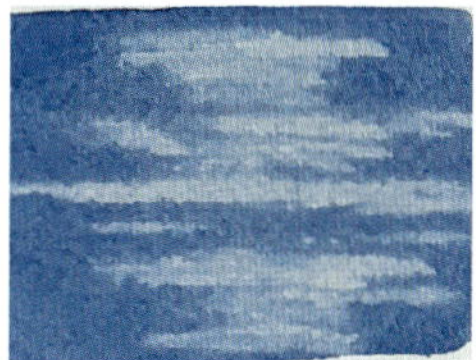

- **Lifting:** Paint in a wash of color and use a completely dry brush to pick up wet paint from the paper. Continuously dry your brush with a paper towel as you're working. This is a great way to add highlights and ripples to your water scene.

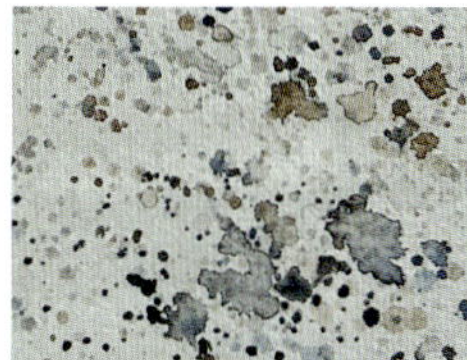

- **Paint splatter:** Load up your brush with lots of paint and tap it over the painting to spray paint droplets over the paper. Do the same thing with clean water to add even more texture, as the clean water mixes with the paint droplets already on the paper. You can either let it all dry naturally or dab some areas with a paper towel for lighter, more subtle textures. This creates an organic pattern great for the rocks on beaches, sea spray, bubbles, etc.

NOTE: Make sure to protect any areas where you don't want droplets with scrap paper or a paper towel, as this technique does not allow you much control over where the paint goes.

BONUS: Use gouache for highlights: White gouache paint is great for adding those final highlights, such as sun reflections on water.

motion of the ocean

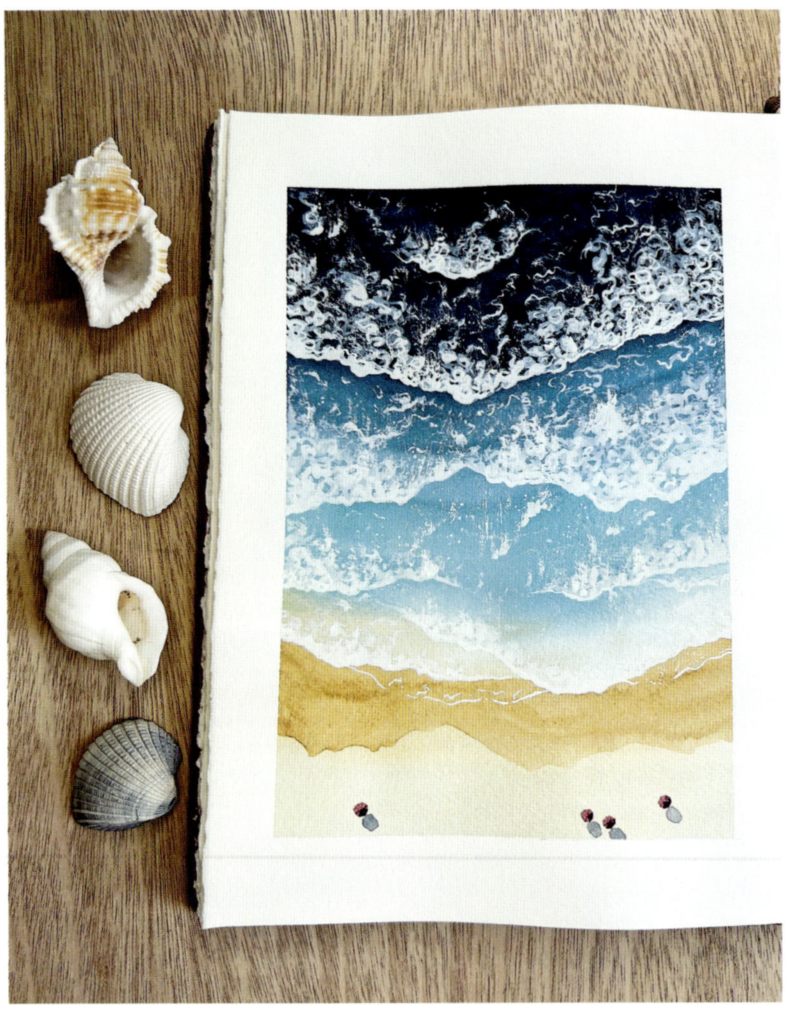

This next project is an incredibly fun way to paint the ocean! I'm not the first person to create a painting like this; it's a fairly common technique in watercolor, as well as resin art recently. That doesn't take away from the fact that paintings like this are super fun and satisfying to make! We will be using vibrant colors to create an overhead view of a tropical beach and white gouache paint to make those waves pop.

materials

Watercolor paints

- Phthalo Blue, Turquoise, Indigo, Burnt Sienna , Yellow Ochre, Magenta and Payne's Gray
- White gouache

Watercolor paper of your choice

- I used my cold press Fabriano Artistico sketchbook size 5.5 x 8 inches (14.5 x 20 cm)

Brushes

- one larger brush (I used a ½ inch oval) and one detail brush (I used a size 0 round)

Orientation

- portrait

Set up your paper as you like and make sure to add a drop or two of water to your colors so they start to soften.

Step 1

The first layer of the painting will be painted all at once, so get your colors prepared before you start according to the color recipes on the following page. Make sure to water down your Sand color! All other colors should be fairly saturated.

PAUSE: Please read through the following instructions before you start, so you can work quickly without stopping to read.

To create the base of our ocean scene, we will be working from dark to light blues and then to our sand color, starting at the top of the page.

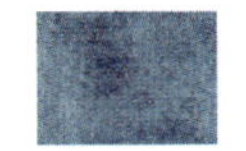

Dark Blue
Indigo + Phthalo Blue

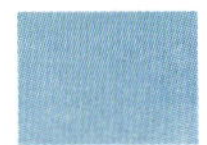

Blue
Phthalo Blue + Turquoise

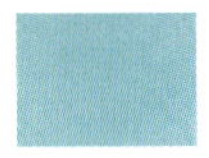

Turquoise
Turquoise

Sand
Yellow Ochre + Burnt Sienna + water

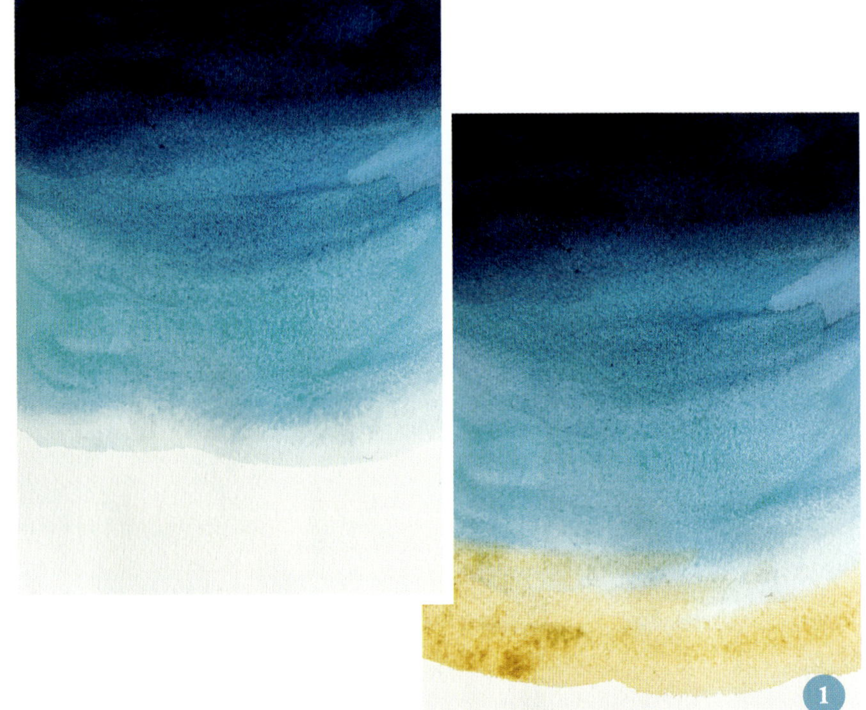

Using a large brush and wavy, horizontal strokes, fill in the top quarter of the page with Dark Blue.

Immediately switch to the Blue color, and continue using wavy horizontal strokes to fill up the next fourth of the page.

Then, switch to the Turquoise color and fill up another fourth of the page with wavy, horizontal strokes.

Then, run a clean, damp brush along the bottom edge of the Turquoise section to soften it.

Lastly, pick up your Sand color and fill in the rest of the paper.

Take a deep breath and dry your page completely.

Step 2 (optional)

Once your painting is dry, you can repeat Step 1 for more saturated and vibrant colors.

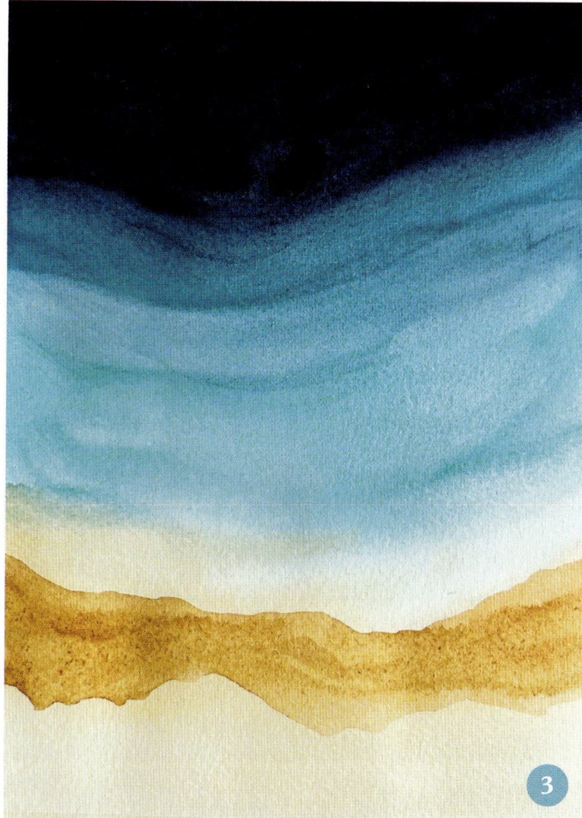

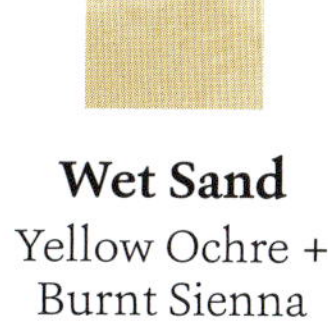

Wet Sand
Yellow Ochre +
Burnt Sienna

Step 3

Mix a slightly darker and more saturated (i.e. add less water) version of the Sand color from Step 1.

Use this Wet Sand color and a large brush to create the darker strip of wet sand at the water's edge. The bottom edge should look like an upside-down mountain range to imitate where waves have lapped at the sand. The top edge will define where the water starts and the sand stops, so make this a more rounded and wavy line.

Step 4

Now we will add the wave details that really bring this piece to life. Grab your white gouache paint and your detail brush.

For the first layer of these wave details, you'll want to *slightly* water down your gouache. This way, the paint is less opaque, and it will blend slightly with the watercolor paint underneath it.

(continued)

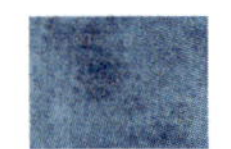

Dark Blue
Indigo + Phthalo Blue

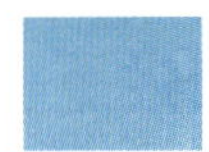

Blue
Phthalo Blue + Turquoise

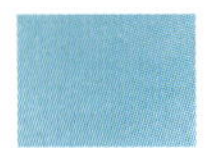

Turquoise
Turquoise

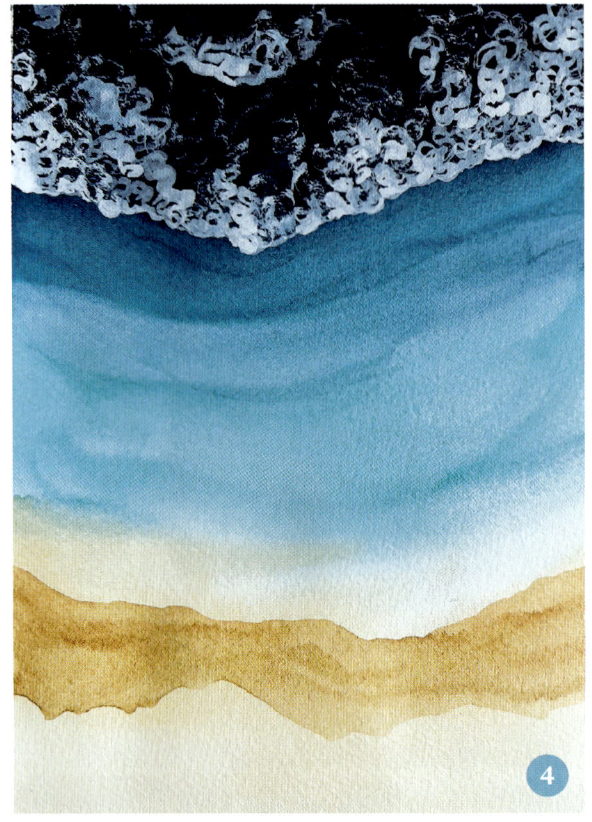

Use your detail brush and start picking out your first wave. I like to place these in the seam between two colors, especially if there are any hard lines left over from the watercolor wash. My first wave is between the Dark Blue and Blue colors toward the top of the page. Don't make this wave a straight, horizontal line—create a wavy edge.

Next, use loose, figure-eight motions with that watered down gouache to add texture extending upward from the wave edge. These figure-eights should overlap, and you should try to vary your brushstrokes a bit so that you have a variety of textures.

Throughout this process, you can add smaller waves above or below your primary waves. You can see the small one I added close to the top of the page.

Step 5

Create two or three more major waves with this same technique, working toward the bottom of your page. The last wave should start at the top edge of the wet sand section from Step 3. Feel free to create breaks in your waves (you can see my third wave has a missing section in the middle) and places where two waves overlap. Be creative and free with this process!

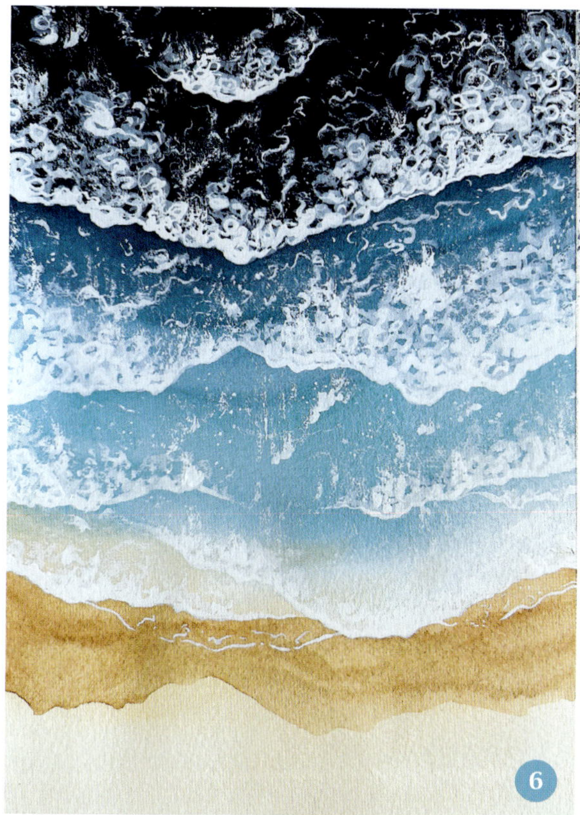

Step 6

Now, we'll use the gouache straight as it comes out of the tube (no watering it down now) and add some new texture on top of these waves.

Continue to add texture in figure-eight or circular motions on top of the figure-eights from Steps 4 and 5, using lighter pressure with your brush to create thinner, more delicate marks. Define the edges of the waves with plenty of white—these are the lightest and foamiest parts of the wave.

You can also add some delicate white details on top of the wet sand section; this will look like waves that have just passed and receded.

The best wave texture to add (in my opinion) is achieved with dry brushing. Pick up a bit of paint, then hold your brush almost parallel to the paper and scrape the side of your brush on the page to drag that paint along the surface of the paper. This will cause the paint to break (especially since we're using thicker gouache paint), and it will create the perfect ocean wave texture. I like to use vertical brush strokes here, starting at the edge of the wave and extending backward through that texture you painted previously.

Lastly, add some dots in random places, just to add some variety of texture.

Magenta
Magenta + water

Pink
Magenta + Phthalo Blue + Turquoise

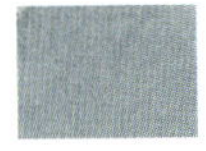

Gray
Payne's Gray + water

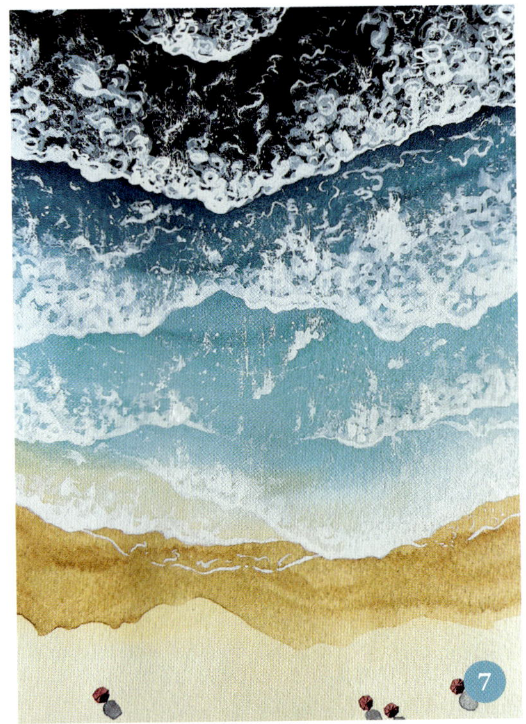

Step 7

The final detail we will add to this piece is the umbrellas on the beach. I used Magenta (though feel free to use whatever color you like) and my detail brush to paint in a few small circles (or octagonal shapes if you want to be fancy) across my beach.

Then, I darkened that Magenta color by adding a touch of Phthalo Blue and Turquoise and added a dark Pink spot on the bottom right sides within those umbrella shapes to give them some dimension.

Finally, I used watered-down Gray to paint an oval diagonally to the right of these umbrellas to create the shadow the umbrella casts.

NOTE: The shadow on the sand should lean in the same direction as the shadows for the umbrellas: to the right.

Feel free to be creative here and add your own beach elements. You could add some small, colorful rectangles for beach towels, a small boat or two on land or in the water using gouache or anything else you can think of!

Once you're happy with your beach, take off the tape, sign and date your painting and admire your work.

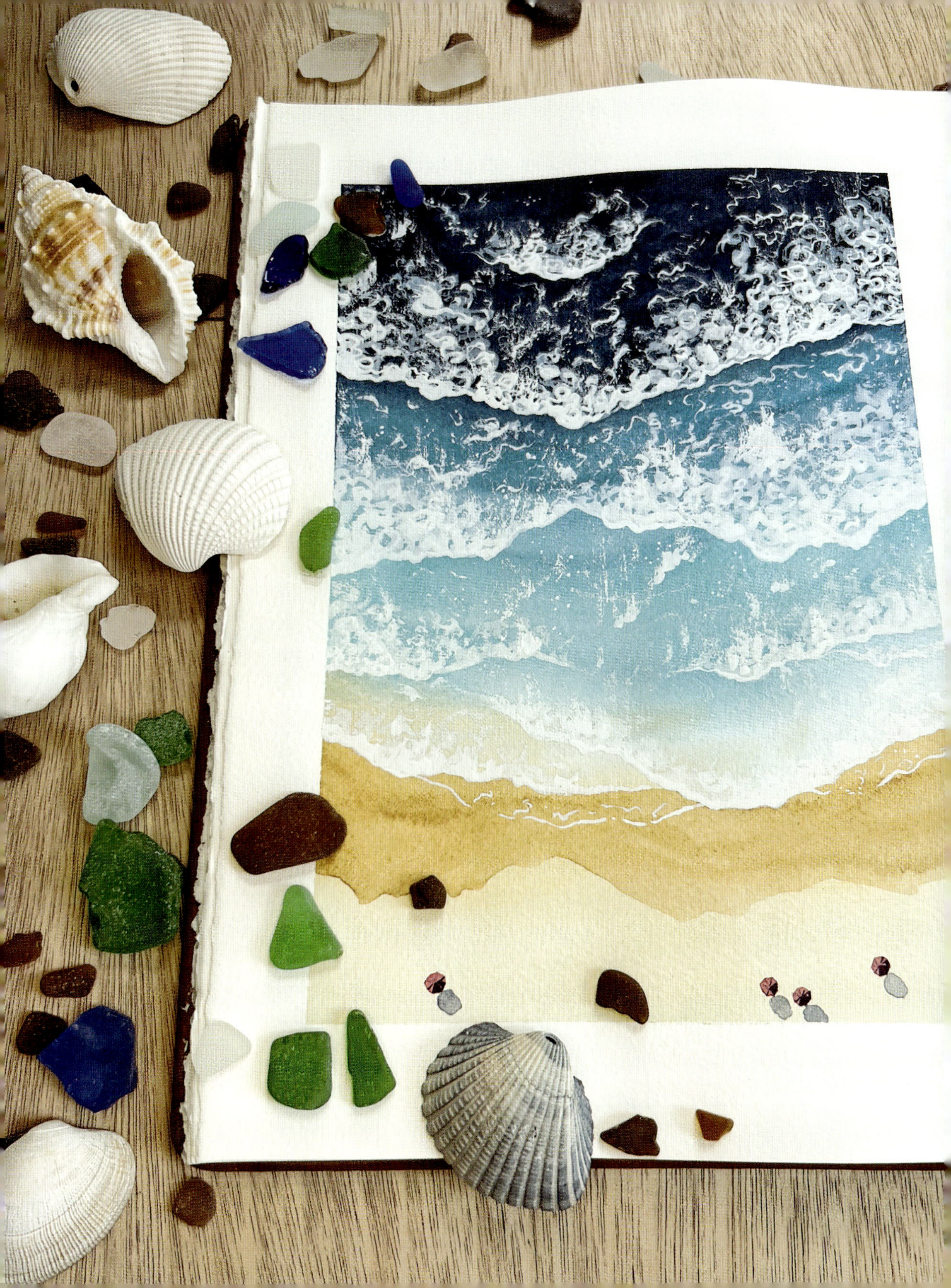

palm tree sunset

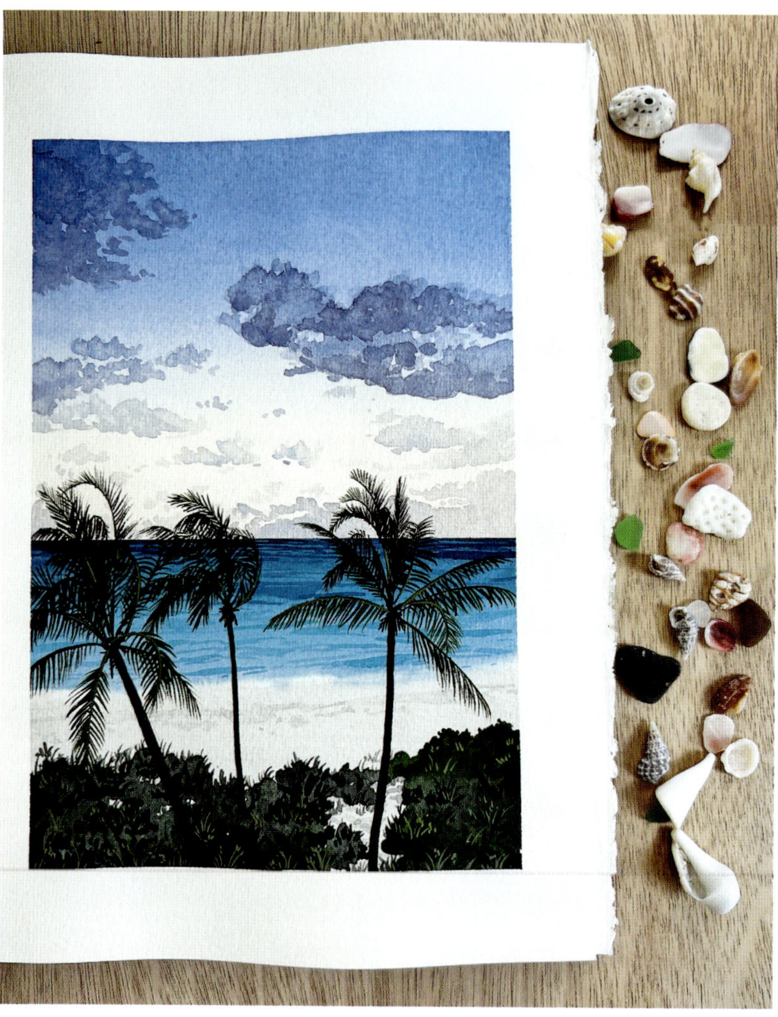

I love a good pastel sunset with palm trees; it makes me feel like I'm on a tropical island. This reference photo was from a trip to Turks and Caicos, and I just adore the soft clouds in the sky, the vibrant turquoise ocean and the palm trees waving in the wind. You'll get some more practice painting the ocean with this one, along with a little introduction to painting palm trees! I hope you enjoy your little tropical vacation with this painting!

materials

Watercolor paints

- Cadmium Yellow, Yellow Ochre, Cadmium Orange, Alizarin Crimson, Sap Green, Ultramarine Blue, Phthalo Blue, Indigo, Turquoise and Van Dyke Brown
- White gouache (optional)

Watercolor paper of your choice

- I used my cold press Fabriano Artistico sketchbook size 6 x 8.5 inches (15 x 21.5 cm)

Brushes

- one larger brush (I used a ½ inch oval), one medium brush (I used a 4 round) and one detail brush (I used a size 0 round)

Orientation

- portrait

Set up your paper as you like and make sure to add a drop or two of water to your colors so they start to soften.

Reference photo

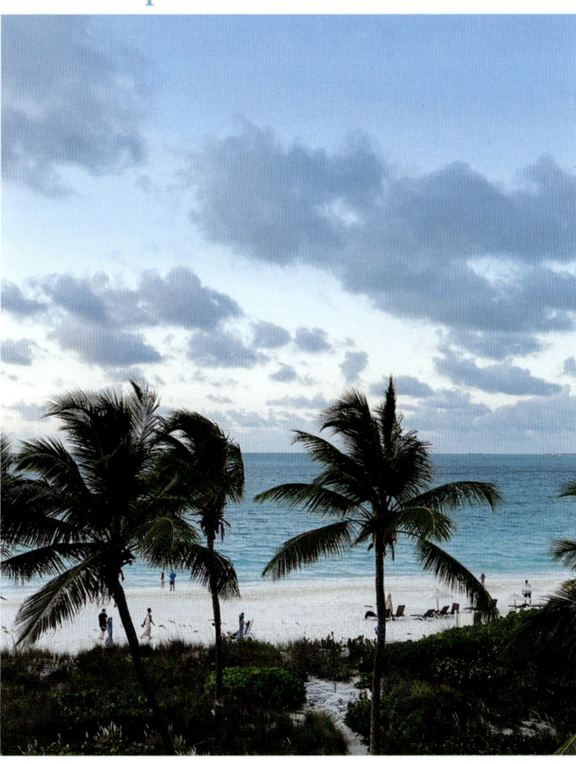

Sketch

Sketch the horizon line a little bit below halfway up the page, along with a diagonal line about a fourth of the way up the paper to mark the ocean edge and a wiggly, horizontal line at the bottom to show where the brush and grass will go. No need to sketch the palm trees yet. Put a piece of tape at the horizon line to get a sharp line there.

Step 1

Let's start by painting this gorgeous pastel sunset. Mix the sky colors first using the color recipes above. The Yellow and Orange colors should be very watered down, while the Blue should stay a bit more saturated.

To fill in the sky, use a large brush and start with the Blue color. Starting at the top of the page, use horizontal strokes to work your way down the paper. Once you've filled about two-thirds of the sky section, clean your brush, and use the damp brush to blend out the bottom edge. Then, paint a stripe below the Blue with the Yellow color and then use the Orange color to fill in the rest above the horizon line.

Feel free to use horizontal strokes and work your way back up the paper from the horizon line to the top to blend everything together. I recommend only doing this once or twice, as it will start creating weird textures if you do it too much. Let this fully dry before moving on.

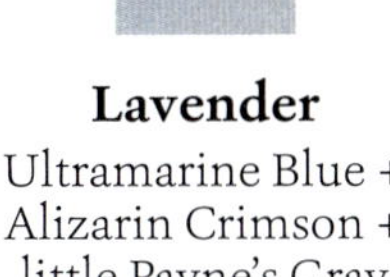

Lavender
Ultramarine Blue + Alizarin Crimson + little Payne's Gray + water

Step 2

Now let's add some clouds to this sky using a watered-down Lavender color.

Use a smaller brush (I used my 4 round) and create some fluffy cloud shapes in the sky with the Lavender color. Put some smaller clouds in the distance touching the horizon line, as well as a few larger ones higher in the sky. Use the reference photo for inspiration here.

As these clouds dry, you can use the same Lavender color to layer and deepen the color in some areas. Use this to add some shadows and contours to the higher-up clouds. Remember, you can always use a clean, damp brush to blend out any harsh lines you don't want.

Once you're happy with your clouds, take off the tape at the horizon line and let this dry completely.

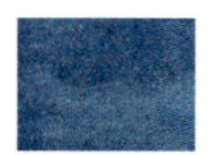

Dark Blue
Indigo + Phthalo Blue + Turquoise

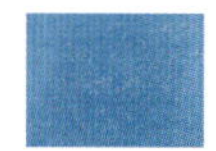

Medium Blue
Phthalo Blue + Turquoise

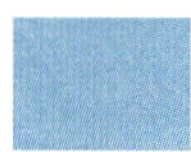

Turquoise
Turquoise

Gray
Van Dyke Brown + Ultramarine Blue + water

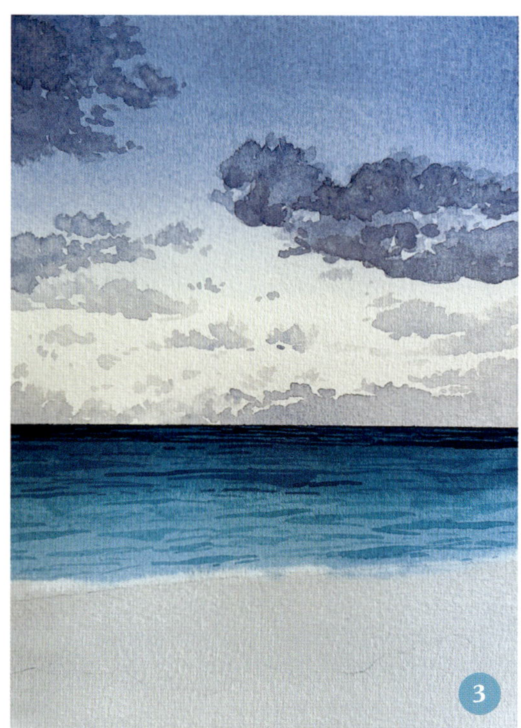

Step 3

Next, let's paint in the ocean and the beach. To preserve the horizon line, I put a piece of tape on the other side of the horizon line. Mix the four colors swatched above for this step.

NOTE: Please read through the following instructions before you start, so you can work quickly without stopping to read.

Using a large brush, work from the horizon line to the bottom of the page. Start with the Dark Blue and add a horizontal stripe at the horizon line.

Switch to the Medium Blue and add more horizontal stripes, allowing the color to blend with the Dark Blue.

Then, switch to the Turquoise and fill in the rest of the ocean section, leaving a small strip of blank paper just above the diagonal pencil line that marks the beach.

Clean your brush and use clean water to fill in the rest of the ocean section.

Finally, use the Gray color to fill in the rest of the page below the ocean (including the grass section).

Let this fully dry before moving on.

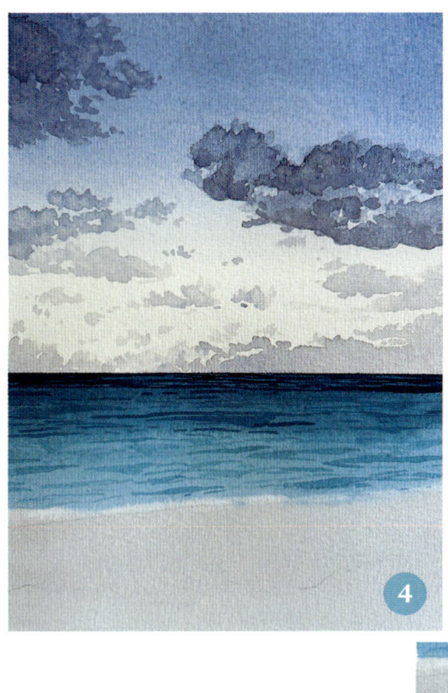

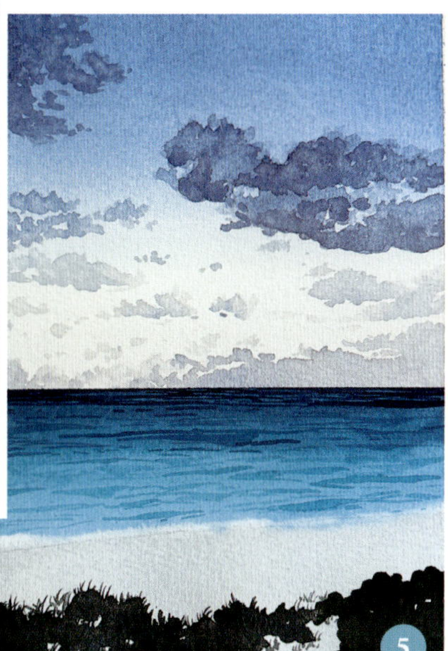

Earthy Green
Ultramarine Blue + Yellow Ochre + Van Dyke Brown

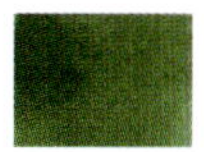

Green
Sap Green + little Ultramarine Blue + little Cadmium Yellow

Step 4

Use the same colors from Step 3 in approximately the same locations to add some texture to the ocean. I used my detail brush for this section and used horizontal strokes closer to the horizon line, then followed the diagonal of the beach once I got closer to it. When doing this, don't use the same brush stroke over and over. Make some shorter and some longer, and use a lighter touch for some and a heavy touch for others, etc.

Step 5

Now let's add the brush and grass at the bottom of the page using the green colors that are swatched above.

Use a medium brush (I used a 4 round) and switch back and forth between these colors, creating little rounded shapes to fill in the grass section. Feel free to leave some sand showing in certain spots. You can also use a detail brush to add some grassy textures here and there.

Let this fully dry before moving on.

Step 6

Let's add some details to the shrubs and the beach. Using the same Gray color from Step 3 and a detail brush, add a little bit of texture to the sand near the ocean. I just stippled on this detail, varying the pressure on my brush and following the shoreline direction.

Then, use the two green colors from Step 5 to add some general detail to the shrubs. Use a dotting motion to add some little leaves or use short upright strokes to add grassy textures. No need to add a ton of detail here—just a bit will help it look more realistic.

Step 7

Now let's add the focal point of this piece: the three palm trees. Use the same Earthy Green from Step 5, plus a Dark Brown.

Use your detail brush to create the three thin, brown trunks of the trees coming out of the grassy section. I add a little bit of spiky texture to the tops of these, which indicates the remnants of the dead fronds.

Dark Brown
Van Dyke Brown +
Ultramarine Blue

Next, use the Earthy Green from Step 5 to start adding palm fronds. This is a great time to observe the reference photo when painting these. Notice how some point toward the ground, some are sideways, some point up and some are bending over in the direction of the wind. Try to mimic this variety in your painting.

Paint the center stem of each frond first and then use a flicking motion with your brush to create the leaves. Allow these to cross over each other or separate in different ways, but don't make them too perfect. Also, the thinner you can make these the better, so use a super light touch with your brush.

Continue adding palm fronds to the trees until they are all filled out.

Step 8 (optional)

For a final optional step, you can mix some gouache into your Earthy Green color and use it to paint highlights on the palm frond stems. This helps to separate them from each other a little bit, and the highlight brings them to life.

Once you're happy with your palm trees, you're all done! Take off the tape, sign and date your painting and admire your work.

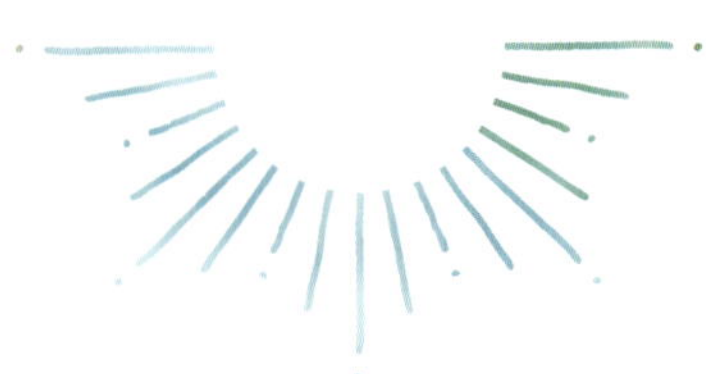

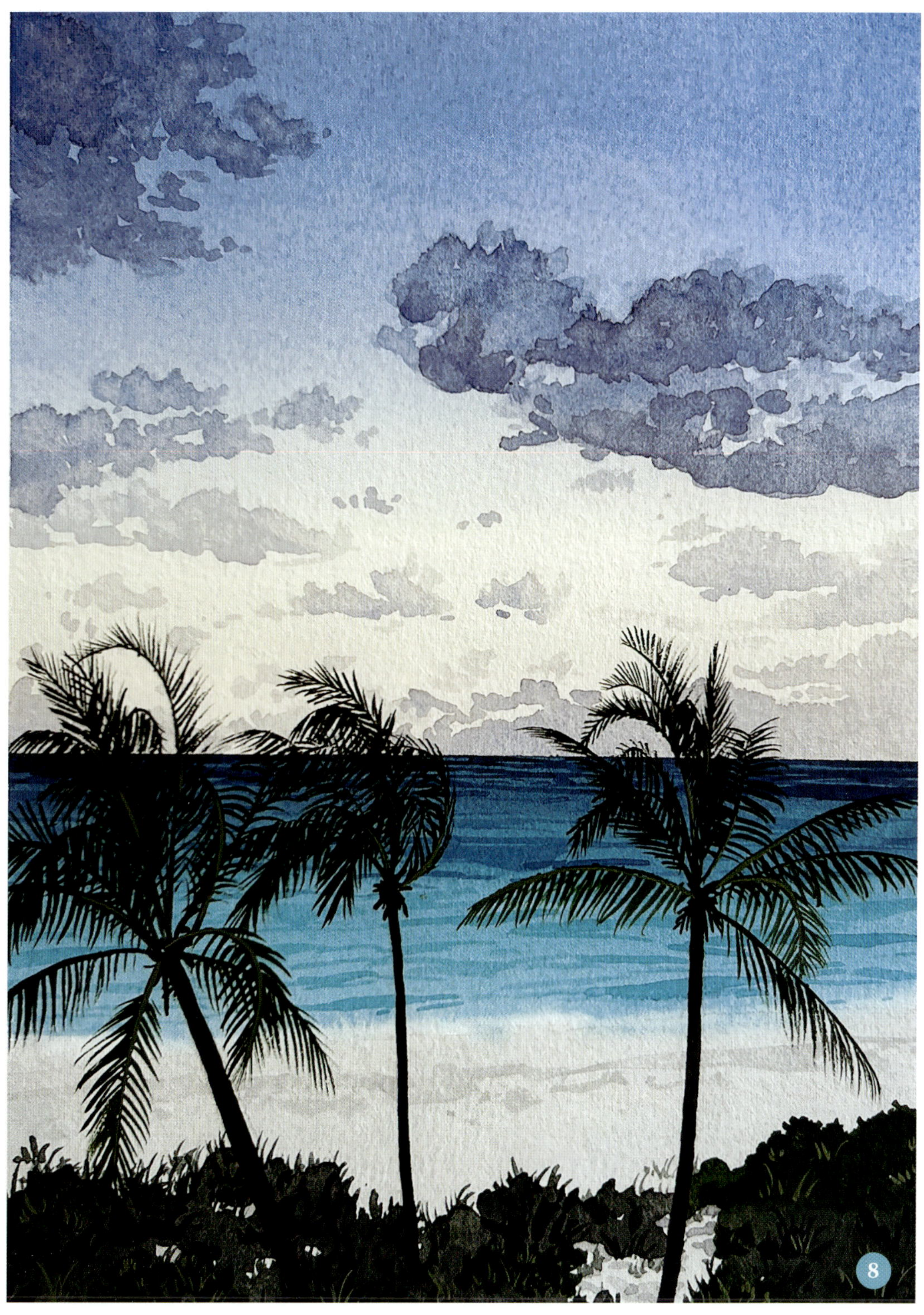
8

violet nafplio sunset

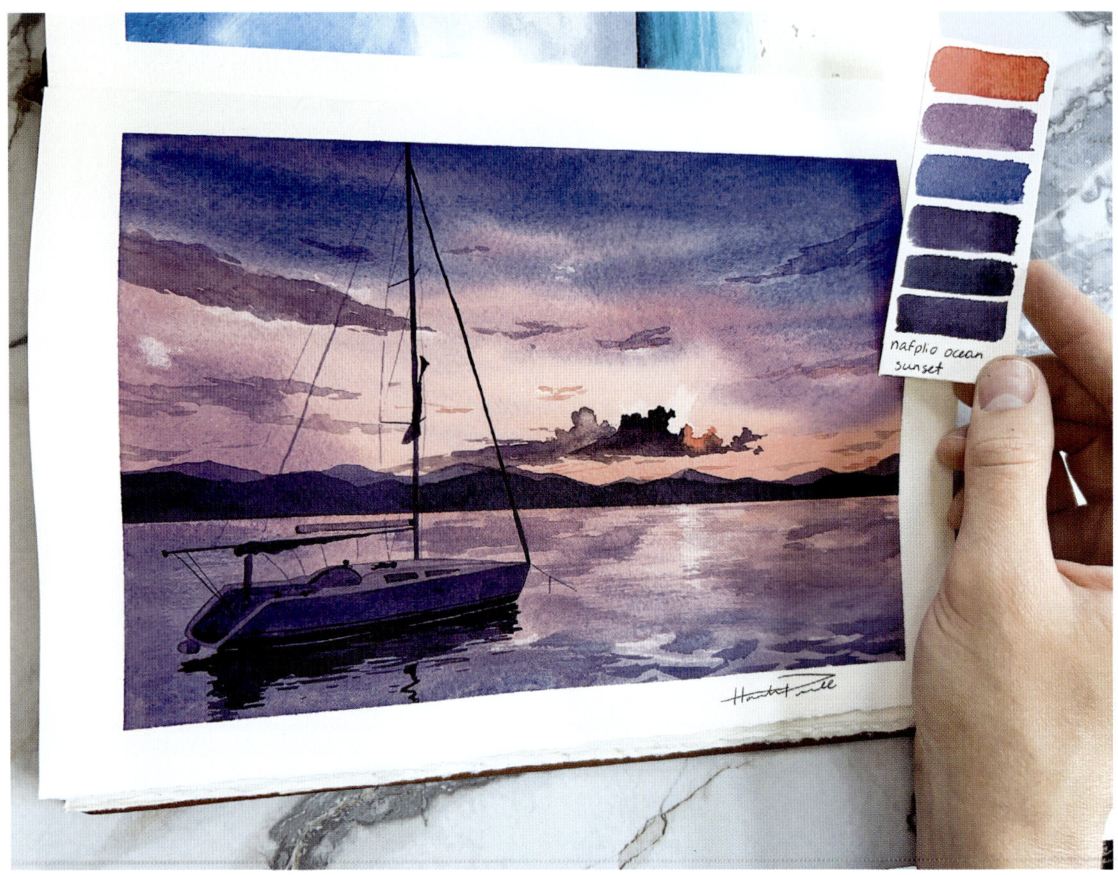

This project is inspired by a gorgeous sunset I saw on a trip to Nafplio, Greece, several years ago. Nafplio is famous for the Bourtzi Fortress, which was built on a tiny islet just offshore in the year 1471. It's a gorgeous place, and I took tons of reference photos there. I actually took this reference photo through my sunglasses because it gave the scene this gorgeous pink and purple filter. I love the reflection of the sky colors in the water, and I love the peaceful look of the sailboat floating nearby. You'll love painting this one along with me.

materials

Watercolor paints

- Cadmium Yellow, Cadmium Orange, Magenta, Ultramarine Blue and Van Dyke Brown
- White gouache (optional)

Watercolor paper of your choice

- I used my cold press Fabriano Artistico sketchbook size 6 x 8.5 inches (15 x 21.5 cm)

Brushes

- one larger brush (I used a ½ inch oval), one medium brush (I used a size 4 round) and one detail brush (I used a size 0 round)

Orientation

- landscape

Set up your paper as you like and make sure to add a drop or two of water to your colors so they start to soften.

Reference photo

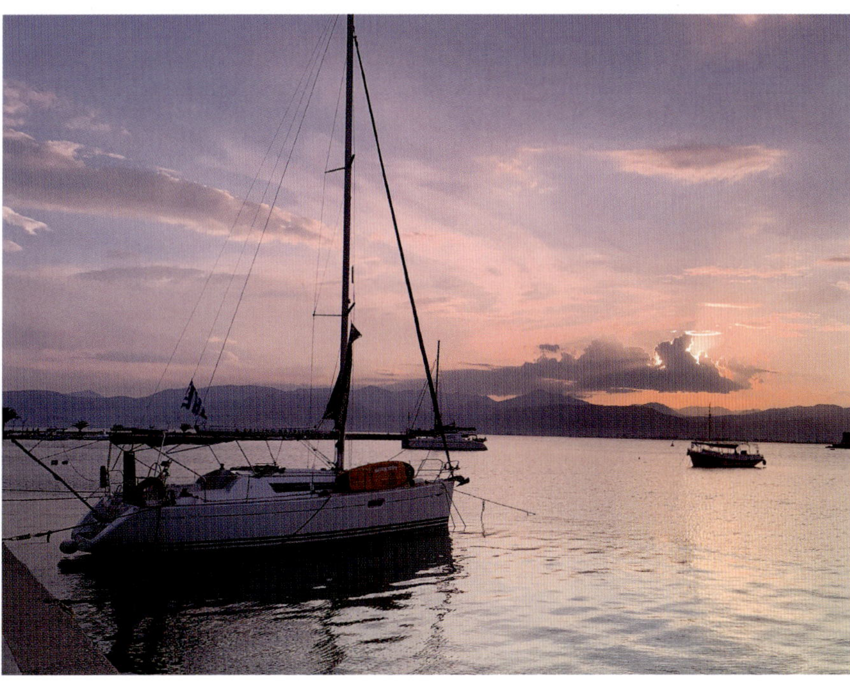

Pink

Magenta + little Cadmium Orange + little Cadmium Yellow

Purple

Magenta + little Ultramarine Blue

Blue

Ultramarine Blue + little Magenta

Sketch

Sketch your horizon line about a third of the way up the paper. Place a piece of tape along the horizon line to get a sharp line.

Step 1

First, let's paint in a beautiful pink and purple sunset! Mix the sky colors first, adding little water to create strong, saturated colors.

PAUSE: Please read through the following instructions before you start, so you can work quickly without stopping to read.

Use a large brush and cover everything above the horizon line with plain water. Then, pick up the Pink color, start at the center of the page at the horizon line and use sweeping motions to create a section of Pink in the center of the page.

Next, pick up the Purple color, and using the same sweeping motions, add Purple on both sides and above the Pink section. The colors should be blending together here!

Finally, use the Blue color to fill in the rest of the page. Feel free to overlap the Purple in some areas!

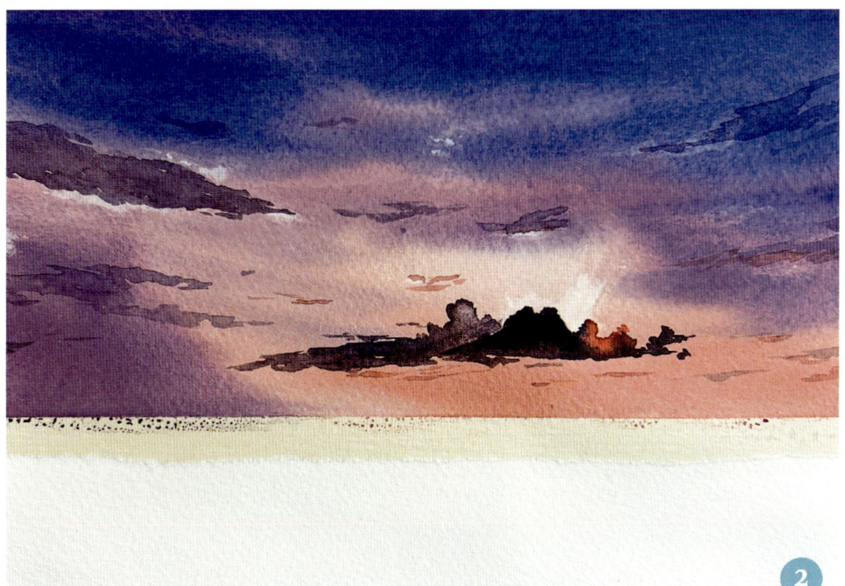

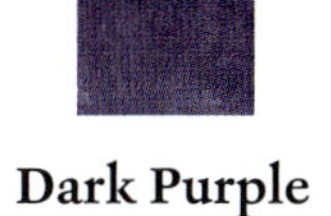

Dark Purple
Ultramarine Blue + Magenta + little Van Dyke Brown

Step 2

Before this sky section dries, use a smaller, completely dry brush to pick up some pigment and create highlights. **The most important part is the spot close to the horizon line, where the sun is shining from behind dark clouds** (note this spot on the reference photo). Use your brush to create a cloud-shaped light spot there, plus some small, lighter sunbeams radiating outward from that spot.

You can also add some more subtle highlights around the sky in the same way. Then, let the sky section dry completely.

Let's add some clouds to this sky! Mix a saturated Dark Purple color according to the swatch above.

Use a detail brush to create the dark clouds close to the horizon line. I started at the light spot we created at Step 1 and painted the outline of the cloud to match the light spot. For extra credit, drop some of the Pink color from Step 1 into the area of the cloud closest to the sun while the Dark Purple paint is still wet.

Next, **water down the Dark Purple color** and add some streaky clouds randomly around the sky, higher up above the horizon line.

Finally, use a watered-down Pink from Step 1 to add some thin streaky clouds close to the horizon line.

Blue-Gray
Ultramarine Blue + little Van Dyke Brown + little Magenta

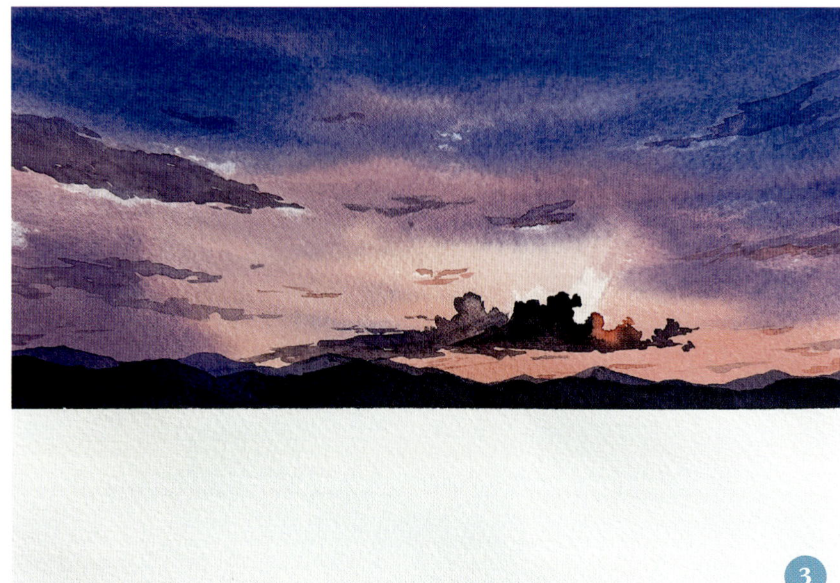

Step 3

Next, we'll add the mountain ranges in the distance. Mix a lighter (add more water) and darker version (add less water) of the Blue-Gray color above.

Start with the lighter Blue-Gray and create a mountain range in the distance, just under those dark clouds we painted in Step 2. Let it dry completely.

Then, switch to the darker Blue-Gray and create a slightly shorter mountain range on top of the first one, letting the first layer peek over in some areas. Let this dry completely and take off the tape at the horizon line.

Step 4

Now, let's paint in the ocean reflection of the sunset. You'll be using exactly the same colors from Step 1, so mix more if you need to.

The process will be very similar to Step 1. Put down a layer of water on the paper below the horizon line and then add in the colors in the same order, creating a mirror image of the sky. Use horizontal strokes to add a Pink area at the horizon line directly under the Pink area in the sky. Then switch to the Purple and fill in the sides and just below the Pink area, and then use Blue to fill in the rest.

NOTE: Instead of using sweeping motions for this section, **use horizontal strokes only.**

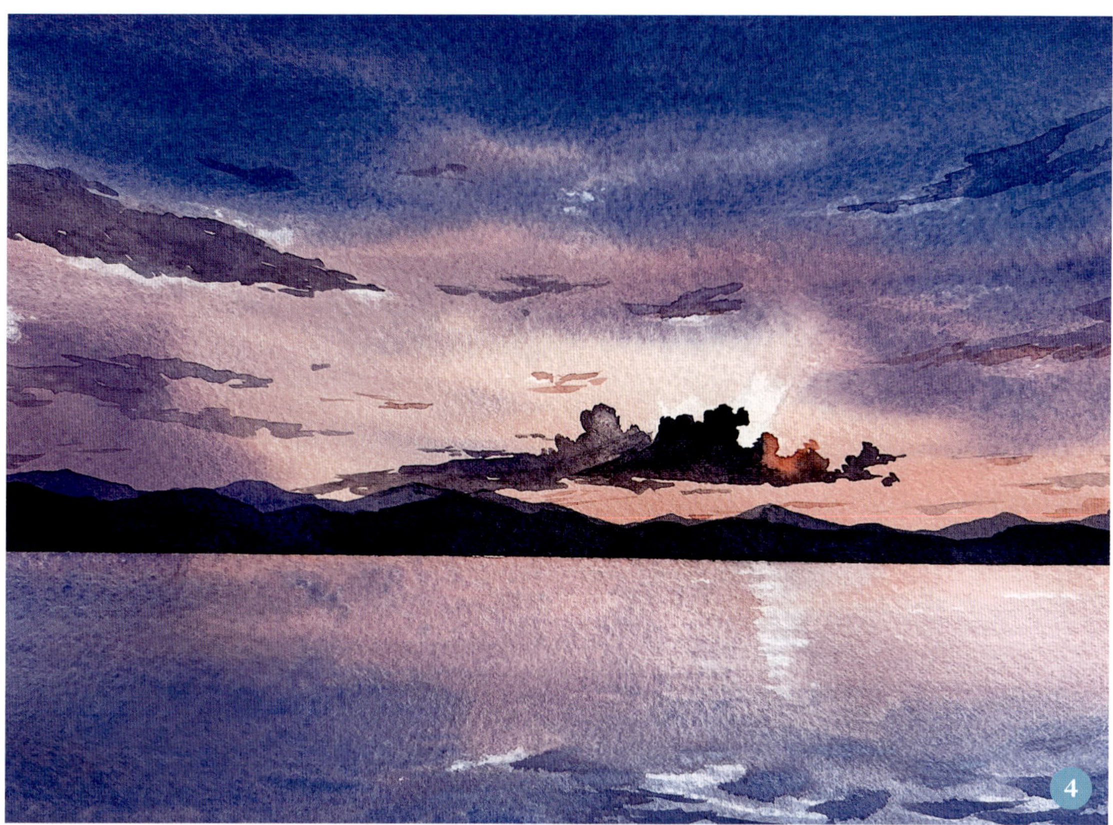

While this section is still wet, use a dry brush to pick up a few highlights directly under the sun. Feel free to lift a few more highlights around the water section, including at the bottom of the page.

Lastly, as the paper is starting to dry, use a smaller brush to add a few ripple details at the very bottom of the page with your Blue color. I like to press and quickly lift my brush in a horizontal direction to create those ripple shapes that you can see in my progress photo. Ideally, some of these will blend out with the wet spots on the paper, and some will stay intact on the dry areas of the paper.

NOTE: If your paper is too wet and the ripples blend out too much, wait a minute or two and try again. If your paper is too dry and the ripples don't blend out at all, use a clean damp brush to blend a few of the ripples immediately after painting them.

Let this fully dry before moving on.

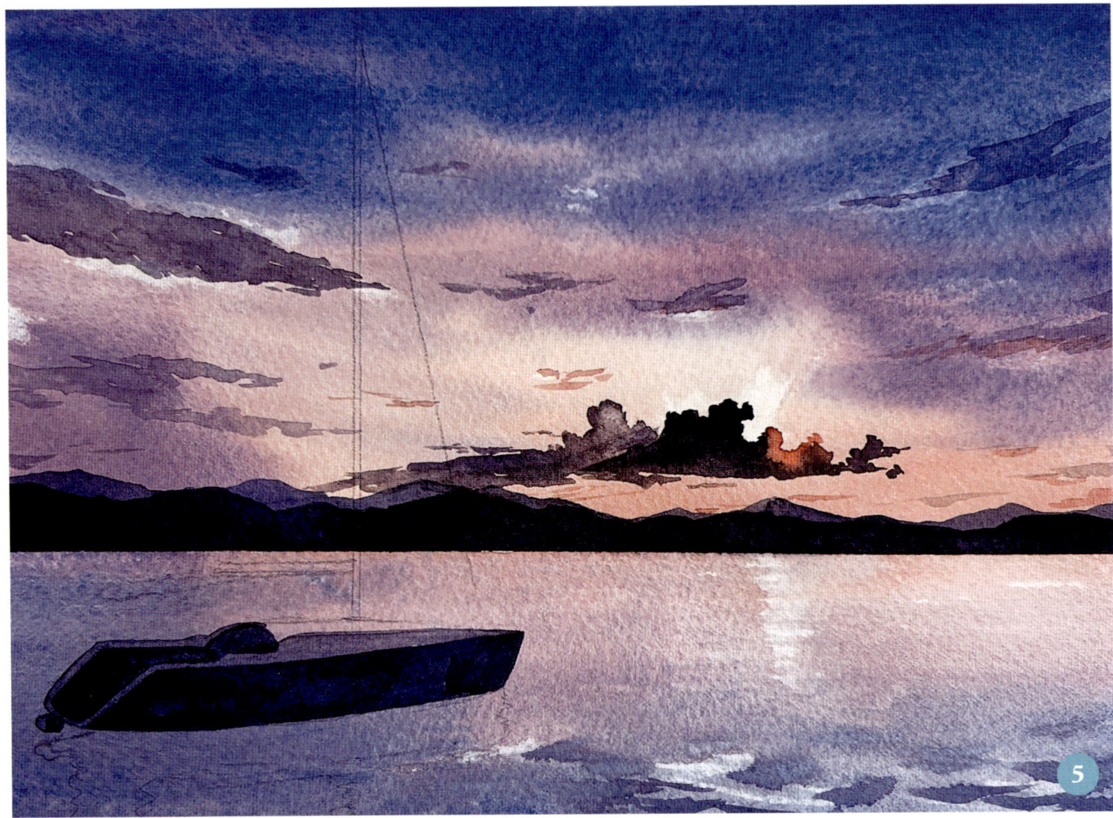

Step 5

Our final step is to create the focal point of this piece, which is the sailboat floating on the water. Use the reference photo here to sketch out the shape of the boat. This doesn't have to be exact at all, and you are welcome to add as much or as little detail as you want. You can even turn this into a silhouette and use a flat wash to fill in the overall shape. I chose to add a bit more detail, sketching the hull of the boat, the top, the mast and some rigging, but there were definitely details I ignored for the sake of simplicity.

To fill in the boat, we'll use different saturations of the Blue-Gray color from Step 3. Use the original Blue-Gray swatched on page 176 to fill in the hull and any dark details on the top of the hull. Then, **water down that color** and use it to fill in the top of the hull, and any areas that are a little lighter like some of the thinner ropes.

Lastly, **mix up an extra dark Blue-Gray** to paint in the main mast and rigging as well as the reflection of the boat on the water. You'll create a mirror image shape of the boat and paint it using wiggly, mostly horizontal lines.

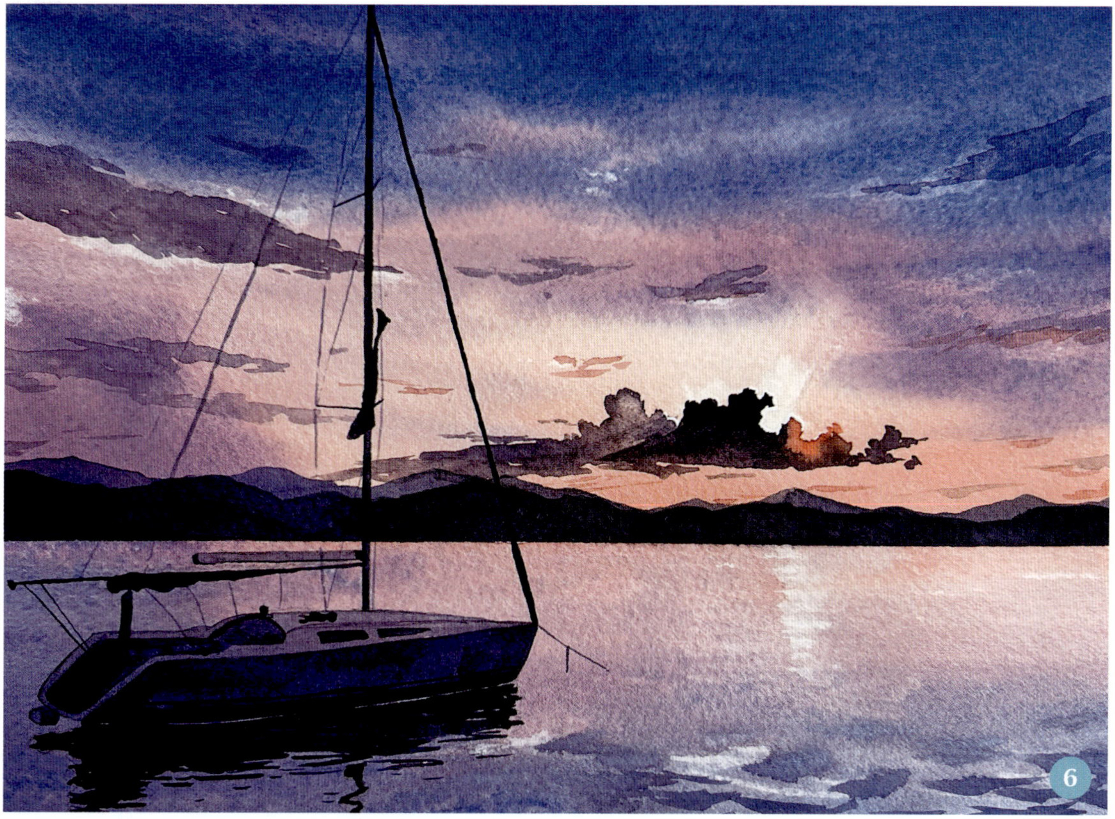

Step 6 (optional)

Our final detail for this painting is to add a highlight to the clouds. I used my white gouache and a detail brush to lightly outline the small section of cloud in front of the sun. This gives that area an extra sparkle and makes it really glow.

Once you're done with your final details, you've completed this painting! Take off the tape, sign and date your painting and admire your work.

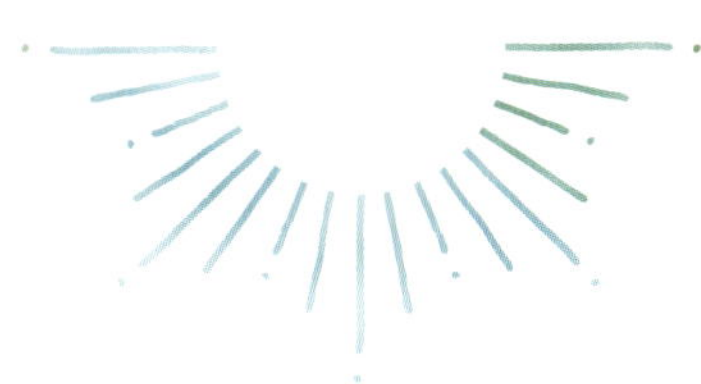

sailboat on sunlit water

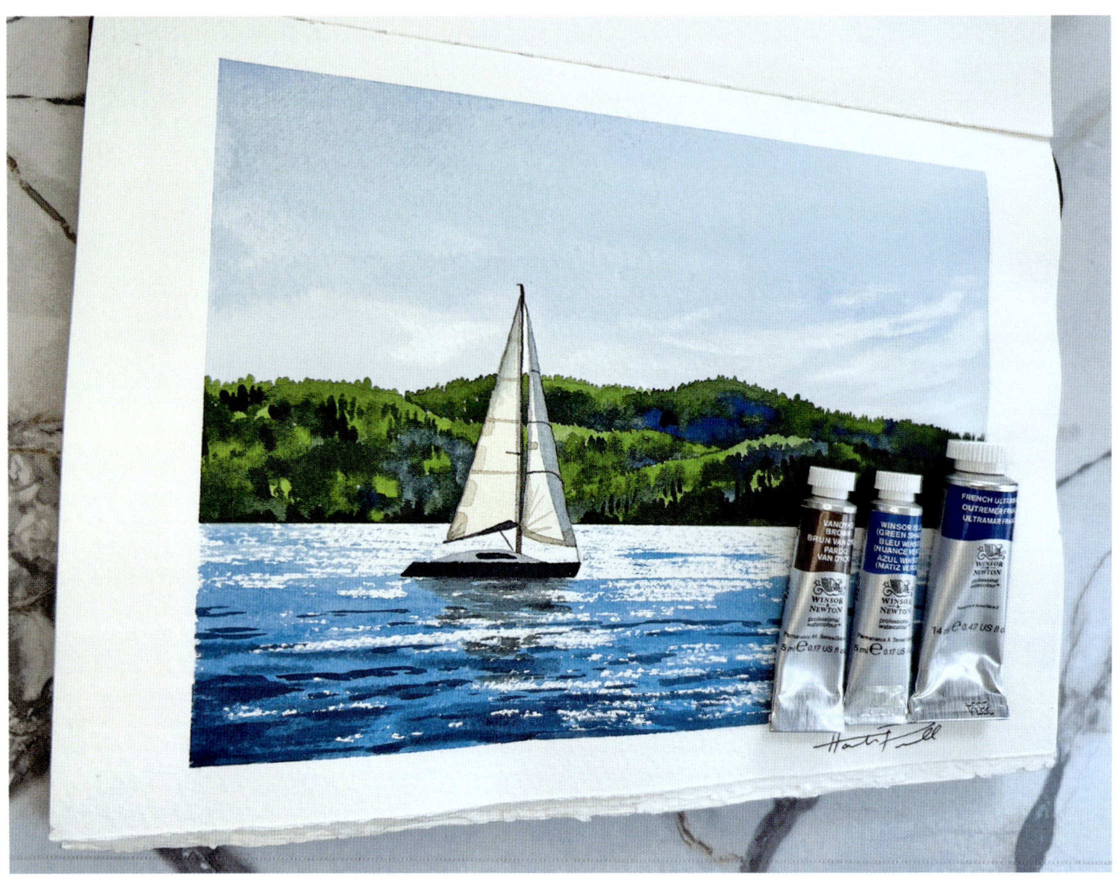

For this project, we will be painting a sailboat on a sunlit lake. I picked out this reference photo because I love the light and texture on the water. This is a great time to practice your dry brushing technique. I love the dark greens and blues in the distant hills and how they contrast with the sparkling water. You'll also get some good practice with your detail work in painting the sailboat. I hope you have fun with this one!

materials

Watercolor paints

- Ultramarine Blue, Phthalo Blue, Indigo, Payne's Gray, Sap Green, Yellow Ochre and Van Dyke Brown

Watercolor paper of your choice

- I used my cold press Fabriano Artistico sketchbook size 6 x 8 inches (15 x 20 cm)

Brushes

- one larger brush (I used a ½ inch oval), one medium brush (I used a size 4 round) and one detail brush (I used a size 0 round)

Orientation

- landscape

Set up your watercolor paints and add a drop or two of water to each of the colors listed above so the paint starts to soften.

Reference photo

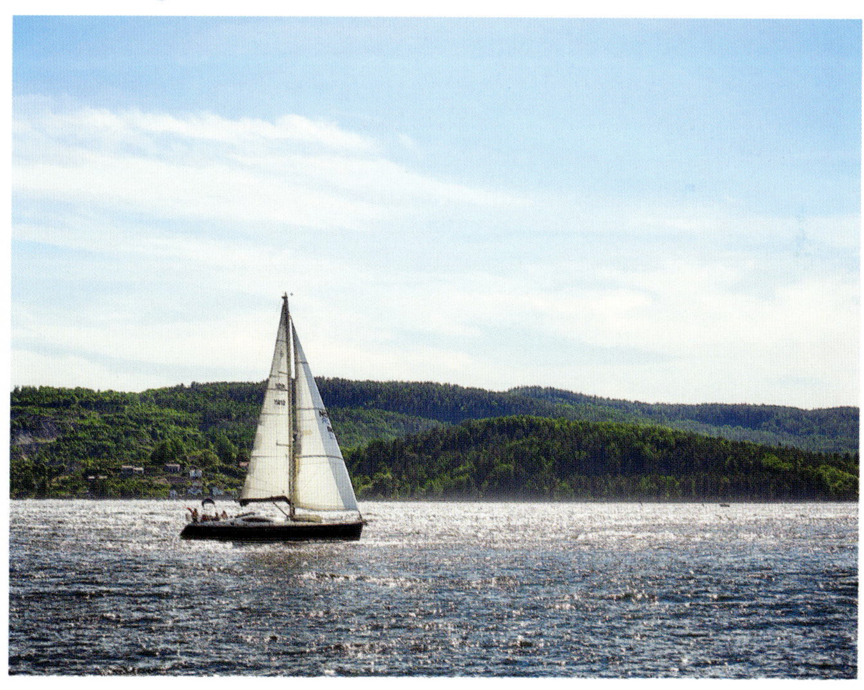

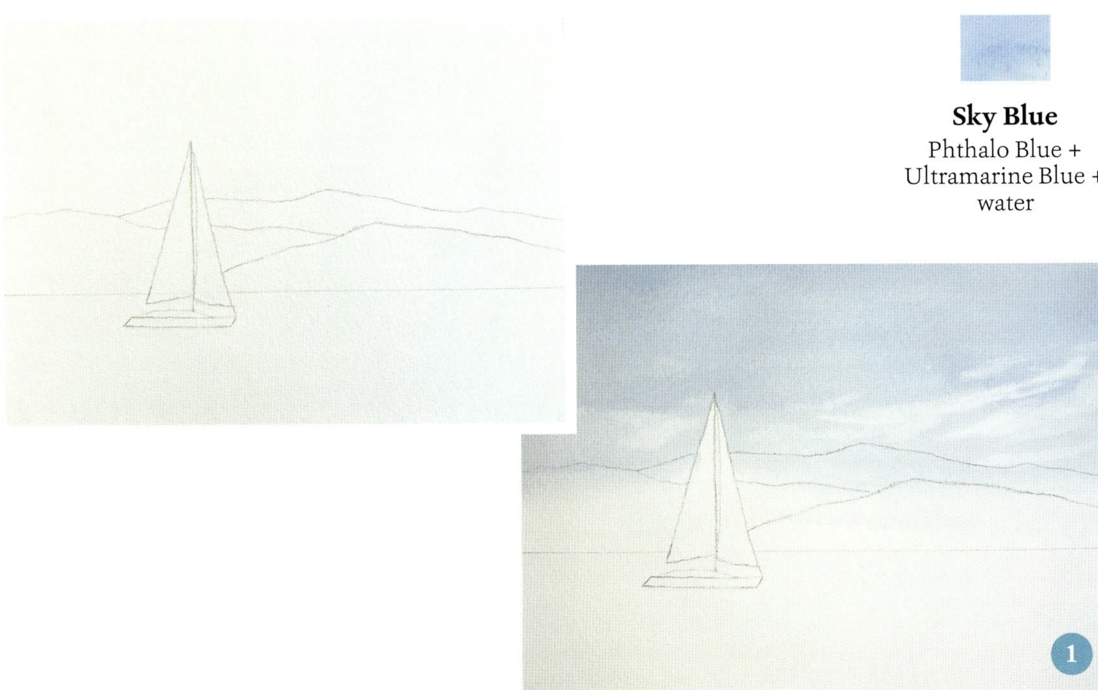

Sky Blue
Phthalo Blue +
Ultramarine Blue +
water

Sketch

Sketch the horizon line about one-third of the way up the page and the three rounded hills in the background. Next, add the sailboat on the water, using a small rectangular shape for the hull, a small, rounded shape on top and a couple of triangles for the sails. I chose to exclude the people you can see on the boat in the reference photo. Feel free to do the same or try including them for an extra challenge!

Step 1

We'll start with painting the sky a pale Sky Blue color.

Using a larger brush and starting at the top of your paper, paint horizontal strokes to cover the sky area with a flat wash. Feel free to overlap the hills a little bit (we'll cover that up later), but try to **avoid painting over the sails on the sailboat.**

While the paint is still wet, use a dry brush to lift some of the Sky Blue color in the sky to create some streaky clouds. Look at the reference photo to get an idea of where these clouds could go and pick up paint there using a sweeping motion for longer clouds or a dabbing motion for shorter and fluffier clouds. Make sure to continuously dry off your brush while you're doing this.

Let this fully dry before moving on.

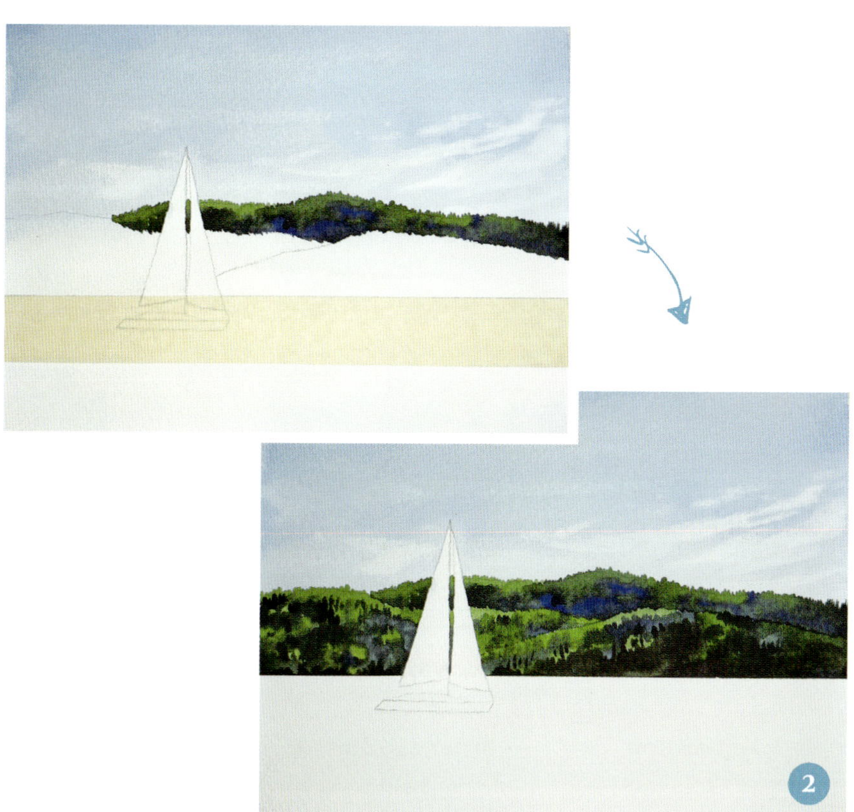

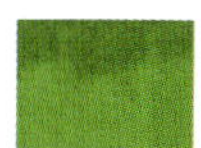

Light Green
Sap Green + little Yellow Ochre

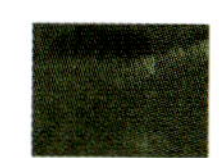

Dark Green
Sap Green + Ultramarine Blue + little Van Dyke Brown

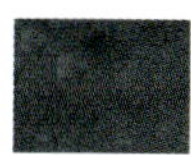

Blue-Green
Sap Green + Ultramarine Blue

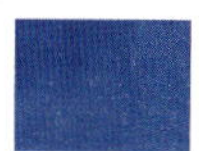

Blue
Ultramarine Blue

Step 2

To paint the hills in the background, you'll need to mix the four colors swatched above. Before you start painting, put a piece of masking tape on the horizon line so you get a perfectly straight horizon line.

Paint one hill section at a time, and switch between all four of these colors to create the texture of a tree-covered hillside. The tops of these hill sections should have more Light Green, and you'll use the Dark Green, Blue-Green and Blue as you move toward the horizon line. Try to do this relatively quickly so that all the colors blend together a bit.

To create this texture, use a smaller brush and make short vertical brush strokes. Once the first layer dries, feel free to go back over it with more vertical strokes if you feel like you've lost too much texture. Once you're done, take off the tape at the horizon line.

Let this fully dry before moving on.

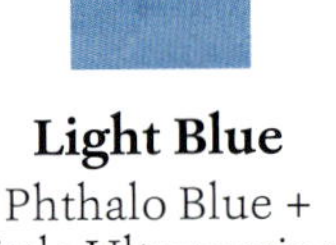

Light Blue
Phthalo Blue + little Ultramarine Blue

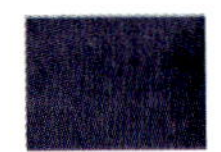

Dark Blue
Indigo

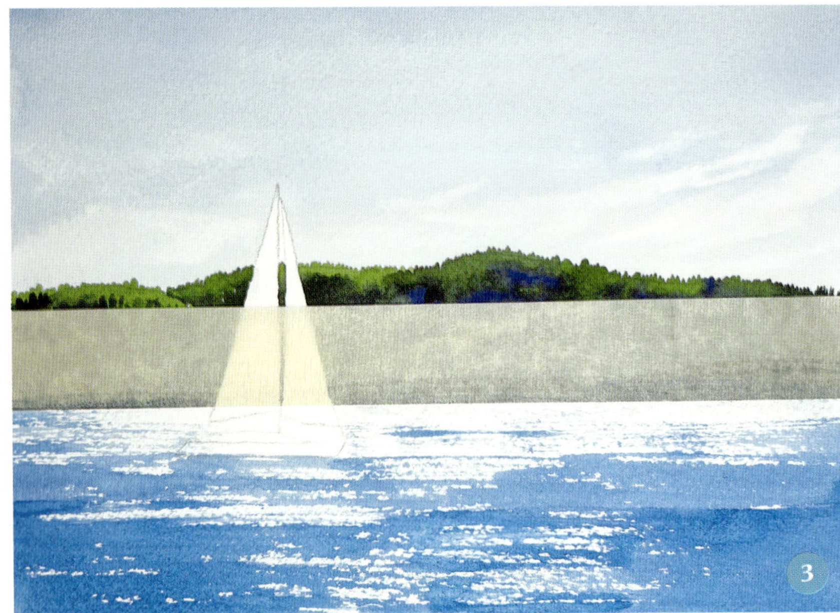

Step 3

Now we can move on to the water section. Feel free to add another piece of tape, this time covering the hills to help keep a sharp horizon line. Start by mixing the three colors swatched above.

We'll be using the dry brushing texture we covered in the One Drop at a Time project of this chapter (see page 154). Load up your larger brush (I used a ½ inch oval) with Light Blue paint. Touch your brush to a paper towel to take some of the paint off, then use the side of your brush to lightly scrape the paint along the paper in horizontal lines. I recommend starting at the bottom of the page and working your way up to the horizon line–you want the color to fade out significantly as you reach the horizon line.

TIP: Start these horizontal strokes from the tape at the sides of the paper; this disguises the beginning of these paint strokes, and it creates the most highlights in the center, which is what we want.

Step 4

Once you're happy with the coverage of the Light Blue color, switch to your Dark Blue and add just a few more dry brushed paint strokes in the bottom half of this water section.

Then add ripple details by using the point of the brush to paint some thin, wiggly horizontal lines. Vary your brushstrokes here–make some ripples shorter and some longer, some thinner and some thicker.

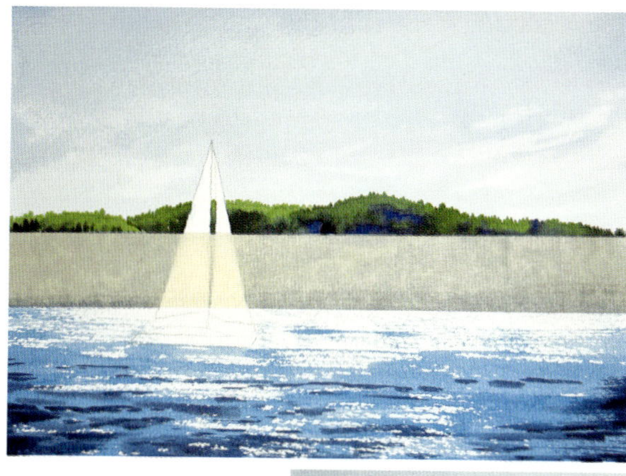

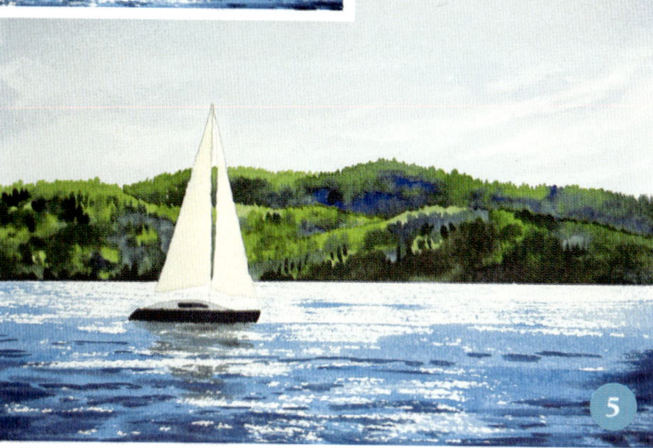

Dark Gray
Payne's Gray

Light Gray
Payne's Gray + water

Light Yellow
Yellow Ochre + water

Gray
Ultramarine Blue + Van Dyke Brown

Step 5

Now let's add the first wash to the sailboat. With your detail brush, paint the hull of the sailboat Dark Gray. Once the Dark Gray paint is dry, paint in the top of the hull with Light Gray, and let it dry. I added the small window you can see in the reference photo with Dark Gray as well. While the hull dries, use your detail brush to paint the sails with the Light Yellow color. Let this fully dry before moving on.

Finally, use the Gray color to add a shadow underneath the sailboat. Use the same dry brushing technique and try to form these strokes in a loose, upside-down triangle shape to mirror the shape of the sails.

Light Brown
Yellow Ochre + Van Dyke Brown + water

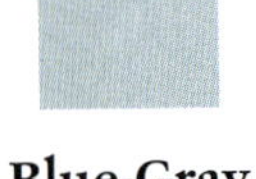

Blue-Gray
Ultramarine Blue + little Van Dyke Brown

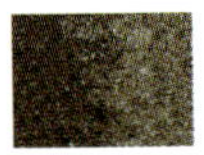

Dark Brown
Van Dyke Brown

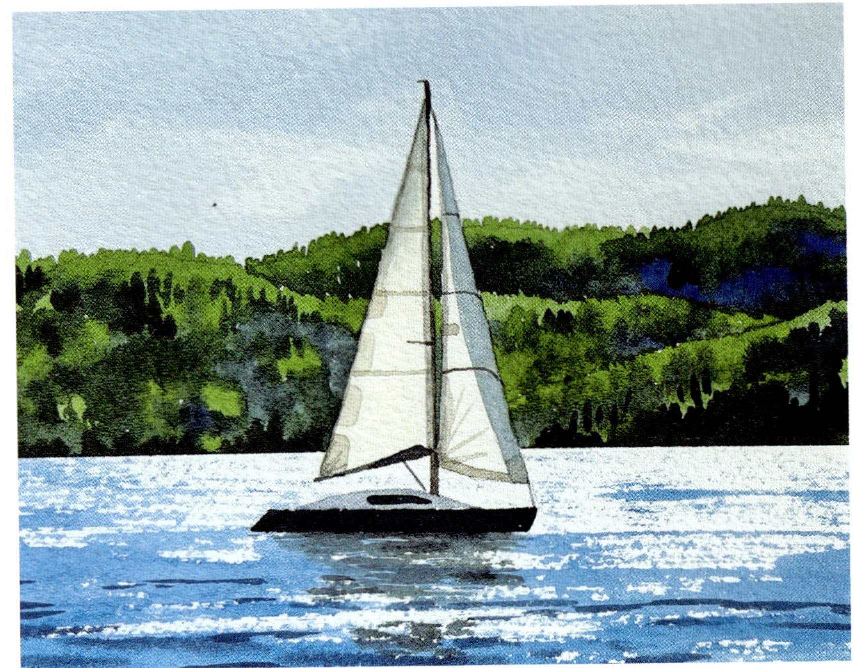

Step 6

Our last task of this painting is to add details to the sailboat. I used a detail brush and a few colors for this section, which you can see swatched on the left.

Use the Light Brown to add the small rectangles that go up the left side of the left sail as well as the horizontal lines that go across both sails. Then, add a rectangle to the left side of the right sail; look at the reference photo for placement. You can also use this Light Brown color to outline the sails, which will give them more dimension.

I also added a few Light Brown lines radiating from the bottom left corner of the right sail to show the tension of the fabric.

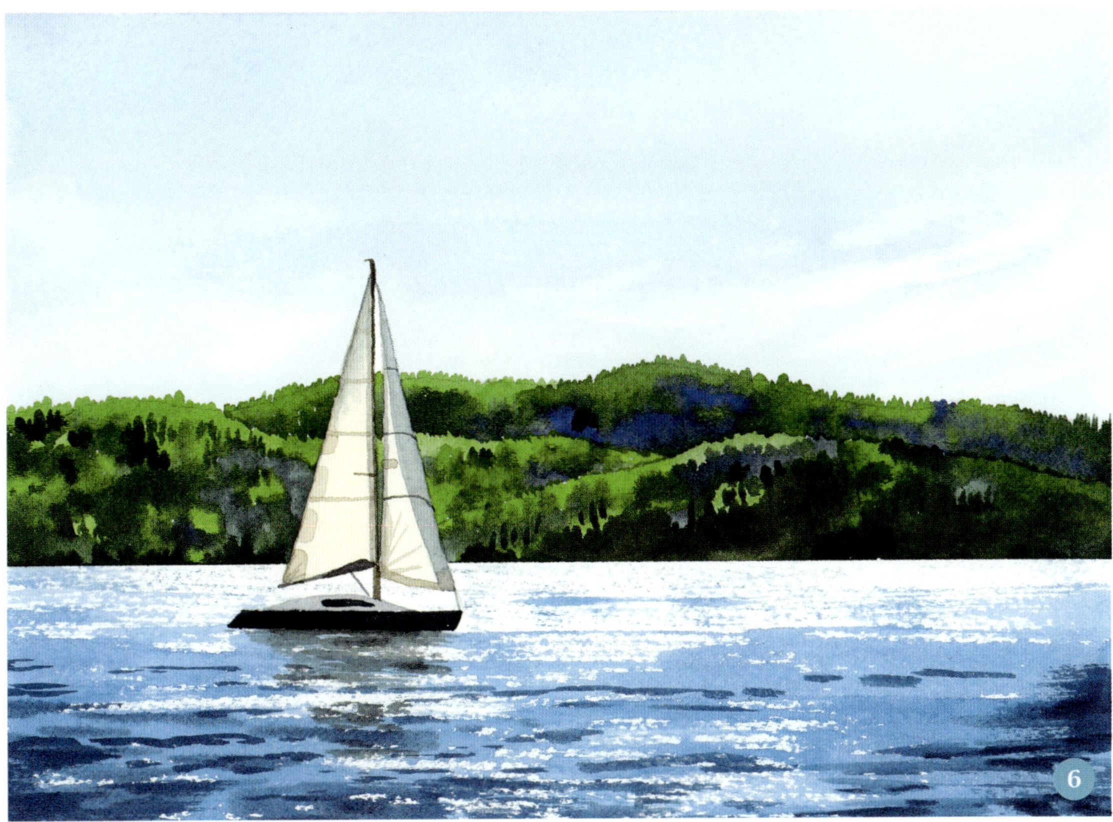

Use the Blue-Gray color to add the shadow on the right side of the right sail.

Use the Dark Gray color from Step 5 to add the lines attaching the sails to the boat as well as the shadow on the bottom of the left sail.

Finally, use the Dark Brown to paint the mast. I also added a short line at the top of the mast to indicate where the rigging ties off. Feel free to add any other details or shadows you see in the reference photo to your painting.

And that's it! Take off the tape, sign and date your painting and admire your work.

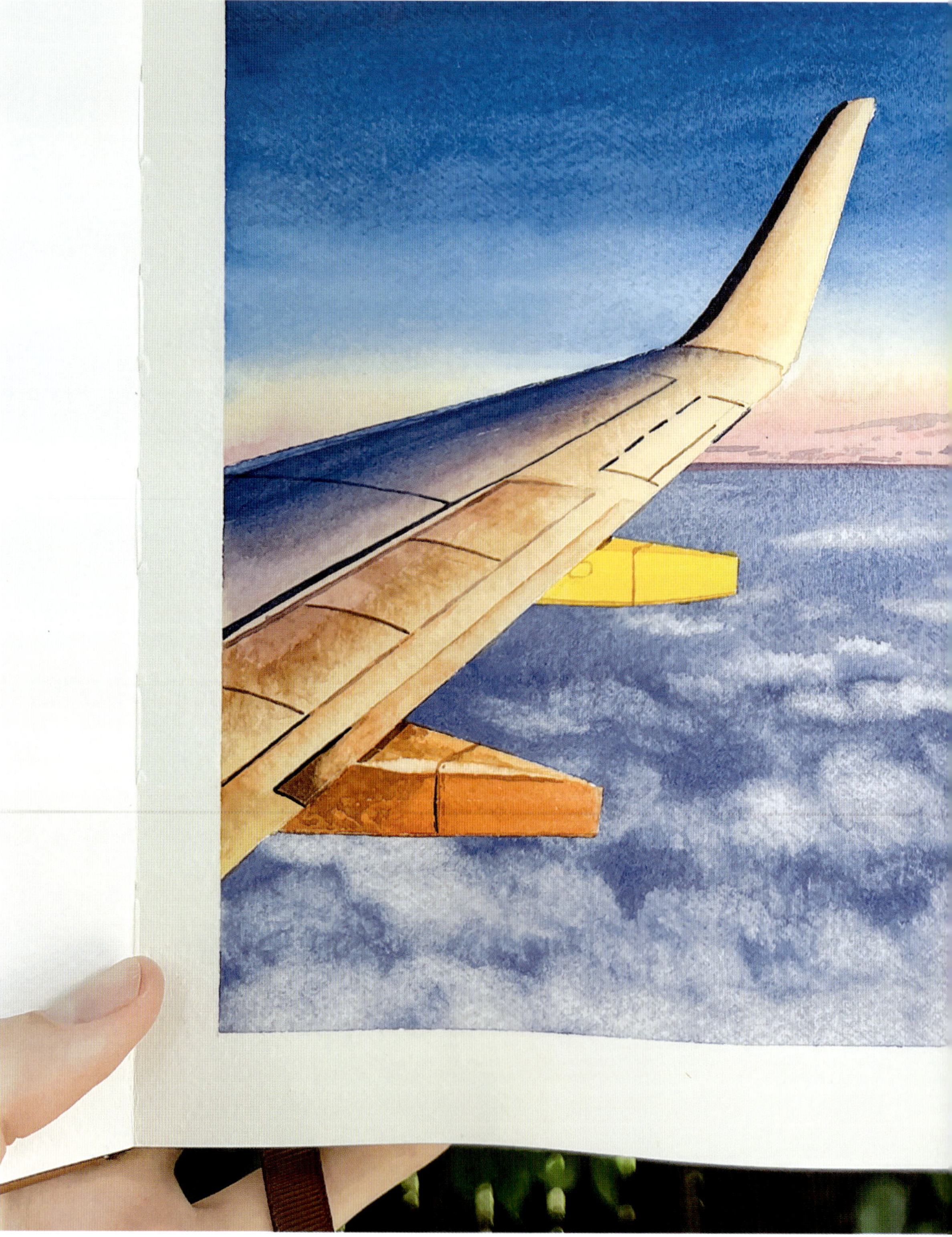

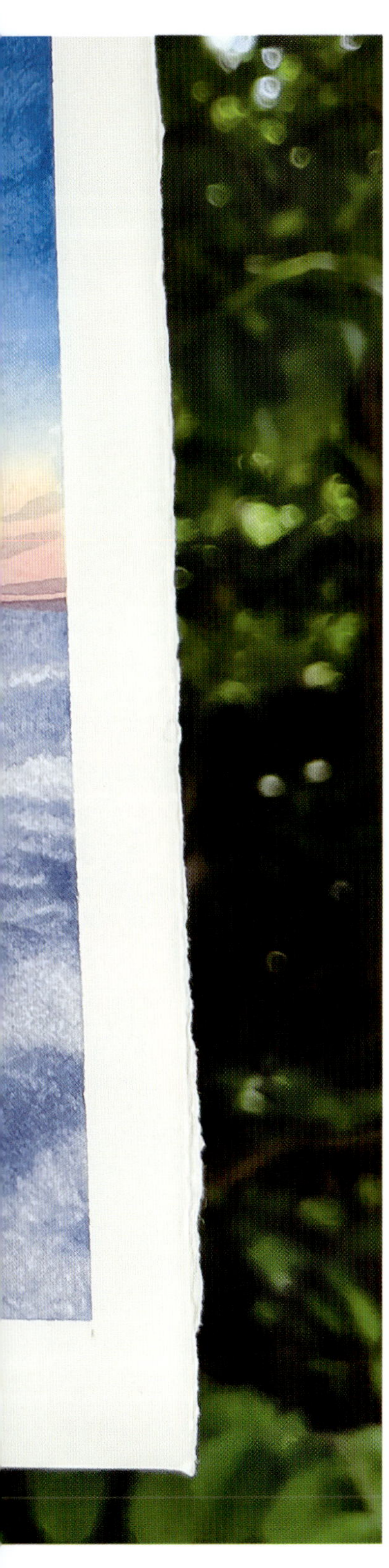

chapter 7
from ground to galaxy

As we reach the final chapter of this book, I wanted to challenge you with a few unique landscapes. To practice form and perspective, we'll paint a Stonehenge scene and an airplane view. To explore outer space, we'll paint a galaxy and visit the deep craters of the moon. I hope you enjoy flexing your painting skills with these exciting landscapes, and I hope they give you confidence to go paint any landscape you love once you're done with this book.

secrets of stonehenge

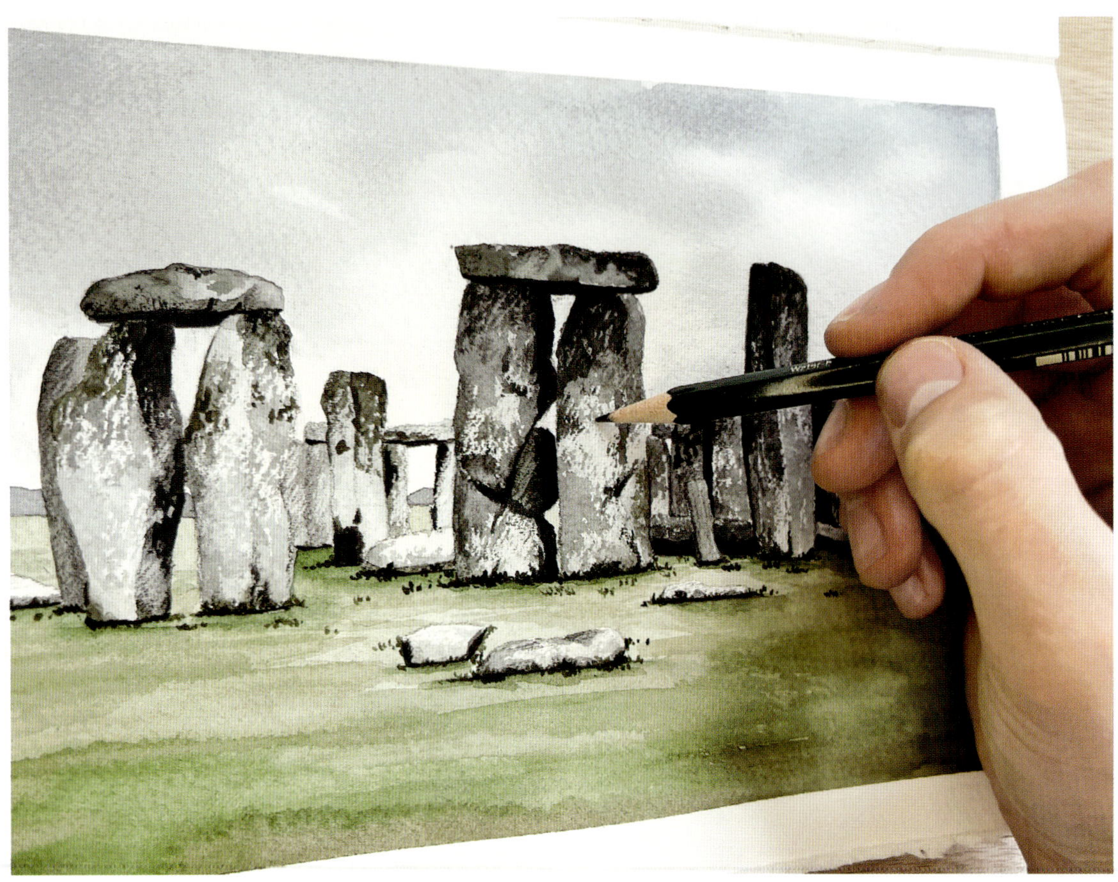

I was lucky enough to visit Stonehenge with my family in 2019. It's a fascinating historical sight, and I made sure to take lots of reference photos while I was there. I've painted Stonehenge a few times since then, and I find that I really enjoy it every time. I love recreating the textures and contours of the stones, and I find the composition really satisfying. We are going to experiment with creating a more finished pencil sketch as a sort of "underpainting," which is a fun technique that you can apply to your future watercolor endeavors.

materials

Watercolor paints

- Sap Green, Van Dyke Brown and Payne's Gray

Watercolor paper of your choice

- I used my cold press Fabriano Artistico sketchbook size 6 x 8.5 inches (15 x 21.5 cm)

NOTE: Make sure to test your pencil by making a few marks and painting over it with some random watercolor paint to make sure it won't smudge.

Brushes

- one larger brush (I used a ½ inch oval), one medium brush (I used a 4 round) and one detail brush (I used a 0 round)

Orientation

- landscape

Set up your paper as you like and make sure to add a drop or two of water to your colors so they start to soften.

Reference photo

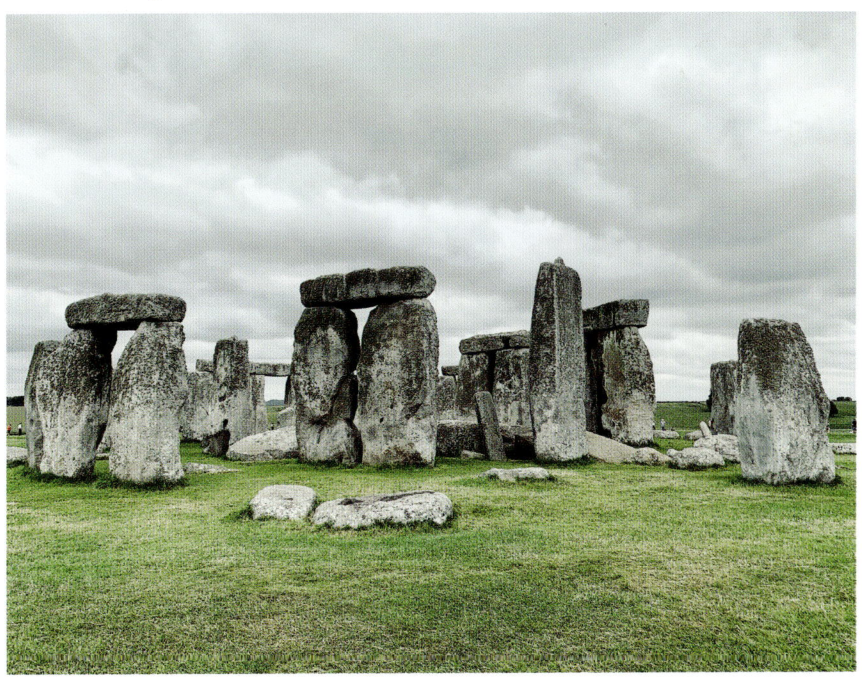

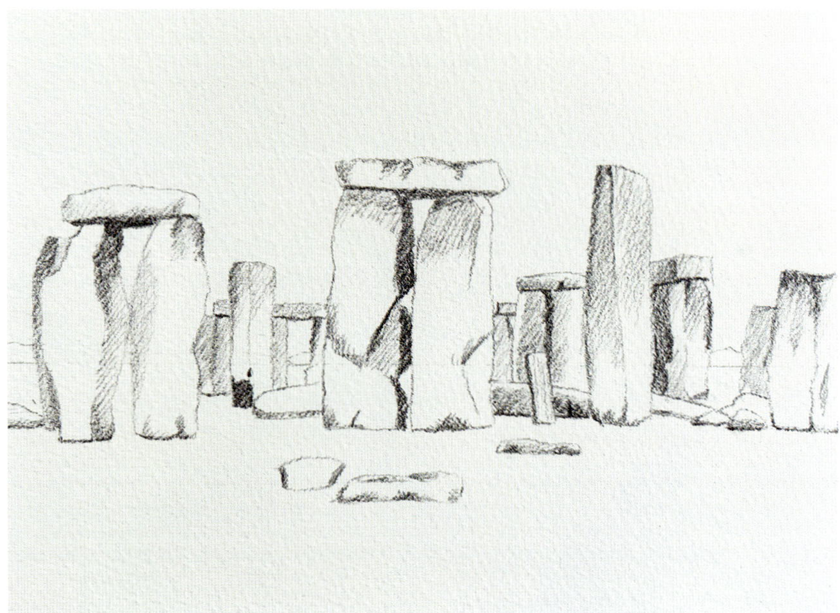

Sketch

This composition can be quite daunting when you're starting your sketch. There's a lot of stones that overlap, and it can get confusing and frustrating. I would suggest starting by lightly sketching the horizon line just under halfway up the paper and then sketching the tallest, most significant stones first. To my eye, this would be the larger pair on the left, the pair in the middle and the single tall stone on the right. Pay attention to the reference photo to estimate how tall and wide they should be. Once those stones are in, you can use them as guides to sketch in the rest of the stones.

Next, shade in some of the darkest areas of the stones and add texture with your pencil.

Don't stress out about this too much—the proportions don't need to be exactly right in order for this painting to look like Stonehenge.

Step 1

With your watercolors, paint in a moody-gray, cloudy sky using a wet-on-wet technique. If you need detailed instructions on this, follow the sky instructions from the Rolling Hills project on page 20, only using Gray instead of Sky Blue.

Use a large brush and put down a layer of clean water over your sky. Then drop in some loose brushstrokes of Gray, leaving some white on the page. Tilt your paper slowly in different directions to blend the paint softly, then use a completely dry brush to lift excess paint and create the impression of clouds.

Let this fully dry before moving on.

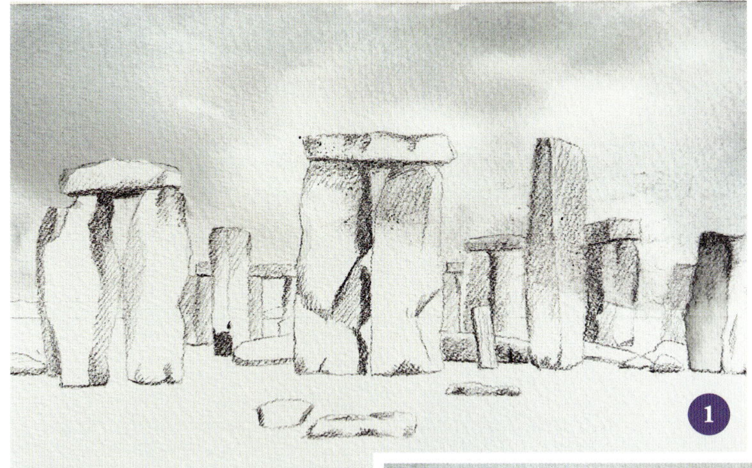

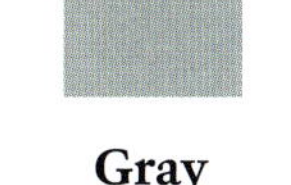

Gray
Payne's Gray + water

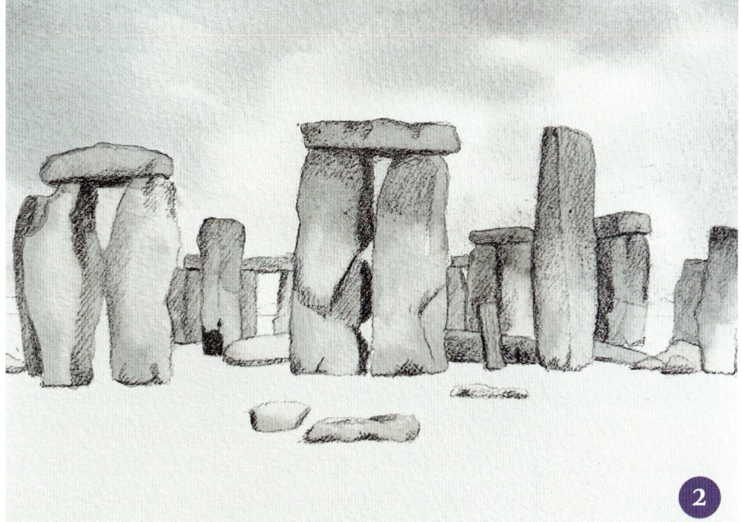

Step 2

Now, we will paint in the initial wash of color on the stones. Use a smaller brush (I used my 4 round) and work in small sections to add the Gray swatched above to the shadowed areas of the stones. Then quickly use a clean, damp brush to blend out the color into the lighter areas of the stones.

Repeat this process for all of the stones. This will give you the varied wash you can see in the progress photo.

Let this fully dry before moving on.

Light Green
Sap Green + little Payne's Gray + water

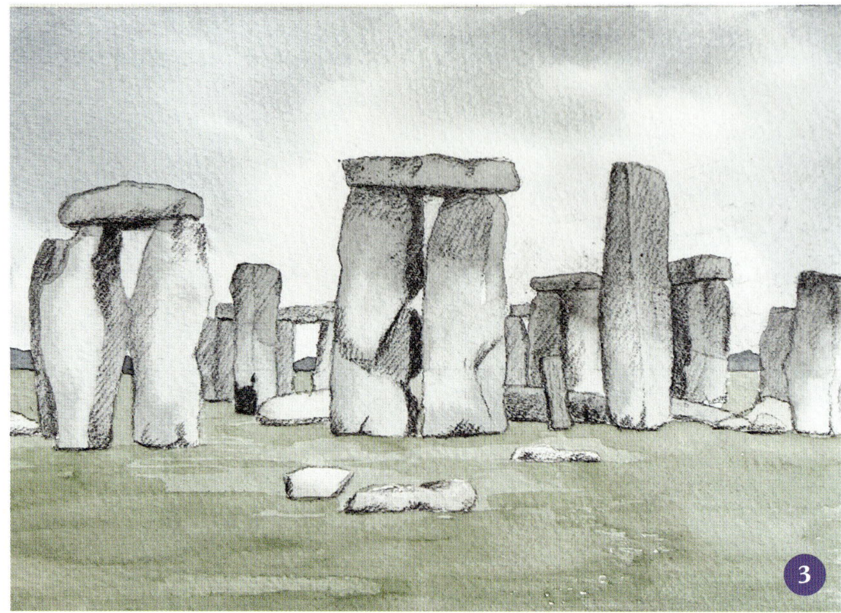

Step 3

Next, we will add in the first layer on the grass with a very muted, Light Green. We will also add the hill in the distance (which you can only see in a few spots) with the Gray color from Step 2.

Use a big brush to fill in the grass section underneath the stones with a flat wash of Light Green. As the paint starts to dry, use the same color to add a bit of texture with horizontal brush strokes. Be careful not to overwork it here—just allow for a bit of texture!

Before moving on, add that distant hill with watered down Payne's Gray and a detail brush in the places where it peaks through gaps in the stones.

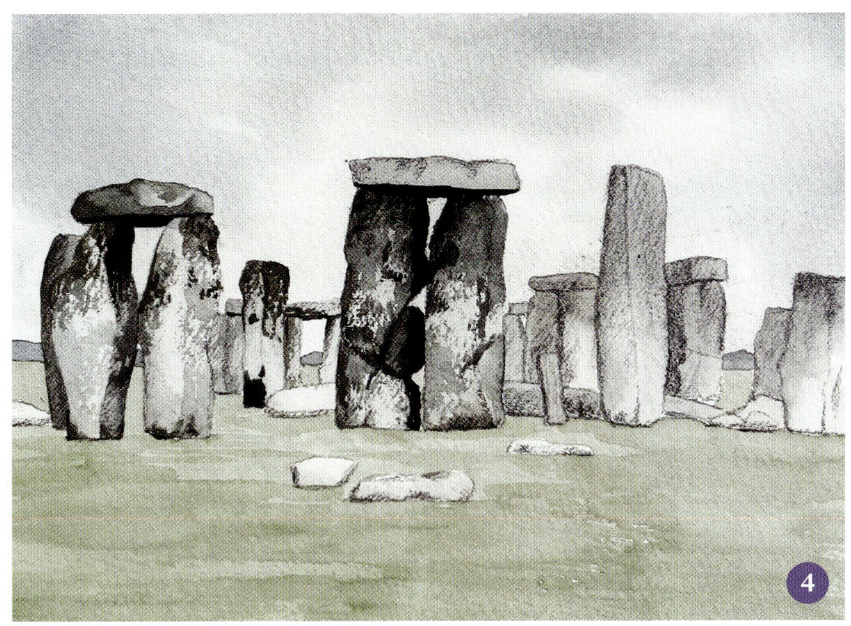

Muted Medium Green

Sap Green + Payne's Gray + Van Dyke Brown

Muted Dark Green

Sap Green + Payne's Gray + Van Dyke Brown

Step 4

Now we will start to really define the stones. Pay attention to the reference photo here; it will help you know where to put the shadows and texture! I used my smallest detail brush for this and a few different colors and textures.

I mixed up several, slightly different dark shades using the three colors of this painting: Sap Green, Payne's Gray and Van Dyke Brown. I did this by slightly altering the proportions of the colors every time with sometimes more green or sometimes more gray, etc. You can see some examples of these colors swatched above, but feel free to create your own unique mixtures!

I used my smallest brush on purpose here. Since it runs out of paint quickly, I can use a dry brush technique to add texture (see page 16 for more details on dry brushing). I also used the same technique from Step 2—adding a little bit of color in certain areas, then using a clean damp brush to blend it out. I used the Muted Medium Green to add mossy areas along the sides of the stones and the Muted Dark Green color to emphasize the darkest shadows I shaded with my pencil.

The overall goal is to create a textured look that also has high contrast (some very light sections and some very dark sections).

Green
Sap Green + very little Payne's Gray

Brownish Green
Sap Green + Van Dyke Brown

Dark Green
Sap Green + Payne's Gray + Van Dyke Brown

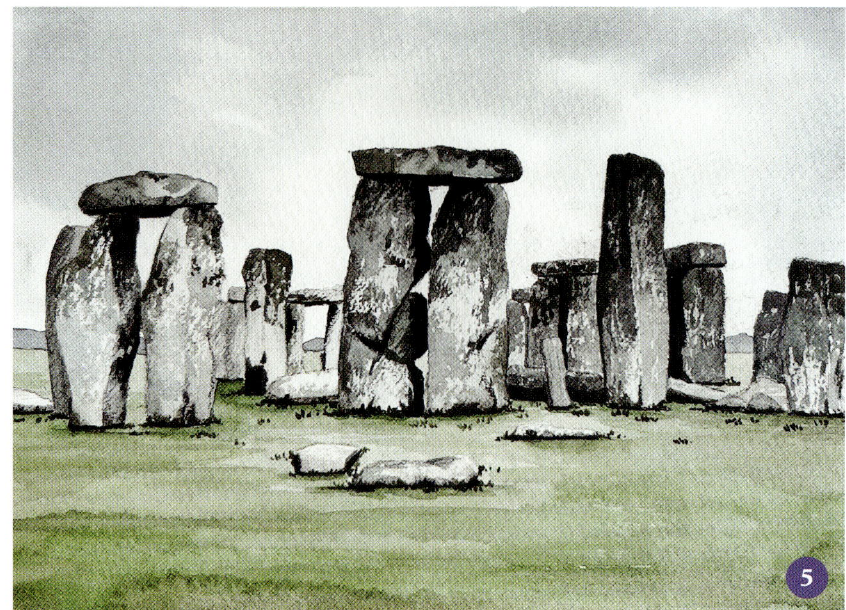

Step 5

Once you're happy with the overall look of the stones, the last step is to add one more layer to the grass. Use a few green variations for this step, like the colors swatched above.

Paint a flat wash of Green over the whole section. While it's still wet, drop in some of the Brownish Green color in a few areas, mostly around the bottom of the page.

Lastly, use Dark Green and a detail brush to add some grass texture around the base of each of the stones. This should make them look fully grounded into the earth.

Once you're happy with your piece, take off the tape, sign and date your painting and admire your work!

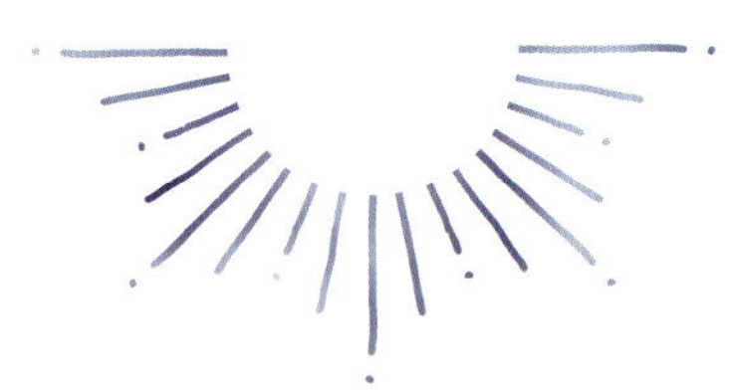

airplane view

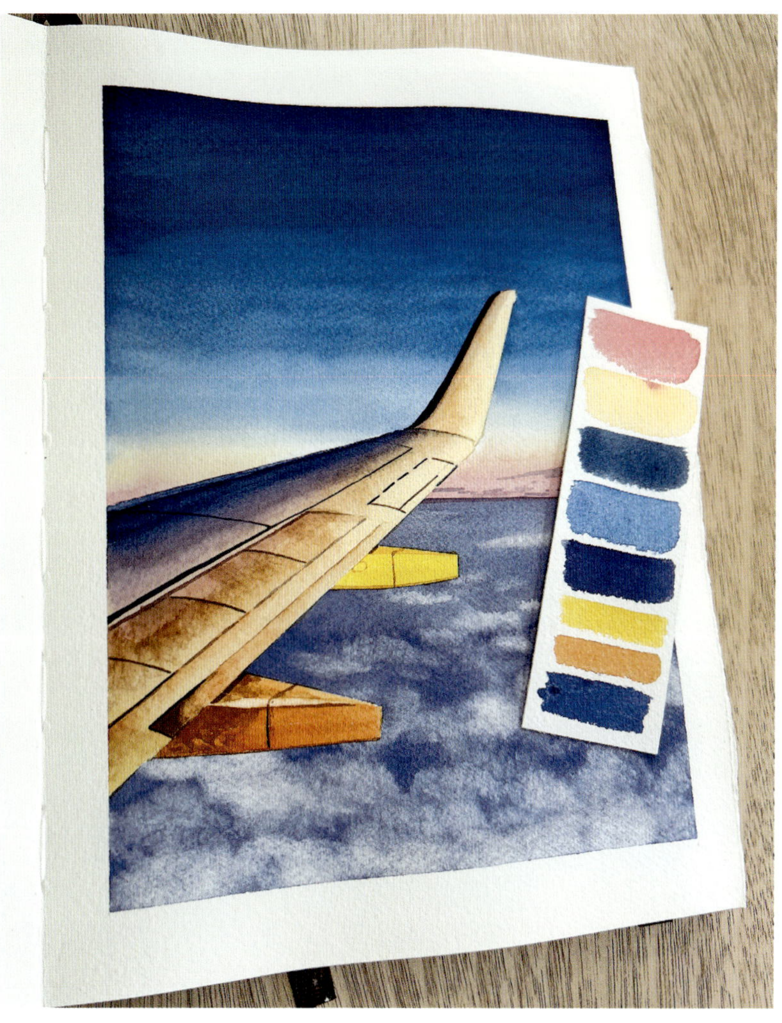

I don't know about you, but I'm a faithful window-seat gal on airplanes. I love watching the scenery go by, picking out landmarks and seeing beautiful sunrises and sunsets from such a high altitude. These can be very fun scenes to paint as well because of the unusual perspective and color. I hope you enjoy this one!

materials

Watercolor paints

- Cadmium Yellow, Cadmium Orange, Magenta, Phthalo Blue, Ultramarine Blue and Indigo

Watercolor paper of your choice

- I used my cold press Fabriano Artistico sketchbook size 6 x 8.5 inches (15 x 21.5 cm)

Brushes

- one larger brush (I used a ½ inch oval), one medium brush (I used a 4 round) and one detail brush (I used a 0 round)

Orientation

- portrait

Set up your paper as you like and make sure to add a drop or two of water to your colors so they start to soften.

Reference photo

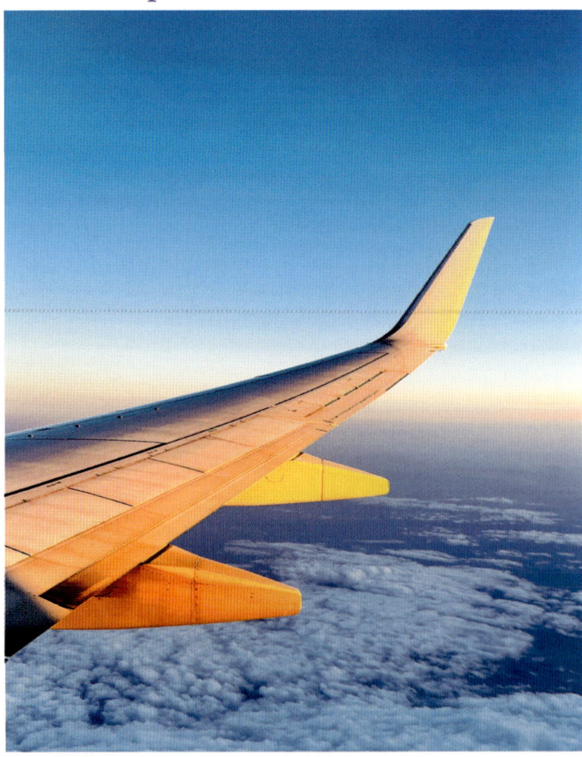

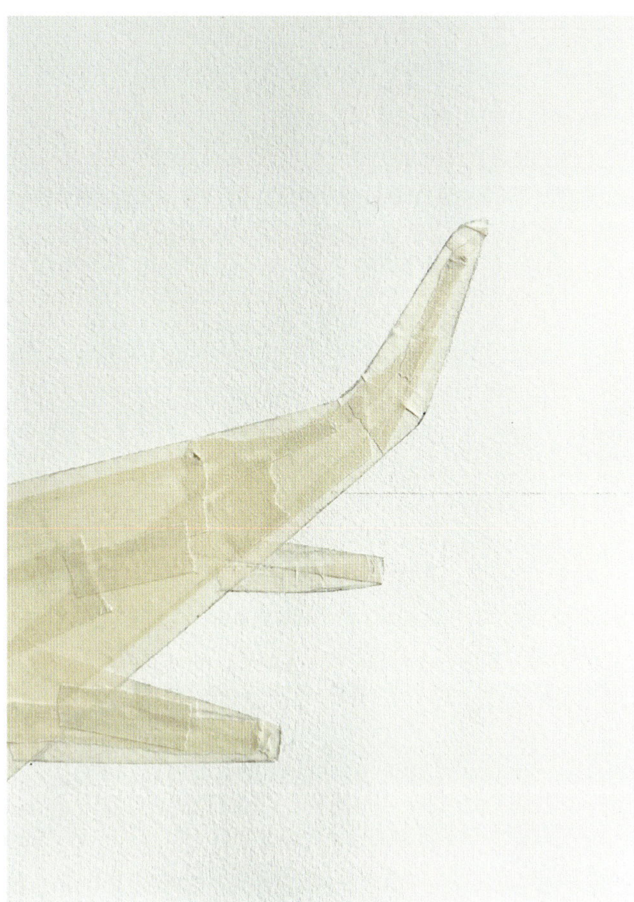

Sketch

Sketch out the shape of the airplane wing, as well as the horizon line just under halfway up the paper. Pay attention to the perspective here; the wing starts out quite wide on the left side of the page and then tapers down to the fin at the end of the wing. Don't forget to include the engines underneath the wings.

PAUSE: Before starting on the painting, I covered the entire wing with masking tape so I can paint the background first without having to carefully paint around the wing. To do this, place masking tape over the entire shape (you should be able to see your sketch through the tape), then use an X-acto knife to gently cut out the shape of the wing. You could also use masking fluid to protect the shape, or you could just paint around the wing shape, though this is a bit more tedious.

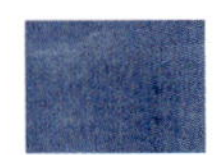

Dark Blue
Ultramarine Blue + Phthalo Blue + Indigo

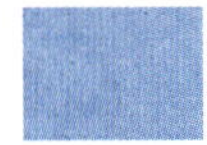

Medium Blue
Ultramarine Blue + Phthalo Blue

Yellow
Cadmium Yellow + water

Pink
Magenta + water

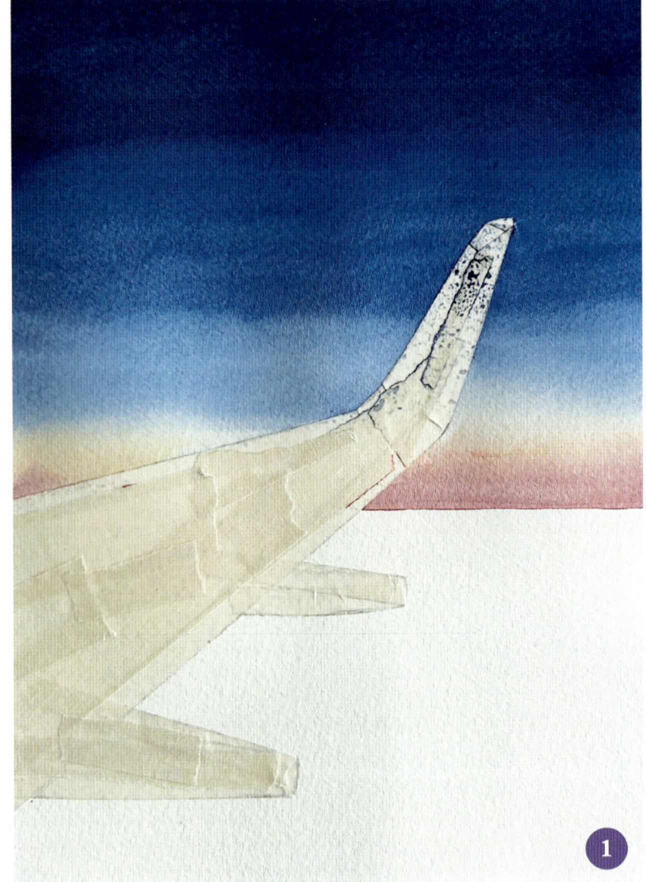

Step 1

First, let's paint the sky using the four colors swatched above.

Using a large brush, start at the top of the page with the Dark Blue color. Cover about one-third of the sky section using horizontal strokes, then quickly switch to the Medium Blue and continue to fill in the page. Once you've filled up about two-thirds of the page, clean your brush and put a stripe of clean water underneath the Medium Blue to blend out the bottom edge. Then add a stripe of Yellow under that clear water and then fill in the rest of the sky to the horizon line with Pink.

You can use a clean damp brush to blend these colors together more if you like–work from bottom to top and only do this once or twice, while the painting is still wet.

Once this layer has dried completely, you can assess the colors and paint another layer in exactly the same way for more vibrant colors if you wish.

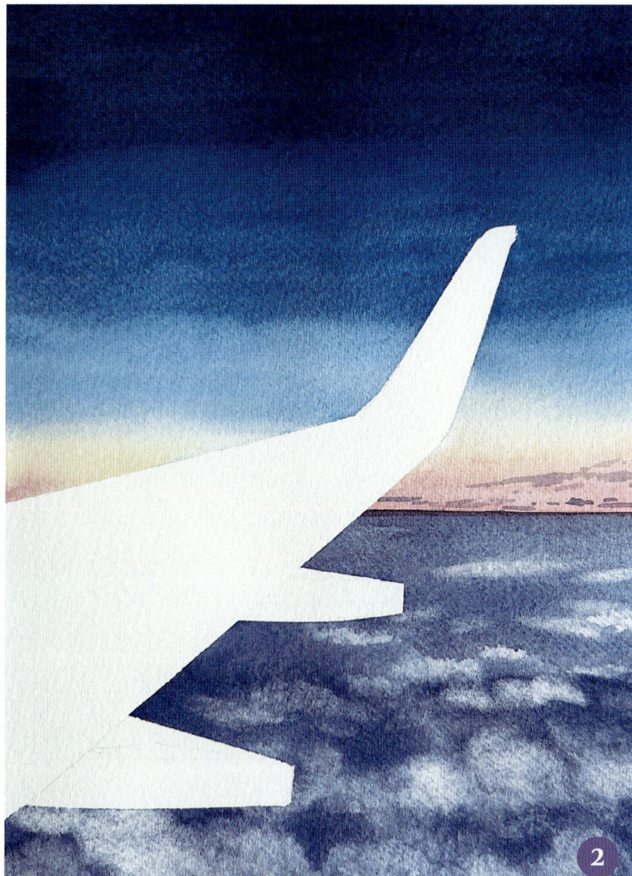

Purple
Ultramarine Blue
+ little Magenta
+ little Van Dyke
Brown

Step 2

Next, we'll fill in the area underneath the horizon line. Mix up a muted Purple color using the color recipe above.

First, water down a little bit of this Purple color and use a detail brush to add some distant streaky clouds just above the horizon.

Then, use a large brush to fill in the section below the horizon line with a flat wash of the original Purple color you mixed. Then, use a completely dry brush and a stippling motion to lift some of the excess color and create some fluffy cloud shapes. Continually dry off the brush as you work so that you can keep picking up paint and work quickly! Once you're happy with the clouds, you can take off the tape or masking fluid covering the airplane wing.

Let this fully dry before moving on.

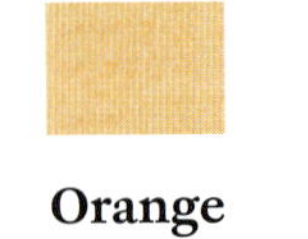

Orange
Cadmium Orange

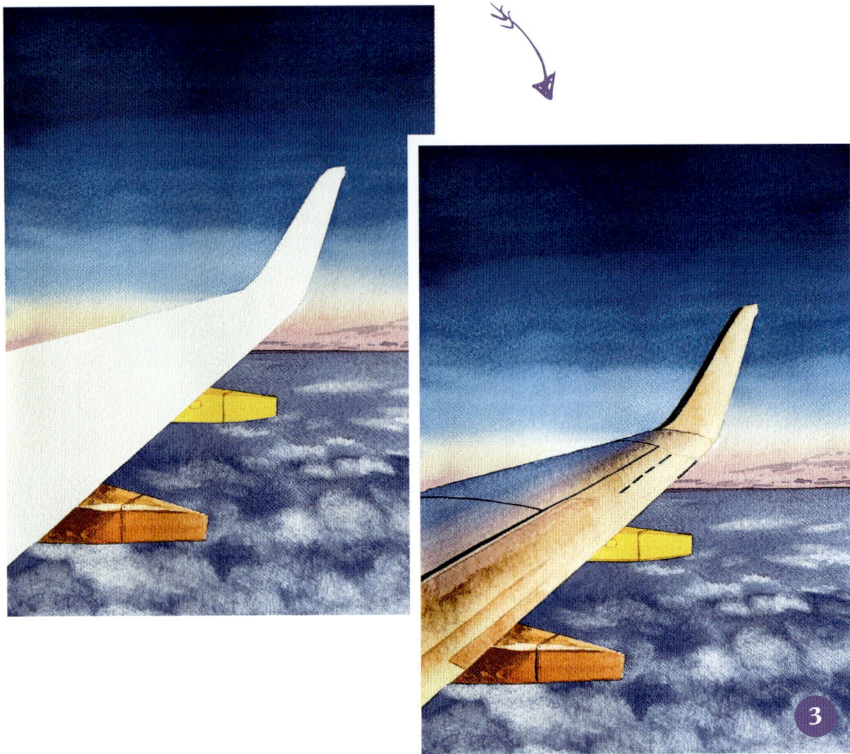

Step 3

Now, let's paint in the airplane wing. You'll need all of the same colors from Step 1 (Dark Blue, Medium Blue, Yellow and Pink), as well as Cadmium Orange.

First, paint in the engines. Fill in the closer one with Orange and the further one with Yellow. Once they're filled in with a flat wash, feel free to **mix a bit of Van Dyke Brown into each of these colors** and use a detail brush to add some shadows and details on the top and sides of the engine shapes. To create the highlight you see on the orange engine, don't paint over that spot anymore, and let the first wash of Orange show through.

Use a smaller brush to create a gradient (see page 15) from the top of the wing to the bottom, starting with Dark Blue, then Medium Blue, then Pink, then Orange and then Yellow. The fin at the end of the wing is just Orange on the left and then Yellow on the right.

I ended up doing two layers of this gradient to deepen the color to my liking, so feel free to do the same. Let this fully dry before moving on.

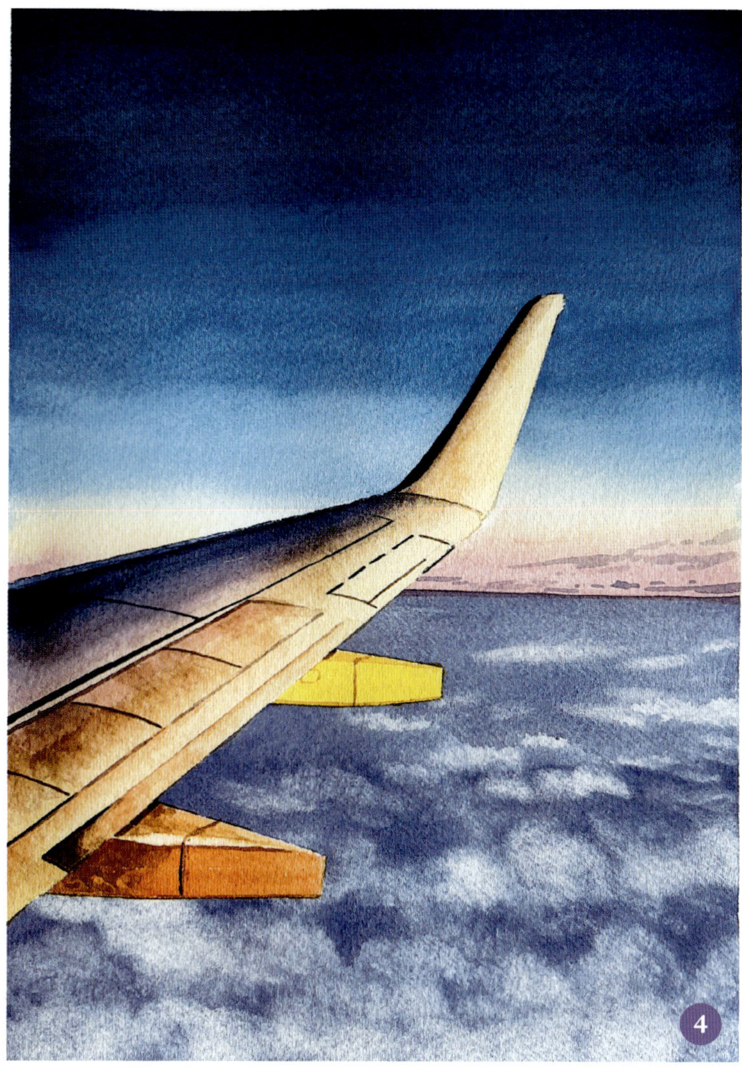

Step 4

Using the Dark Blue and a detail brush, add some more details to the wing: the dark line on the front edge of the fin, the straight lines on the wing and some of the gaps between panels. Observe the reference photo here and use it to inspire your detail at this point.

You can also use some Orange or Pink to add some shadows where those panels are; you can see those on the bottom left side of the wing in my progress photo.

Once you're happy with your airplane wing, you're all done with this painting! Take off the tape, sign and date your painting and admire your work.

colorful galaxy

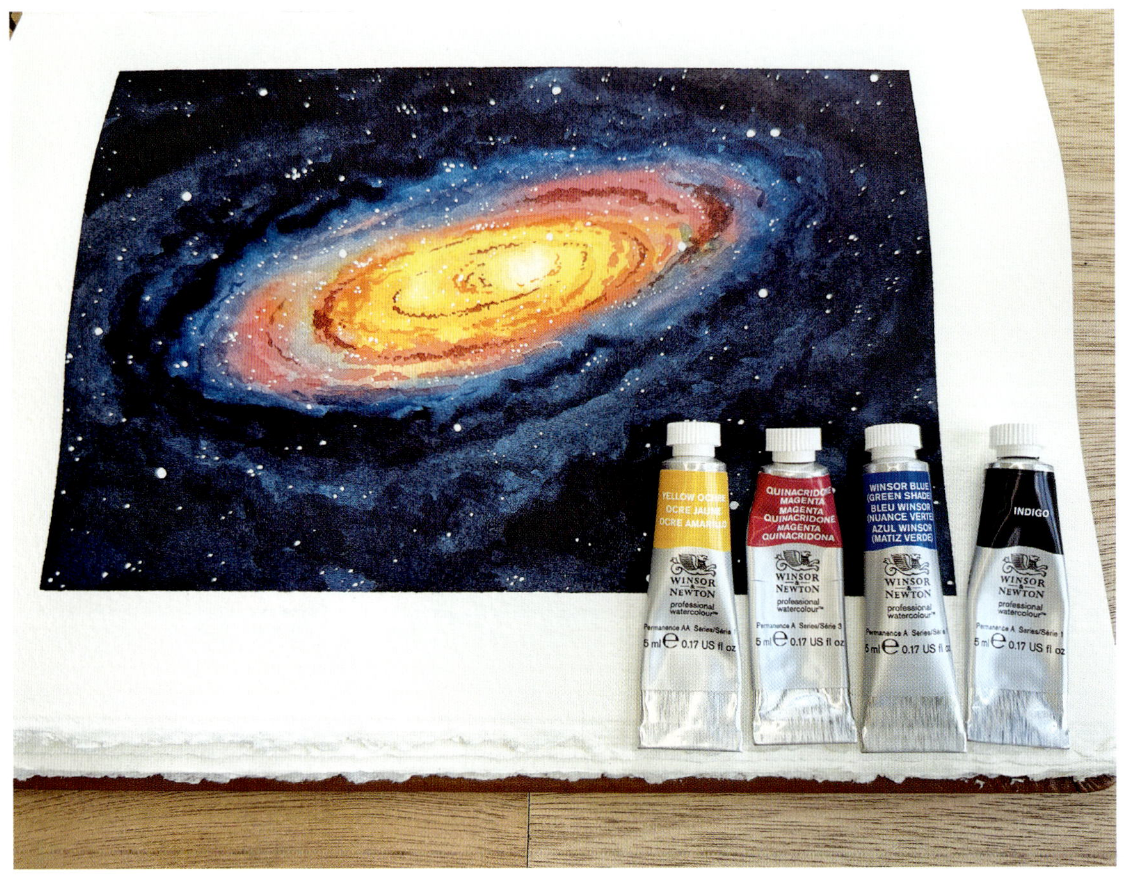

Galaxies are one of the most fun and free subjects to paint with watercolor! You get to use whatever colors you want and let them all blend together to make a beautiful impression of the cosmos. I researched a few different photos of galaxies to prepare for this painting and landed on a NASA Hubble image to inspire this piece. I took some liberties with more vibrant colors and many more stars because that's what art is for!

materials

Watercolor paints

- Cadmium Yellow, Cadmium Orange, Magenta, Phthalo Blue, Indigo and Payne's Gray
- White gouache

Watercolor paper of your choice

- I used my cold press Fabriano Artistico sketchbook size 5 x 7.5 inches (12.5 x 19.25 cm)

Brushes

- one larger brush (I used a ½ inch oval), one medium brush (I used a 4 round) and one detail brush (I used a 0 round)

Orientation

- landscape

Set up your paper as you like and make sure to add a drop or two of water to your colors so they start to soften.

Reference photo

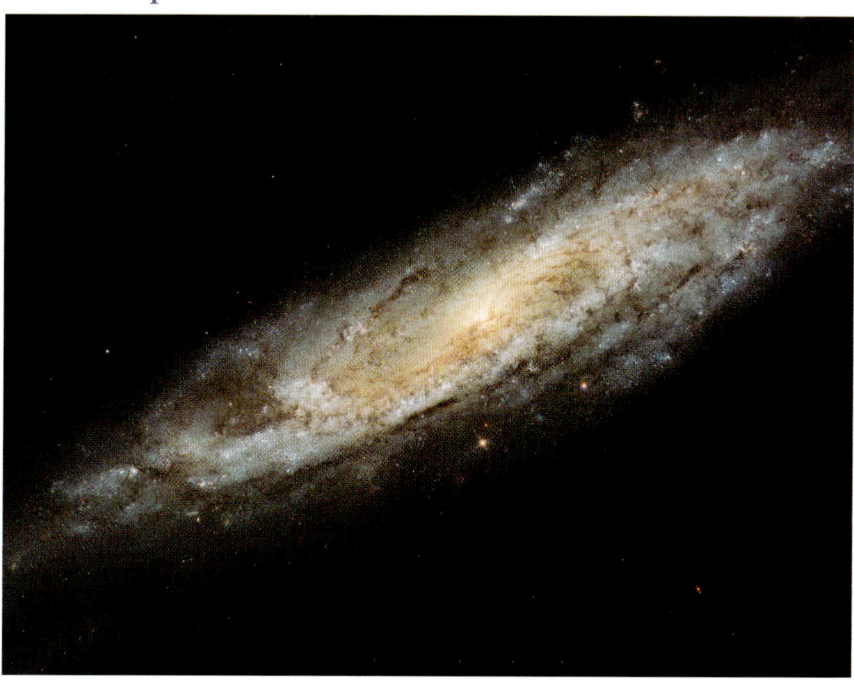

Yellow
Cadmium Yellow

Orange
Cadmium Orange

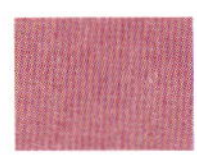

Magenta
Magenta

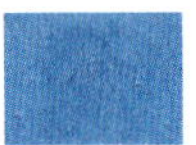

Blue
Phthalo Blue

Dark Blue
Indigo

Gray
Payne's Gray

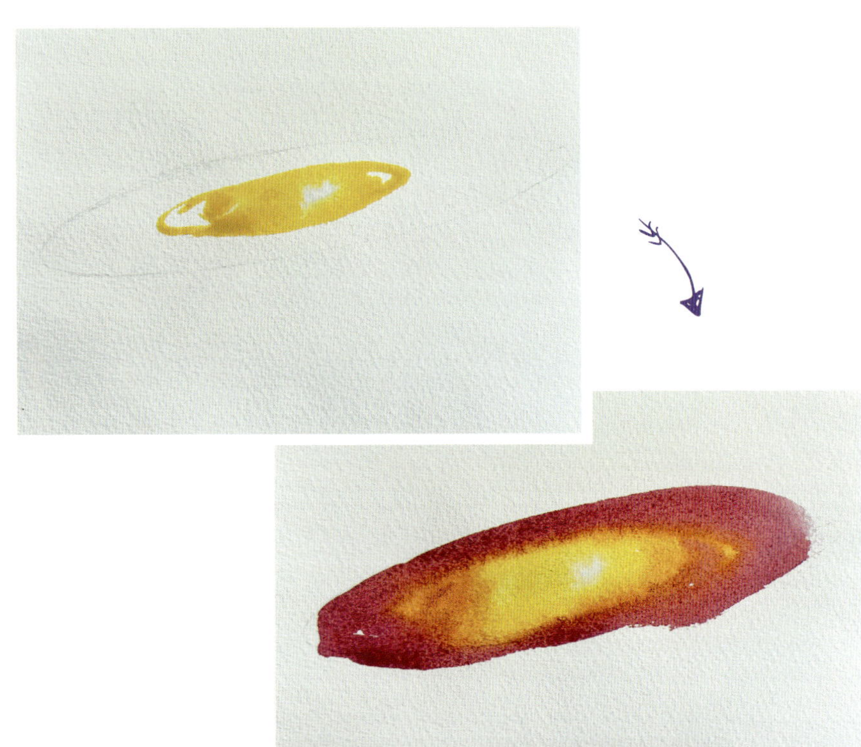

Sketch

Sketch an oval in the general area you want your galaxy to be. Use a light touch with your pencil or slightly erase your lines before painting, so that the pencil doesn't show through later.

Step 1

This painting doesn't require much color mixing, as most of the colors will blend together on the paper. But it's always good to prepare your colors in separate pans before starting so that you get an even mix of colors. Prepare some fairly-saturated versions of the six colors swatched above.

NOTE: For the first layer, we will be working (mostly) on dry paper so that we get bright, saturated colors. Therefore, it's important to work quickly and loosely so that the previous color won't dry up on you. Don't worry about cleaning your brush between colors (they're all mixing on the paper anyway!) and make sure you read through the following instructions before starting so that you know where we're going!

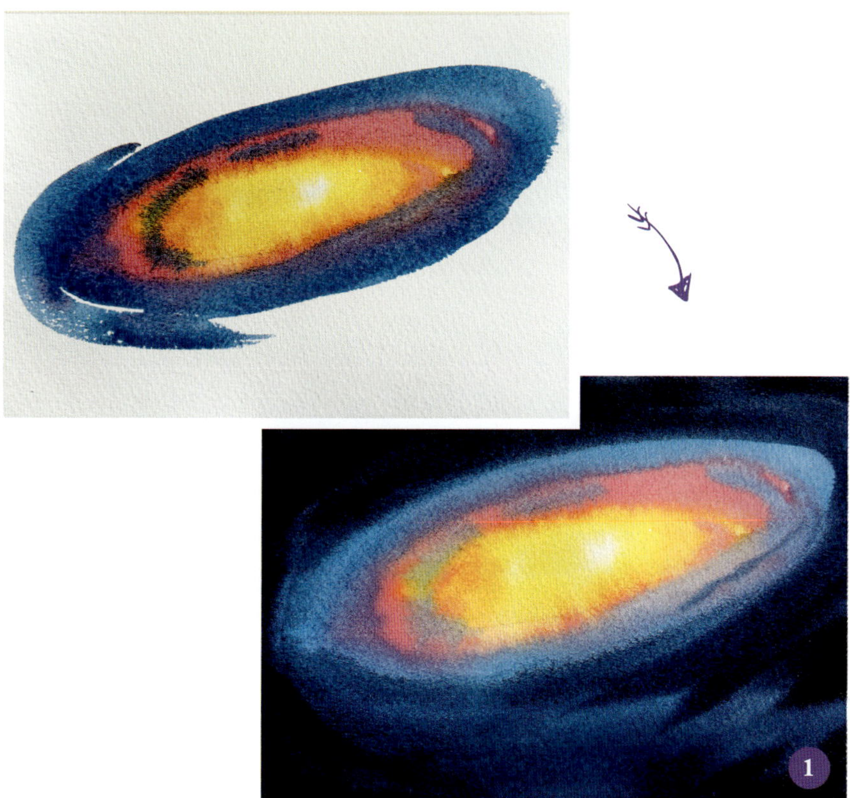

We will be working from the center outwards, so first paint a small circle of clean water in the center of the galaxy. This will give you a light spot at the center.

Use a large brush and start with your Yellow color. Create a small, loose oval shape around the circle of water in the center of the galaxy.

Switch to the Orange color and add to the oval.

Switch to the Magenta color and add to the oval.

Switch to the Blue color and add to the oval. You now should be overlapping your initial pencil sketch of the galaxy.

Switch to the Dark Blue color and add to your oval, taking this color almost to the edges of your paper.

Switch to the Gray color and fill in anything still blank.

Take a deep breath. If the center of the painting is still wet, use a clean, dry brush to lift some of the paint from the center to make it lighter.

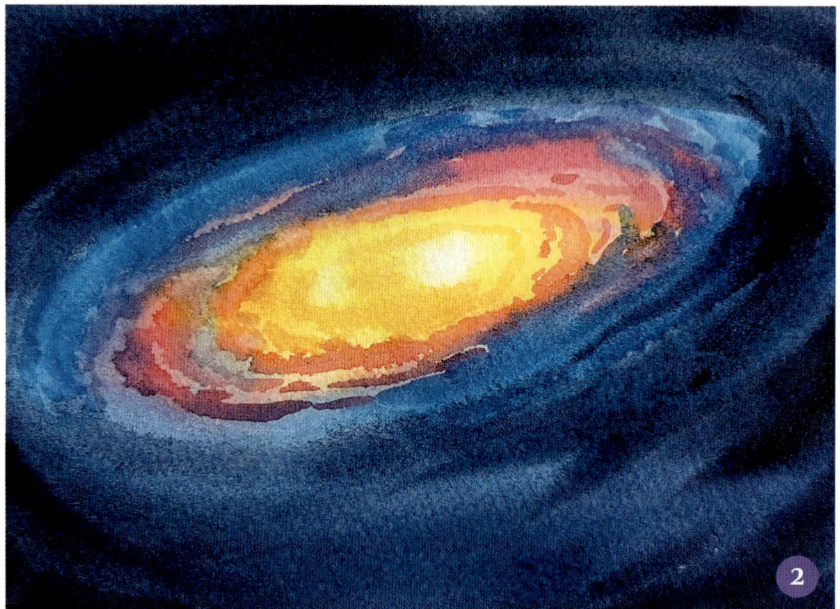

Step 2

No need to fully dry the painting yet. We are going to take advantage of the damp painting and add a little bit of texture. Use a smaller brush (I used a 4 round) and drop in some colors within your galaxy in different places. I again started from the center and worked my way outwards, dropping in some Orange over the Yellow and then some Magenta over the Orange and Blue and then some Blue around the outer edge of the galaxy. Follow the direction of the oval and wiggle your brush randomly to create some fun textures.

Let this fully dry before moving on.

Step 3

Now let's add some texture to the outside of the galaxy. Use your Dark Blue and Gray colors and begin adding cloud-like textures. Work in sections here and there, adding some color and then using a damp brush to blend it out. You can also use your Blue color to add some of these cloud textures around the outer edge of the galaxy so that everything looks cohesive.

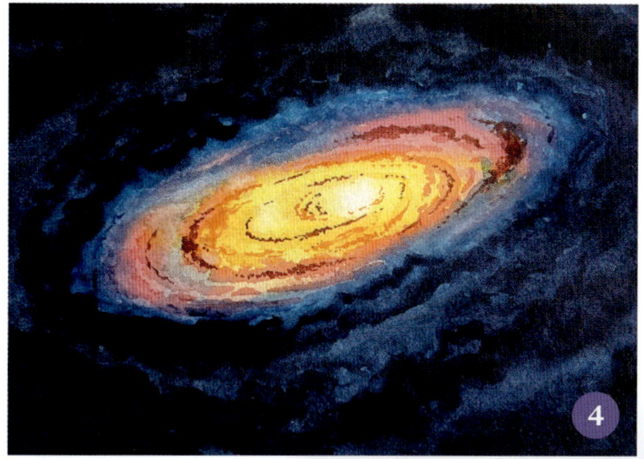

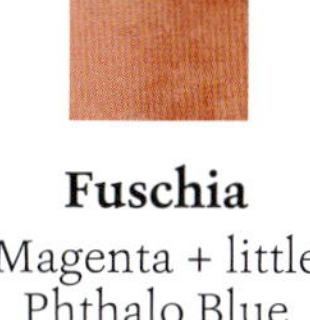

Fuschia
Magenta + little
Phthalo Blue

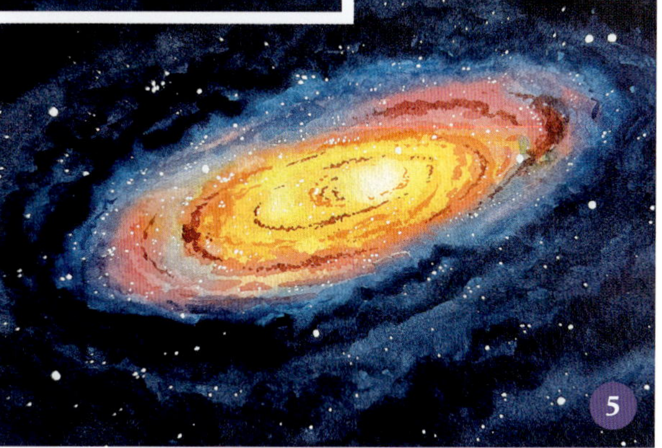

Step 4

Now let's add some final details within the galaxy. You'll notice in the reference photo some "spiral arms" where the space debris has collected and is rotating around the center. I used my detail brush and the Orange color for these details closer to the center, then I mixed a Fuchsia color for those details further away from the center. I heavily simplified this from the reference photo on this step!

Step 5

For the final detail, let's add some stars! I used my white gouache and a detail brush to add in little dots all around the painting, including inside the galaxy. Vary the sizes of your stars; make some really small and make some a little larger. Cluster them together sometimes and spread them out randomly—this will help with the effect!

Once you're happy with your piece, take off the tape, sign and date your painting and admire your work!

mr. moon

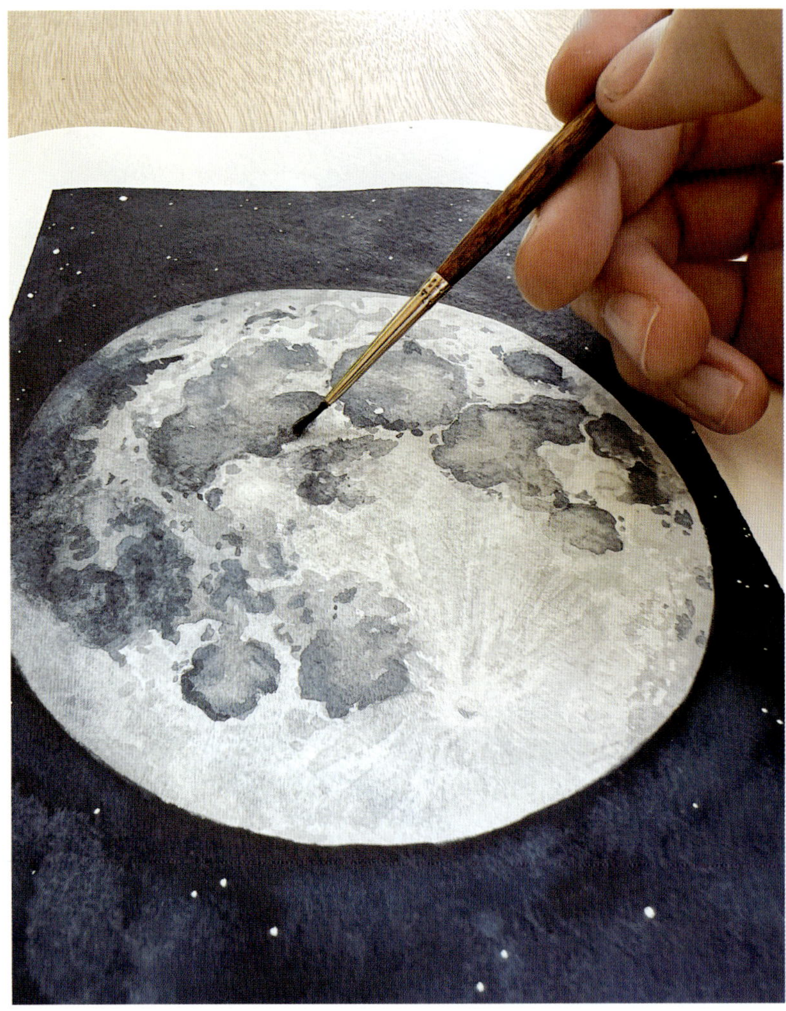

I've always loved looking up at the moon on clear nights. One time as a child, I even woke up my dad in the middle of the night to tell him, "Mr. Moon is shining through my window." It turns out the moon is quite fun to paint, as well! I loved creating the well-known craters and shadows on the surface, and I think you'll find it to be a fun and inspiring project. This is a limited palette painting, as we'll just be using three colors to create this piece.

materials

Watercolor paints

- Ultramarine Blue, Van Dyke Brown and Payne's Gray
- White gouache

Watercolor paper of your choice.

- I used my cold press Fabriano Artistico sketchbook size 5 x 7.5 inches (12.5 x 19.25 cm)

Brushes

- one larger brush (I used a ½ inch oval), one medium brush (I used a 4 round) and one detail brush (I used a 0 round)

Orientation

- portrait

Set up your paper as you like and make sure to add a drop or two of water to your colors so they start to soften.

Reference photo

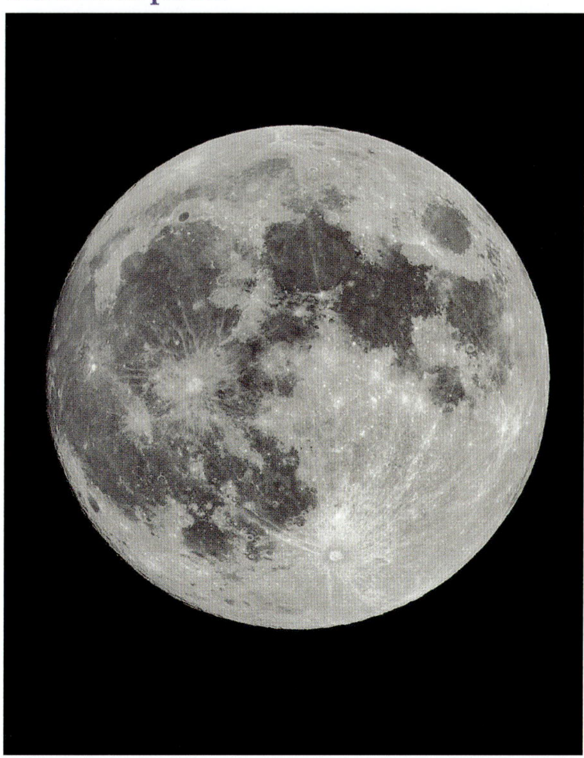

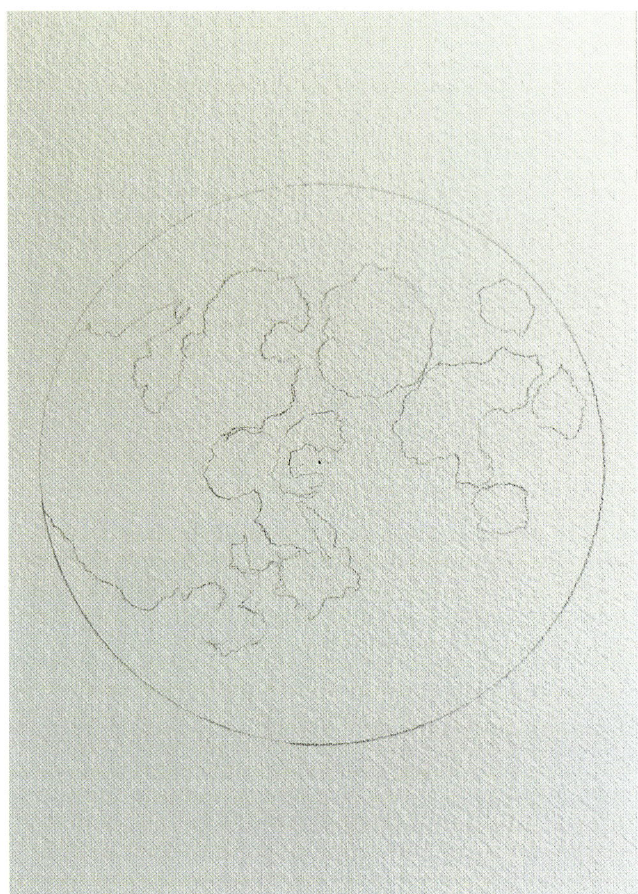

Sketch

For the pencil sketch, find the middle of your paper with a ruler and then use a compass or round object to draw a circle in the center of your paper. Then sketch out the major shadow shapes on the moon using the reference photo. Feel free to shade some of the shadows with your pencil if you wish!

Step 1

To start, mix a light, Warm Gray (use a little more Van Dyke Brown than Ultramarine Blue to warm up the color).

Add plenty of water and then use a large brush and fill in the entire moon shape. Don't worry about coloring in the lines; the background will be much darker, so we can fix the circle shape later.

Let this fully dry before moving on.

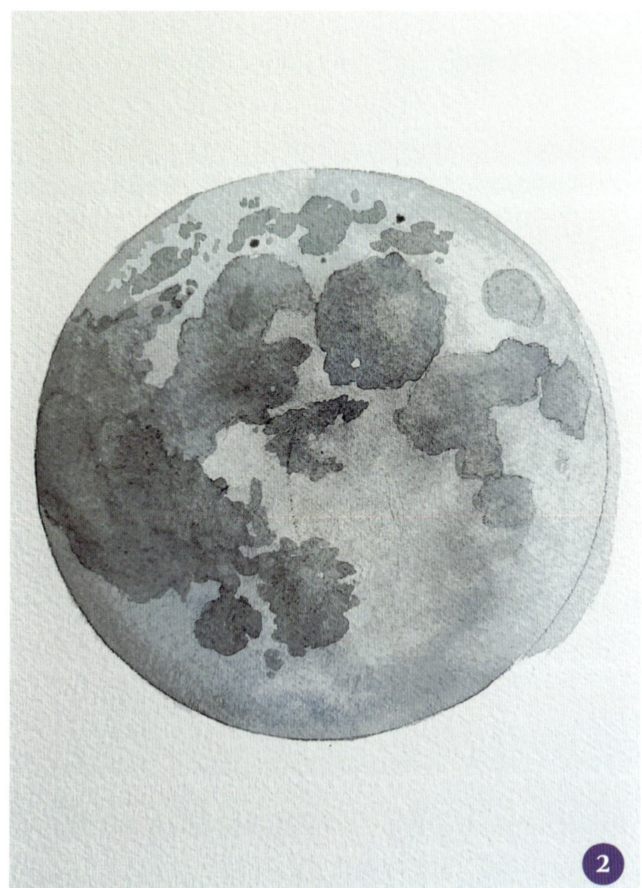

Warm Gray
Van Dyke Brown + Ultramarine Blue + water

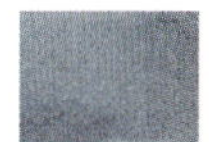

Cooler Gray
Van Dyke Brown + more Ultramarine Blue + a little water

Step 2

Next, create a cooler (add more Ultramarine Blue) and more saturated (add less water) version of the Warm Gray color from Step 1. Keep this original Cooler Gray handy for Step 3.

Water down a bit of this Cooler Gray and use a smaller brush (I used my 4 round) to fill in the crater shapes around the moon. Feel free to add random smaller dots and details around the moon, as well, for texture!

Step 3

Use the original Cooler Gray color mixed in Step 2 to start building up the shadows in the craters. Work in sections, putting down small areas of color and then use a clean, damp brush to blend the color out. I focused these shadows around the edges of the crater shapes, but I also continued adding some random smaller dots and textures around the moon.

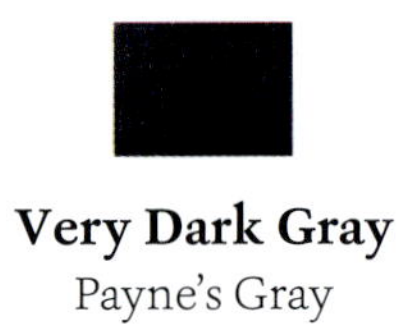

Very Dark Gray
Payne's Gray

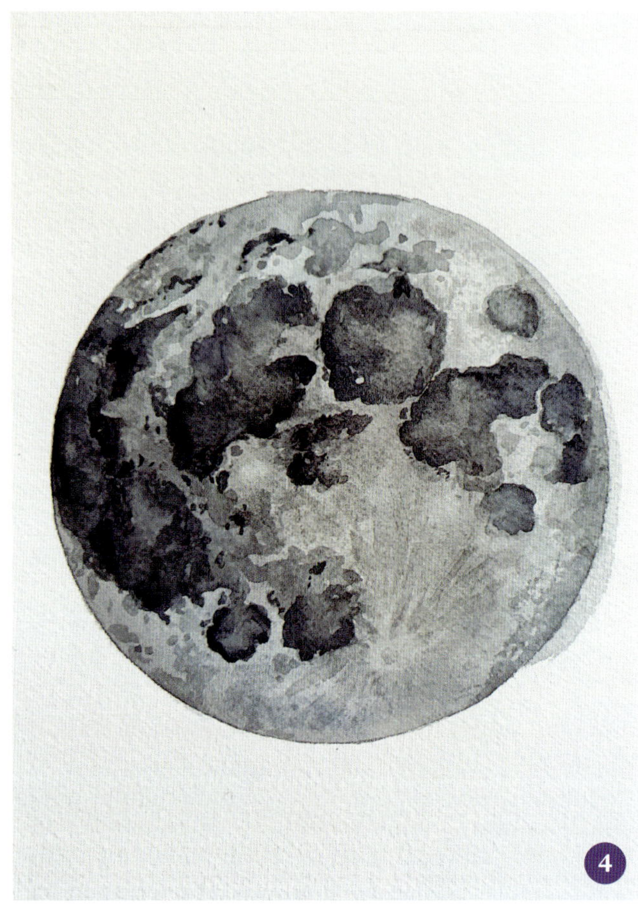

Step 4

Let's use a new technique to lighten some spots up! There are a couple of spaces (like the crater toward the bottom of the moon) where there are some highlights expanding outward from a point. To imitate this, use a clean, damp detail brush to scrub a small area of the paper where you want a highlight. Do this for three to five seconds and then immediately dab the area with your clean paper towel. This should lighten up the space gradually. Repeat as often as you need to and wherever you need to add some highlights to your moon.

Step 5

Once you're happy with your moon, paint in the background using a saturated Very Dark Gray and a larger brush. This is when you'll carve out the final shape of the moon, so take some time to carefully outline it. Don't worry about getting blooms or textures in the background; in my opinion, that just makes it look more realistic!

I ended up doing two layers on the background to get the darkness I wanted. Make sure the first layer is completely dry before going over it with another layer of paint!

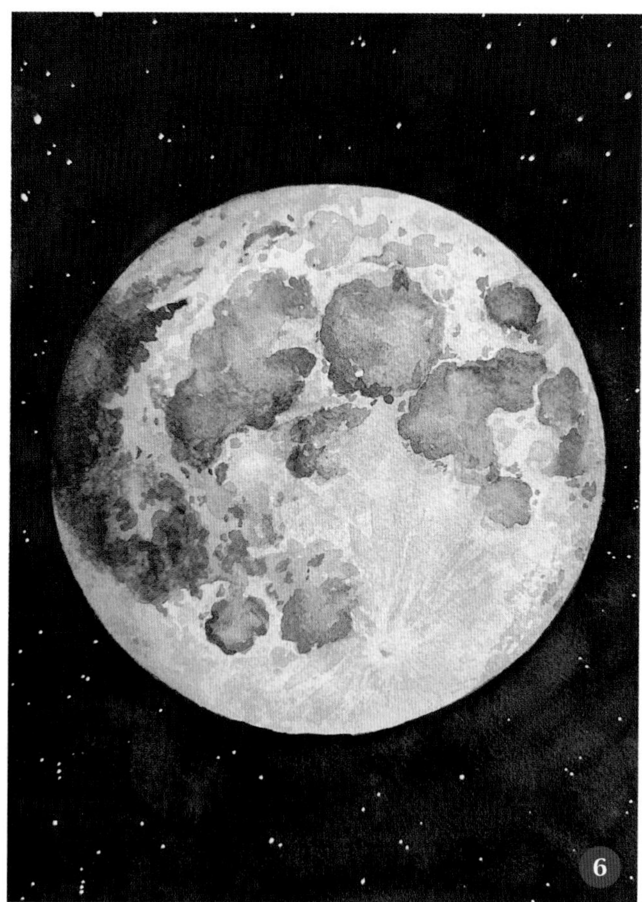

Once your background is filled in, take a look at your moon. If your shadows suddenly look too light, circle back to Step 3 and deepen your shadows.

Step 6

For our final details, let's add some stars! I used my detail brush and white gouache to add some small dots in the background. Make sure to vary the sizes of the stars and spread them out randomly.

Once you're happy with your piece, take off the tape, sign and date your painting and admire your work!

acknowledgments

Thank you to my family, friends and my partner, Michael Payne, for your constant love and support.

Thank you to everyone who contributed reference photos to this project: Alan Pickerill, Dianne Pickerill, Adrienne Pickerill, Donna Payne, Jarred Decker, Div Pithadia, Vidar Nordli-Mathisen, ESA/Hubble & NASA, A. Filippenko and Mike Petrucci. An artist is nothing without good reference photos.

Next, thank you to my editor Sadie Hofmeester and to everyone at Page Street Publishing Co., for making this dream a reality for me.

A huge thank you to everyone who has ever supported me on social media or purchased my art. Without you, this book would not exist, and I would not be living my dream as a professional artist, so I can never fully express how much I appreciate your support.

And finally, thank you to you, dear artist, for sharing your creativity with me here.

about the author

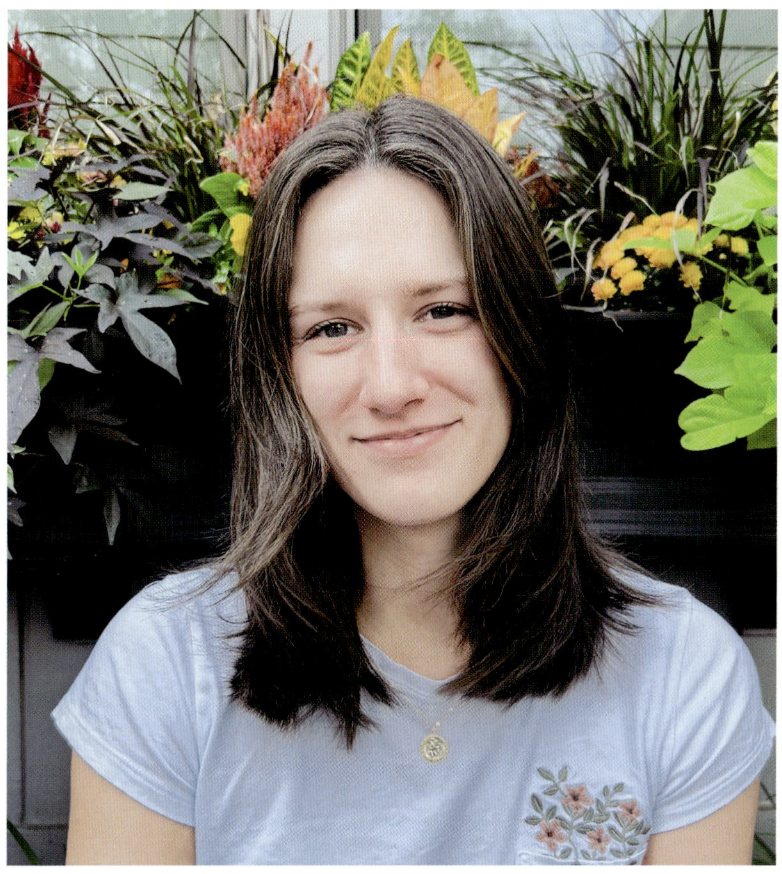

Hannah M. Pickerill is a professional artist currently working in Cincinnati, Ohio. She has been drawing and painting from a young age and was able to transition to a full-time artist in the fall of 2021. Hannah focuses her work mainly on landscapes but also enjoys painting plants, animals and cityscapes. She is a multi-disciplinary artist, working with watercolor, gouache, acrylic paint and oil paint interchangeably. She is passionate about teaching art and often posts instructional videos on TikTok, Instagram and YouTube with the hope that she can inspire others' creativity and passion for art.

index

d

e

f

g

h

i

l

m

n

o

p